D0873863

Audacity to Believe

Audacity to Believe

SHEILA CASSIDY

COLLINS ✸ WORLD

Published by William Collins + World Publishing Co., Inc.
2080 West 117 Street, Cleveland, Ohio 44111

Published simultaneously in Canada by
Wm. Collins Sons & Co. Ltd., Toronto, Ontario, Canada.

First published in the U.S.A. January 1978

Library of Congress Cataloging in Publication Data

Cassidy, Sheila, 1937-
  Audacity to believe

  Autobiographical.
  1. Cassidy, Sheila, 1937-   2. Political prisoners—Chile—
  Biography.   3. Surgeons—England—Biography.
  4. Catholics—Chile—Biography.   I. Title.

HV9598.C37   1978   364.1'34   77-18195
ISBN 0-529-05464-7

Manufactured in the United States of America.

Contents

Contents

Dedication

To the people of Chile,
of every class and creed;
that they may be united
in peace, freedom and love.

I have the audacity to believe that peoples everywhere can have three meals a day for their bodies,
education and culture for their minds, and dignity,
equality and freedom for their spirits. I believe that
what self-centered men have torn down other-
centered can build up. I still believe that one day
mankind will bow before the altars of God and be
crowned triumphant over war and bloodshed, and
nonviolent redemptive goodwill will proclaim the
rule of the land. And the lion and the lamb shall lie
down together and every man shall sit under his own
vine and fig tree and none shall be afraid. I still
believe that we shall overcome.

Martin Luther King,
Nobel Peace Prize Acceptance Speech

Preface

On the day that I left Chile, one of my fellow prisoners told me that since she had known me her opinion of Catholics had fallen even lower than it had been before. This hit me especially hard not only because she was a woman whom I deeply respected but because I had secretly imagined myself to be living a life of splendid Christian witness among the Marxists. She said that when I decided not to speak about my prison experiences because of the risks involved she could hardly bring herself to speak to me. Her condemnation of me was for professing to be a Christian without having the courage to act like one.

It was then that I realized that I owed it to the members of the camp to speak out on their behalf; it became clear to me that, whatever the diplomatic or personal repercussions, I must speak the truth quite openly to those who were prepared to listen.

This book, then, is written as the final stage of the fulfilment of a pledge made to the women of Tres Alamos prison in Santiago. These women are now free in Chile or living in exile but other Chileans have taken their place, for Chile remains in a state of siege.

I have written the story of what happened to me, not in a spirit of vengeance or bitterness but of love and hope, for my experience in Chile has convinced me of the incredible and unconquerable goodness in people. My encounter with the Catholic Church in Chile, and with the men and women who showed me the face of Christ among the dispossessed, has changed my life and I do not have words to express my gratitude. Because of my work with the Christians I had the privilege of sharing the suffering of another group of Chileans: men and women equally, though differently, committed to the liberation of the oppressed. Their courage, integrity and selflessness remain a reproach and an inspiration to me.

There is a phrase much used in these times of hardship in Chile: *entrega total* – total commitment. It is a phrase which links Christian and Marxist for they have both answered the call of that Greater Love whereby a man is granted the strength to lay down his life for his friends.

My deepest thanks are due to the many people who have helped this book to come into being, especially:
Pierre Collins, who had greater faith in me than I had in myself; Marjorie Villiers, without whose wise counsel and skilful editing it would not have been written; Pat Cassidy, my sister-in-law, who fed and supported me during the long months of writing; Ken Fox, Kate Davis, Helen Chilton and the girls from Planprint in Kingsbridge, who transformed a doctor's hieroglyphics into manuscript; Peter McIlhenny, who helped with the research; Brendan Smith, Bonaventure Knollys and Michèle Byam who corrected the proofs but who take no responsibility for my lack of punctuation; John McDonnell who corrected my singular Spanish; Marcel Montecino, Peter Hellmich, the Columban and the Maryknoll Fathers who lent me photographs; Anthony Sheil and Gill Coleridge, for their advice and encouragement; and lastly to all my friends in England, Scandinavia, France, the United States and Latin America who have provided material, ideas and encouragement.

July 1977

Introduction

Towards midnight one autumn evening in the early 1960s
the Roman Catholic Archbishop of Birmingham, whom I
had been entertaining, said it was time he went to bed. I was
chaplain to the Roman Catholics at Oxford University and
lived in the beautiful and ancient building opposite Christ
Church meadows known as the Old Palace. My room overlooking St Aldate's was joined to the rest of the house by a
narrow passage leading to a small oblong room used for
television and sitting about; from there another door led to
the bedrooms.

Going ahead through the passage, I opened the door of
the television room for the archbishop to precede me. He
moved past, gasped and withdrew. I peered in. Close to
where he had stepped was a three-bar electric fire, full on;
beyond was a mass of long fair hair spread out towards the
heat; beyond again the recumbent figure of a young woman.

My polite cough made her raise her head. Quite unperturbed she sat up and explained. She had heard I was to
appear on TV giving a late night epilogue; unable to get to
a set in Somerville where she was reading medicine, she
came to the Chaplaincy. Being early, she had decided to
spend the time washing her hair; having no hair drier, she
put on the electric fire and lay happily in front of it.

I was highly amused; the archbishop was not!

Sheila Cassidy enjoyed the whole incident, watched the
epilogue over a cup of coffee and went cheerfully back to her
digs with dried hair and laughing eyes.

This episode I recount at length to illustrate Sheila as she
then was and still is – a real person – alive, enthusiastic, good
at her studies and her medical practice, efficient, impetuous,
starry-eyed, down-to-earth-practical, emotionally unin-
hibited, politically a child, spiritually liable to climb to

heights and plumb the depths, good with her hands and mind, a maker of toys and other things . . . but always God-based even when she has periodically neglected him.

The story she writes is unadulterated Sheila. I simply verify that the true Sheila comes through – honest, mixedly humble and opinionated, undoubtedly brave because she accepts her fear, her cowardly feelings, the 'betrayal' of her friends under torture. She is outspoken in her condemnation of Chile's present regime, stark in her description of torture, prison conditions and her general treatment after she had been seized. She spells out the complex pattern which weaves from utter despair to a vivid faith in God and hope for mankind.

Some people may well say that no one could walk into a situation so naively. I can only say – 'Sheila Cassidy could!' I say that not disparagingly but in admiration. Some could then come back at my own naivety in accepting Sheila . . . in believing the truth of her testimony. My reply – I know Sheila.

The interesting fact for me is that I have known Sheila before, during and after what she tells here. I have seen her in a smock painting the outside of the Chaplaincy at Oxford, prayed with her, listened as she poured out the sadness of the loss to another girl of the man she loved. At her request with other graduates I first gave a series of talks on prayer. I met, talked to, liked and became a friend of Consuelo. Visiting Leicester I met – but did not have time to become a friend of – the chows! There we discussed the voyage away from National Health pressures to a new life in Chile. Afterwards by letter from Latin America and by word of mouth when she visited her dying father, I heard of Consuelo's illness and death, of life in Santiago, of Sheila's return to God. For weeks in England, she teased out, alone and with me, God's call and her return to Chile.

In a way it was a shock to hear of Sheila's arrest; in a way always utterly possible. By coincidence Reginald Secondé, the British Ambassador in Santiago, had been my life-long friend from school and army days. When I approached him he was enormously kind and helpful, though he did not hesitate to tell me off for writing in protest to Chile's President – one of very many letters the President received. Anyhow, one way or another, Sheila was released and the Foreign Office alerted me to meet her at Gatwick.

She arrived very 'high'. It was immediately clear she had been through 'something', though at that time torture was still not publicly accepted. In subsequent weeks and months she stayed often in Southall where I am living and working. On several occasions she asked my advice about how to cope with her intense fear. The world now knows the publicity she received. Voices have been raised for her and against.

It can sometimes happen that a particular person – almost by chance – causes an eruption. I think Sheila Cassidy did this, because without politics she behaved as a Christian and a doctor in going to the aid of a wounded man. I would ask the reader to ponder what she has written and the implications of her story.

My personal political stand is to follow Jesus Christ, and preach his message to each and every political party – backing here, questioning there, chastising somewhere else – according to the policy and morality of what is 'happening'. Sheila's reaction to a situation of human need blew up, created a situation and hit many people in the world. We are all subject to our sense of right and wrong, sensitive or dulled in reaction. All too often our own comfort and safety outweigh the claims of justice and humanity. Where we see someone else making a stand for goodness, peace and love, we may well immediately label them as 'revolutionary' or 'reactionary' – thus feeling released from sharing their views or their involvement.

Yet by our own action or inaction we are taking part in the life of the world, for better or for worse. The testimony of Sheila Cassidy, backed by a mass of other verified evidence, is that in one country of our world there are serious attacks on human rights, attacks which brutalize those in power and undermine the essential freedoms of mankind. Sadly, we know that such indictment as she is making can and has been made much nearer home – in Northern Ireland. All too often the ordinary person feels powerless. I sincerely hope what has happened so suddenly and dramatically in the life of a British doctor may act as a conscience-pricking reflection, a further insight into the good and evil possibilities in human nature and an encouragement to many others to have the audacity to believe.

Southall   Michael Hollings

I

How it Began

I fled Him, down the nights and down the days;
I fled Him, down the arches of the years.
Francis Thompson
The Hound of Heaven

In December 1971, wearying of the academic rat-race of surgery in England I set off on a cargo boat for Chile. In the cabin I took my dog and thirty-three pieces of hand luggage among which was included my sewing machine and my gramophone, while in the hold travelled such other of my worldly goods as seemed important. Finding that the cost of professional packing was greater than the value of my possessions I packed them myself, securely, if a little unorthodoxly. The sheets and blankets travelled in the box which had been the home of the mynah bird, the fridge was wrapped in an eiderdown and my clothes came quite simply in their chest of drawers. The more fragile articles such as a mirror and two anglepoise lamps were carefully sandwiched between two mattresses which like some unwieldy packed lunch were enveloped in a large piece of brown carpet, and tied up with rope. I lost only a box of silver fruit knives and the mirror was broken, otherwise my home arrived with me and was I think my salvation in the first difficult months of adjusting to life in a foreign land.

On 29 December 1975 I was expelled from Chile by the government because I treated a wounded revolutionary and I returned to England by air with a suitcase packed for me by the British consul and without my dog.

Ever since I came back from Chile people have been asking me why I went there so I have developed a glib little answer about going in search of an easier life. This has sufficient truth for me to be prepared to say it, and for the people who do not know me it makes lots of sense because so many young doctors get fed up with the rat-race and go abroad. It is a useful phrase too, in that it makes it clear that I went neither for political nor for humanitarian motives and that is a very important truth to convey, especially when one half of the world sees me as a machine-gun toting marxist revolutionary and the other half as a cross between Florence Nightingale and Joan of Arc.

As so often happens in decisions which change one's life, my decision to go to Chile was made for various mixed and rather undramatic reasons. It is difficult to explain to people outside the British medical profession just what the rat-race is all about and how energetic, enthusiastic young doctors get caught up in a machine which does things to their lives and their love of medicine which they had never thought possible. This is not the place to describe the problems of the British junior hospital doctors, but during the first six years of my life in the National Health Service I was resident in hospitals and worked between sixty and eighty hours a week. I spent six months on the dole in London studying for a post-graduate examination in surgery because I could not make time to study while working, and then along with all but ten per cent of the entrants I failed. After a further year of studying while teaching anatomy at Oxford University I passed the Primary Fellowship exam. This made me in theory eligible to apply for a job as a surgical registrar in which in addition to working a ten-hour day I would be expected to work all night every third night and all night and all day every third weekend. By 1971 I had lost none of my early love of medicine, but I was extremely disillusioned about the way junior hospital doctors were expected to work and I doubted my capacity to live a humanly fulfilled life while working full time in the hospital service.

I had decided to become a doctor when I was fifteen. All I remember is saying to my father, 'I wish I were a man and then I could become a doctor', and he said, 'But darling, you don't have to be a man.' My father was happy for me, I think, not only because he considered medicine an honourable profession but because he wanted one of his children to 'make good' in the academic world and I was his last chance; my sister was happily married and my brother a contented young farmer who was blissfully happy on our five-acre Australian poultry farm working from six o'clock in the morning until he dropped from exhaustion at eight at night.

I, on the other hand, was a rather idle but clever little girl of fifteen who came pretty near the top of the class without doing any work worth mentioning. This was not really surprising as I had at the age of thirteen announced firmly that I was going to be a dress designer and so entered the course at school which studied drawing and sewing and cooking and a minimum of the three Rs. Perhaps this accounts for the fact that now, as an Oxford graduate with an MA degree, I still don't know the names of the kings of England, let alone when they lived or what they did, and the other day when I went to Helsinki I had to buy a map to see where it was!

I don't know why I decided to become a doctor but I suspect that it was born out of a mixture of hero-worship for our family doctor, and the reading of the A. J. Cronin's *The Citadel*. (Why *The Keys of the Kingdom* did not inspire me to be a missionary in China I don't know: or perhaps it did because at seventeen I knew quite well that I wanted to be a priest.)

After deciding to become a doctor, I duly entered fourth year of high school with a lot of ambition and very little book learning. The next two years were very difficult ones as I joined up with people who had already done three years of chemistry and higher mathematics. Nevertheless, by dint of very hard work and a great deal of special help, I managed to get University Entrance when I was seventeen. I was jubilant. My chemistry and botany books were ceremoniously burned and I prepared for medical school, only to receive a rude awakening when I found that my marks did not merit a university grant and that my father did not have enough money to pay my fees. Furious and humiliated I returned to school to repeat the year and re-sit the University Entrance.

Again, as has so often happened to me later, this dreaded year was one of the happiest and most important in my life. Instead of setting off on my father's old bicycle, catching the train and then walking half a mile to school, I became a boarder. My brother, ever generous and loving, paid the difference in my fees so that I should not have to spend two hours a day travelling. The combination of the extra time available to me, the companionship (a much nicer group of the girls) and the fact that I was better able to cope with the work, made for a much happier year. I worked with less strain and greater success and was able to take part in the various extra-curricular activities such as debating and acting and weaving and what have you. (Shall I ever forget the smell of the tomato sauce that filled the auditorium as we threw it over Julius Caesar prior to knifing her!)

About halfway through the year something happened to me which I had not expected: I began to wonder if I had a calling to the religious life. I was appalled.

From the moment of decision to become a doctor I had been radiantly happy and now, on the threshold of this brave new world, it seemed that I was being asked to give up all that I loved and embark upon a way of life which appeared from the outside not only stupid but alien and distasteful. It is difficult to explain how it first was. I saw no visions, I heard no voices, but somewhere, deep inside me, I knew that God was calling me to work for him in a special and demanding sort of way. In retrospect I think that I felt the need to do the greatest possible thing with my life, and I had no doubts that this meant a life devoted without reserve to the service of God, and that this in its turn meant the renouncing of marriage, of medicine and of my liberty. It was as simple and as devastating as that. I hadn't asked to be called and I didn't want to be. I had my life all worked out; I was going to be a successful woman doctor, happily combining marriage with a career and a small family.

I took my problem to one of the nuns and then I went, afraid and desperate, to talk to a priest. Now, twenty years later, I see how God arranges things or makes use of circumstances; anyway, however one sees the workings of fate or the gentle hand of the Lord, I was lucky to find a very kind and patient priest who guided and supported me during those turbulent months. I suppose people must have suggested medical mission orders because it was such an obvious solution. I don't remember. I recall only that I was awed and desperate at a summons that I didn't understand and didn't wish to follow.

I said nothing to my father. It was unthinkable; I knew instinctively that my parents would be hurt and totally unable to comprehend my state of mind. (When, many years later, I told them I planned to become a nun I found that my fears were quite justified.)

Somehow, I survived. I prayed a fair bit and I worried a great deal. I knew quite well that this was an all-or-nothing decision, that there was to be no compromise about medicine and anyway I had no desire whatsoever to be a missionary. I didn't know much about poor people in foreign lands and what I did know did not attract me in any way to go and serve them; especially not in a long white habit and veil. Somehow I've always had a phobia about wearing a veil; I've always hated hats and simple sensations like the wind in my hair or the feel of the sandy beach or a lawn under my bare feet have been important to me. I used to find that the place where I prayed best was on the back of my brother's motor bike where, blissfully innocent of crash helmets, we would speed around Sydney. I would love the rush of the wind and be filled with an excitement and joy that moved me to such a love of life and its creator that I felt I should burst.

I could not believe that this same God should have made me with such a zest for life and yet want me to give up those very things which spoke to me most vibrantly of his presence.

When the year ended and I secured University Entrance I was no nearer making a decision so I was advised to go ahead with medicine. Thus, in March 1956 I entered medical school, full of joy at the thought of university and of pursuing a career that appealed to me in every way. It is perhaps interesting to record that apart from the uneasiness about my call to the religious life I never have contemplated any other career; during eight years as a medical student and twelve years as a doctor I have never once repented of my decision. I have complained about working conditions, wept with exhaustion, been afraid, humiliated, desperate, but I have always loved medicine both as an ideal and as a way of life.

In 1958 I transferred from the University of Sydney to Oxford and in 1963 I qualified as a doctor. Twice during these eight years of medical school I had a violent return of the call to be a nun. On both occasions my feelings were just as I have described them earlier: a powerful sense of calling to serve God totally and without condition as to where or how, but accompanied by extreme distaste for the way of life of nuns as I understood it and a terror of losing my liberty. So great was the unrest that came upon me in my second year at Oxford that I made tentative plans to enter the Dominican order and I got as far as telling my parents. The anger of my father as he saw me throwing my life away moved me less than the tears of my mother who could not understand my folly.

Ironically, all this drama was wasted because I fell deeply in love with a fellow medical student, and was thus again thrown into a state of conflict. It was a completely one-sided business and when he became engaged to be married to someone else I took refuge in long hours of work in the Radcliffe where I was beginning my years as a clinical student. These three years passed very happily and in 1963 I qualified as a doctor. After two years residency I decided to follow plastic surgery as a career.

It was during my six months as resident in plastic surgery in Oxford that I met Consuelo. She was a young Chilean doctor who had a British Council scholarship and who was working in an honorary capacity in the department. We became close friends and when our paths crossed again in Leicester two and a half years later we shared a hospital flat. It was through my contact with Consuelo and her friends that I came to know about Chile and I was so fascinated by what she told me that when in 1971 I decided to go abroad, it seemed natural that I should go there.

By 1968 I was working as senior casualty officer in the Leicester Royal Infirmary. It was a good job, well paid and I had a permanent contract; I worked from nine till five and was responsible for the day-to-day running of one of England's biggest casualty departments. After two years, however, I realized that I could not be happy for ever in a job with so much administration and so little surgery; although I was in charge of the department I had no responsibilities within the hospital proper and thus had no opportunity for further training in general surgery, which was a necessary step to a career in plastic surgery.

I gradually realized that, lured by easier hours and better pay, I had gone into a blind alley; and that if I was to do work which was sufficiently technically satisfying to me I must return to the highly competitive field of general surgery and get the second part of my FRCS, the qualification without which it is impossible to work as a surgeon in England. I had a trial run at the exam and though I did quite well in the papers I failed two of the oral exams. I realized that it was not worth sitting again without further surgical experience. This meant returning to the semi-slavery of the junior hospital doctor's life: alternate nights and alternate weekends on duty with no time off in lieu. The other possibility was to go abroad for two years to gain operative experience in an underdeveloped country where there was less competition and easier hours; and then return to England, take the exam and re-enter the plastic surgery world. Daunted by the prospect of the return to so much night work, I decided to seek my fortune in Chile.

So I resigned my job, sold my car and furniture to pay the fare and set off.

2

To Chile

> They went to sea in a sieve,
> they did,
> In a sieve they went to sea,
> In spite of all their friends
> could say,
> On a winter's night and a
> stormy day
> In a sieve they went to sea.
> Edward Lear
> *The Jumblies*

On 4 December 1971 Winston and I sailed from Antwerp on the s.s. *Brandenstein*, a small German cargo boat. Winston is my dog, a chow, and he and I had travelled squashed in my sister's car from Birmingham to Dover and then to Antwerp. My family had to return to England so I embarked alone. I went to the docks by taxi and we just walked along the dock until we found what seemed a very small and old boat called *Brandenstein* and as there was no one around we climbed the gang plank.

The first week at sea was not much fun because of the weather and I wondered if my anti-seasick pills would run out before the calm. But when we entered the Caribbean they erected a wood and canvas pool and we swam several times a day. I have always loved the sea and would be happy sitting for hours on a pile of old rope, watching the green waves and listening to the singing of the Chinese laundry-man who led a solitary existence in a tiny wash-house at the end of the ship.

As we drew nearer to South America the sunsets became more exotic and I drank deeply of the peace and beauty around me. Although I prayed little at this time I was very conscious of the presence of God in the sea and the wind and the sky around me, and I was curiously peaceful as we

neared this brave new world which I was entering so unprepared.

All I knew about Chile was that it was a long, narrow
country flanked by the Andes on one side and the sea on the
other. I also knew that the people spoke Spanish but in my
British way I suppose I thought I'd get by with English
shouted. I knew that Chile had recently elected a marxist
coalition government but it did not occur to me that this
would affect my life in any way. I had always been bored
by politics and had never bothered to educate myself
politically. In England governments came and went but I
had never noticed any difference and I had never used my
right to vote. It may seem incredible that an Oxford
graduate should be so ignorant but I had always found so
many things to occupy my leisure hours and politics had
not been one of them.

Two days before Christmas we arrived in Valparaiso.
There was a heavy storm but, eager to set foot in Chile, I
went ashore with Winston in the pilot's launch. We arrived
on the beach and I found that Valparaiso is a very big port
indeed. I was not able to ask 'Where had the *Brandenstein*
been due to dock at before the storm delayed her?' This was
not something expressible in sign language so the pilot
kindly took me to the office of the shipping agents; they were
likewise confounded but sent me firmly off to the Ministry
of Agriculture to have Winston's entrance into Chile
legalized.

Bewildered, we followed the messenger along the streets
and then went into an enormous office. We waited where
they put us and I had visions of being forcibly parted from
the dog who by now was my only contact with my previous
existence. I thought they would take him away to quaran-
tine or even shoot him for having set paws in such a dirty
city as Buenaventura. After a while a man came out and
said 'What a lovely dog', and patted him and then went
away. After another half hour I was presented with six
copies of an impressive looking paper in Spanish which bore
my name and Winston's and a lot of stamps and we were
dismissed. Heartened by this success I returned to the office

of the shipping agent. I decided that the only thing I could do was return to the ship for the night and hope that there would be someone to meet me the next day when we docked in the official place. In the hour before the launch was due to return to the ship I was walking aimlessly about the streets when quite suddenly I heard my name called. I turned round and was greeted by a friend of Consuelo's who had recognized both me and Winston from a photograph!

My new acquaintance swept me off to have a sandwich. I was confused but delighted to find a friend and an hour later we walked down to the wharf, where I heard a shriek and there was Consuelo. She had been waiting with other friends in a car since early morning. They had spent the day watching my storm-tossed boat unable to dock and it was only because her companion happened to notice Winston and say, 'Oh there's a nice chow', that she looked up and saw me.

3
Consuelo

You become responsible, forever, for what you
have tamed. You are responsible for your rose. . . .
                    Antoine Saint-Exupéry
                        The Little Prince

Consuelo Silva had returned to Chile several months before
me and had bought herself an old and rather decrepit house
not far from the centre of Santiago.

She was the daughter of a Chilean civil engineer who,
after being educated at Harvard, returned to his own
country and eventually became the first Chilean head of the
Chilectra, the American-owned hydro-electric company.
Consuclo's mother had suffered from tuberculosis from the
age of fifteen and had spent six years in a sanatorium in
Switzerland. When she returned to Chile she fell in love and
married against the will of her parents. Stubbornly refusing
to obey medical advice she had three children and died
when she was in her early thirties; Consuelo was then four.
Terrified that his little girls would also die of tuberculosis
their father kept them very sheltered and Consuelo was
taught by governesses until she was sent to an exclusive
English school in Santiago at the age of eleven.

Over the years of our friendship Consuelo had told me
much about her youth. An English education and a lonely
childhood and adolescence had turned her into a passionate
reader. She was a tremendous devotee of Evelyn Waugh,
Winnie the Pooh and P. G. Wodehouse, and during the
years we shared a flat in England had persuaded me to read
books other than the whodunnits which were then my only
fare. She had read widely in the fields of philosophy, politics
and psychology and would patiently explain to me how
Karl Marx wrote his book in the British Museum and how
wars were necessary to countries which sold arms so that

business should be maintained. Consuelo was politically aware, though too idle to work in politics; she tried to explain political theories to me but I got bored and would change the subject and she did not try to convert me. I remember much more the psychology she taught me, especially about human relationships, how precious they were and that they must be protected. An agnostic, Consuelo had her own very strict code of behaviour. She had been greatly traumatized by the apparent suicide of a friend who had been turned away from her door by a protective maid at three o'clock one morning and this had made her intensely vulnerable to people. She had trained as psychiatrist but changed to plastic surgery later because she became too involved with her patients and burdened by their problems. She was a very good surgeon and had a wonderful manner with patients and nursing staff though she tended to be shy with other doctors. She had that rare gift of gentleness with underlings that made the men and women nurses love her; she had also a flair for rapid diagnosis which was both respected and envied by her colleagues.

It is perhaps important to explain at this juncture that although I long to write about many of the people who filled my life during my four years in Chile, that is not possible. Chile is a divided land, a country in a state of siege, and therefore to be mentioned as a friend of someone who has been expelled from the country is, to say the least, undesirable.

Consuelo, however, is dead. There can be no knock on her door at one in the morning, and she cannot be led away to be hurt and humiliated and perhaps killed as she surely would have been had I spoken about her in her lifetime.

Although in some ways an eccentric, she had many qualities which were typical of her countrymen. A passionate anglophile, educated at an English school, she remained Chilean. Intensely proud of her country, of its natural beauty and of its rich resources, she was prouder still of its people. Chileans are naturally generous and welcoming to strangers; there is a very Chilean expression: '*tu casa*' which means simply 'your house', or rather, 'My house is your house, please feel at home.' Although Consuelo had often told me of this hospitality I had not imagined the extent of it before I came to Chile and received an unbelievably warm welcome from her friends. Over the months to come I was to receive unending hospitality and warmth from all the Chileans I met until they became a part of me and I of them.

Consuelo was passionately pro-Allende and her main reason for returning to Chile in 1971 was to be in her country during the time of the Popular Unity Government. Like many doctors she had been forced, whilst a medical student, to face the reality of the bad housing and malnutrition of the majority of Chileans and she was acutely aware that this state of unfair distribution of wealth was tolerated by most middle class Chileans and actively maintained by others. As happened to so many Chilean university students awakened to the injustices in her country, she found in Communism a constructive vision for the future. For a while she worked with the Young Communists but eventually wearied of their discipline and intensity and left them without ever becoming a party member.

Instead, she threw herself into medicine and chose to work in the poorest, dirtiest emergency hospital in Santiago, the '*Posta 3*'. Here she worked happily, treating the *rotos*, 'the broken ones'. Confident of her personal dignity and upper class background she had no need to put on the airs and graces of those less secure. She would madden her more class-conscious colleagues by coming to work on a scooter in jeans and by being on christian name terms with the nurses and orderlies. By nature compassionate, she was particularly gentle with the drunks and prostitutes and would treat them most lovingly of all.

Consuelo was both clever and idle. Had she chosen to study she could have become successful in whatever branch of medicine she chose because she was a 'natural', by which I mean she had a brilliant diagnostic eye combined with clever hands and a lot of common sense.

In 1965 she came to England as a British Council scholar to study plastic surgery. They sent her to the Churchill

Hospital in Oxford and it was there that I found her when I joined the plastic surgical unit as resident in February 1966.

When I moved to the Churchill I was given a week's holiday by a benevolent chief and Consuelo acted as my locum. I had installed myself with all my belongings before departing for Devon and she stayed in my room. It was an oasis. Here were books and a gramophone and records and pictures and rugs and cushions and all the clutter that I firmly moved round the hospitals of England during my resident years.

Had we not been thrown so closely together in our work we would probably never have become friends. I was well accustomed to working in hospitals with a mixture of English and foreigners and automatically sought out my fellow countrymen for friends and politely but firmly ignored the others. When told that I would be working with an Armenian lady doctor in my new job I thought, 'God, how tedious!' and hoped there would be a nice British registrar. Why I should have been given the idea that she was Armenian I still don't know, but what I see now is my own appalling insularity and conviction that wogs began at Calais. At 27 I didn't know anything about Latin America and I didn't particularly want to. If anyone had told me in 1966 that less than ten years later I would be using my surgical training to operate on the leg of a wounded Marxist in a convent of some North American nuns in a country which I had virtually never heard of, I would have told them they were quite mad.

So it was that, quite by chance, I met Consuelo and in her I met Chile. She gradually introduced me to English literature, to classical music and to the poetry of Chile's Pablo Neruda. More important by far, she taught me about people. She made me read *The Little Prince* and taught me to be responsible for my roses. She also made me aware of the existence of injustice and inequality, although I never really understood what she meant until a year after her death when I came face to face with people who were hungry and who had no doctor, and worked alongside colleagues who daily wrote prescriptions without being

troubled by the knowledge that their patients had no money
to buy the drugs or even for the bus home.

I still prefer, as did Consuelo, to work in medicine, but
now I understand more about the difference between those
who are happy to live in a system of self-propagating social
misery and those who are prepared to die to change it.
Knowing her as the peaceful idealist that she was, I am glad
that she is not alive to suffer with Chile now; there are many
Chileans who are being reborn in the fight for their country's
liberty but I cannot visualize Consuelo amongst them, for
she was a thinker, not a fighter.

> The man of action
> Shall have satisfaction,
> The man of peace
> A leaf's release

Douglas Stewart
The Fire on the Snow

4
Cultural Shock

When we leave the limits of the land in which
Our birth certificates sat us,
It does not mean just a change of scene,
But also a change of status.
The Frenchman with his fetching beard,
The Scot with his kilt and sporran,
One moment he may a native be,
And the next may find him foreign.

Ogden Nash

I don't know quite what I imagined I would do on arrival in Chile: work as a doctor I suppose. I was a good doctor, and Chile needed doctors, so somehow I'd manage; but it wasn't like that at all. Consuelo took me with her to the *posta* (the emergency hospital) to do a night and there I saw the sheer impossibility of it: they didn't speak English and I didn't speak Spanish, and that was that. We could smile and shake hands and I could watch what was going on and try to guess from the look of someone what ailed them, but there was zero communication. There was another factor, too, which I hadn't reckoned on—the different pattern of disease. I had only read about half the cases that were being treated here: there were people with advanced tuberculosis, alcoholics in terminal cirrhosis, people under forty dying of pneumonia because they were undernourished, men with stab wounds in the heart, bullet wounds in the head and so on. I, who had been in charge of a similar department in England, was completely useless in Santiago.

And yet they were so patient with me and practised what English they knew, and took me into the operating theatre to assist and explained to me how their system worked and tried to enquire about how it was in England. I was humiliated and desperate and marvelled at my incredible folly in leaving the security of a country and a system that I knew for this strange and alien land.

At least in the house I was needed. Consuelo was doing overtime work to raise money to pay off the mortgage, so it fell to me to run the place and manage the workmen. Here again I was in deep water but, determined to survive at all costs, I got by. There was a supermarket one block away and every day I would solemnly go to buy the food. We had no fridge, for the one I had brought from England was broken, and in the hottest part of the Chilean summer the difficulties of catering were considerable. We were desperately short of money. In Chile the National Health Service does not pay its doctors until they have worked for about four to five months. This is due to some curious piece of bureaucracy but it has the distinct value to the employer that the salary when eventually paid is worth about 25 per cent of what it would have been at the time it was due. Consuelo, having been working only three months, had not yet received her salary. She was living on money earned from occasional private practice or borrowed from friends. There was no question of a bank loan to someone so impecunious but she borrowed money from a moneylender at enormous interest.

Not long after I arrived I realized that being in debt was making Consuelo quite desperate and the thought of what she owed to the moneylender was stopping her from sleeping. I had brought with me all the money I had: 900 American dollars, neatly stitched into the collar of my anorak. This was riches, and sold on the black market would have kept me in food and spending money until I could earn; but I decided it was better to help Consuelo get out of debt and, saving fifty dollars for an emergency, we went together and paid off the moneylender. I think that day I learned the meaning of the word usury. The moneylender was a fat lady with an oily way of speaking and I was happy that Consuelo need have no more to do with her.

Although this nightmarish debt was settled we still lived from hand to mouth. We had no furniture except two deck chairs and two stools and a table which I made out of an old cooker with a sheet of formica-covered chipboard (brought from England) on top. We had one bed and a mattress on the floor and the rugs and pictures and cushions which I had brought.

When the kitty was empty Consuelo would go cap in hand to her friends to borrow enough for the week. To add to the cost of housekeeping was the feeding of the dogs. Consuelo had brought her two dogs with her by air from England. Joshua was a large, black, handsome and very stupid chow and Jericho his mate was a fat, clever and charming bitch. They lived together with Winnie in a state of intermittent mutual tolerance and respect.

Feeding these beasts was no mean work. I discovered that pedigree dogs in Chile were kept by rich people with maids and were fed a carefully prepared diet of cooked meat and vegetables with rice or spaghetti. There is no canned dog food and no dog biscuit but the owner does not miss this because the dog's food is lovingly (or crossly) prepared out of sight and the dog is presented, rather like a Victorian child, when required by his owner. The *quiltro* or mongrel dog of the poor has long since adapted to live on whatever he can find and survives. I could not afford meat so fed the dogs on fish.

In addition to my duties as housekeeper and kennel maid I was overseer of the workmen. Consuelo had chosen her house well, centrally placed and on the bus route, but it was greatly in need of repair. It had belonged to an architect and had been lived in by his elderly mother and it seemed that nothing had been done in the way of maintenance for many years. When I arrived José was installed and the roof was off. In Chile it does not rain between the months of November and February so we had some time in hand. José was a general handyman but more especially a plumber and 'gas fitter', which meant basically that he was a man who understood about pipes and cement and corrugated iron roofs. He worked with Juan, his young assistant, and the three of us soon became good friends. I learned the key words for bricks, sand, nails, cement and tiles and, firmly getting my bearings by the block of flats near the house, would set out to buy materials.

Little by little I established a beat, always within sight of the tower block near my house. It is hard to explain the terror I had of getting lost because of my inability to enquire the way home or understand the directions which well-meaning people would give me. I became like a child, afraid to take a bus because it might not stop where I wanted it to, and my world was limited by the distance I could walk and still see the purple tower.

A kind friend came every day for three months and gave me private lessons in Spanish in exchange for English conversation and slowly I began to communicate with the patient tradespeople of our district. My first 'friend' was José the plumber. He would arrive at eight when I was making my breakfast, Consuelo having left for work at seven thirty. I don't know what he had for breakfast, but I suspect it was very little because he would radiantly tuck away a plate of scrambled eggs before he began his day's work. José was a man of about forty. I learned that he was married and had two children but as practically all our communication was in sign language I was never learned more than that about his background. He was a gentle, charming little man and, practically friendless, I lavished attention on him which he enjoyed. He seemed to be a good worker, arriving early and toiling till dusk, but he would have strange periods of absence about every three to four weeks. I remember vividly how he dug up the tiled floor of the bathroom one day and then didn't come back for a fortnight. I didn't understand it at the time and Consuelo, apart from cursing daily as she fell into the hole, did nothing about him. I realize now that he was an intermittent alcoholic; he would stay 'dry' for three weeks or a month and then go on a week's bender and, after a further week's convalescence, return to work.

There are many workers such as José in Chile. They live in tiny shanty town houses with their wives and children and rise at six to travel in crowded buses to be at work at eight. They go home at six or seven to a harassed wife and wailing children and often turn to wine for comfort and oblivion. Wine in Chile is good and plentiful and a litre of cheap wine costs about the same as litre a of milk. Drunkenness is both a product of and an escape from subhuman living conditions and Chile has an incidence of cirrhosis second only to France.

In February I was invited for a week to the south of the country. Consuelo could not come so I went off with two of her friends to stay on a farm near Osorno. The south is breathtakingly lovely. In contrast to Santiago there is heavy rainfall and acres of rich green land, well farmed by wealthy, skilled farmers mainly of German descent. For me it was a fairy-tale land with snow-capped volcanoes and still lakes. I could visualize myself working as a country doctor in such an area. We spent a happy week with generous hosts and I thought that their house and garden, full of hydrangeas, was like my own family house thirty years ago when there were maids and gardeners for the asking.

The visit gave me an insight into the extent of the wealth of certain Chileans, for our hosts owned five farms, an island, two aeroplanes and five motor launches and ran a quiet little tourist business for rich Americans who came to shoot the deer with which they kept their island well stocked.

After a week we drove back to Santiago along dirt roads until we and all our luggage were covered with fine red dust.

Back in Santiago I returned to my routine of shopping, and Spanish lessons and sank daily deeper into my slough of despond. In March Mary Jane, another friend of Consuelo's, arrived from England to spend six months studying for a higher exam in medicine. In theory we should have been company for each other but it didn't work out that way as she studied all night and slept all day so I just got lonelier and lonelier. I took to reading as an escape and would read a novel a day; luckily Consuelo had a library of about a thousand paperbacks so I could have survived in this way for some time.

In April, however, I was taken in hand when Consuelo's friends, berating her for her neglect of me, sent me to work with the only doctor they knew who spoke English. He worked in a nearby hospital. The fact that he was a cardiologist and I a half-trained plastic surgeon mattered nothing to these kind laymen; we were all doctors to them, so I became an honorary member of the best cardiology unit in Santiago and from that day things started to look up.

5

Hospital San Borja

For to be idle is to become a stranger unto the seasons,
and to step out of life's procession that marches in
majesty and proud submission towards the infinite.
Kahlil Gibran, *The Prophet*

The Hospital San Francisco Borja is an old colonial style
hospital in the centre of Santiago and when I went to work
there I was both appalled and enchanted by what I found.
It is built around a central patio of grass with palm trees
and bushes and there are miles of covered tiled passages
from which the wards lead off. By English standards it was
all very primitive and not really very clean but the actual
standard of medicine was high and to my surprise I found
myself working alongside men who had done their post-
graduate study anywhere from the National Heart Hospital
in London to the Johns Hopkins or Massachusets General
in the USA or the Karolinska Institute in Stockholm.

I was attached in an honorary capacity to a team of
general physicians and worked in particular with one of
them who spoke English. Every day we went on ward
rounds; he examined his patients and taught his students
and patiently translated what seemed important for me.
Luckily I am an enthusiastic physician so although it was
six years since I had done any internal medicine I was delighted to be faced with patients again and to indulge in the
intellectual gymnastics which are part of the diagnostic
process. Always proud and a shameless name-dropper, I
pretended to understand more than I did and, when in
doubt, would mention the name of one of my old chiefs in
Oxford, all of whom were world famous figures. I was
treated with great deference, it being assumed that an
Oxford graduate must be learned, and I got away with a lot
in those early days.

Fate provided me with a friend in the form of Liza, a delightful German girl who was also working in an honorary capacity. She however was quids in because after three months she spoke very good Spanish and with a teutonic determination attended all lectures for the students and kept copious notebooks. I discovered that she also spoke English, French, Italian, Russian and Indonesian so I reckoned that she was out of my class and refused to compete.

Used to a system where housemen spoke only to registrars, registrars to senior registrars, senior registrars to consultants and consultants only to God, I was captivated by the classless society of our unit. Later I was to realize that this was a rather special pro-Allende unit I had fallen into, but at the time I thought that this was just Chilean medicine. There was a spirit of friendship between the doctors which was something quite new to me. From being 'Doctor Cassidy', or at the best, 'Sheila', I became '*la Gringuita*', 'the little English one'. I should explain that all English and Americans and often Europeans are known as *gringos* in Chile; it is, I suppose, the equivalent of 'wog', but is used as a term of endearment. Accustomed also to a shake of the hand (perhaps) upon being appointed to a job, I now found myself in a society where I was hugged and kissed by anyone whom I had not seen for a few days.

After a month 'working' with my physician friend he decided I would be better off in surgery and I was therefore apprenticed to a lady plastic surgeon. Although firmly convinced of the place of women in medicine I have secretly always preferred working with men. Doctor Margarita however was a honey. She was a happily married lady about twelve years my senior and she adopted me. Although officially a plastic surgeon there was no plastic surgery department in San Borja, and as Margarita enjoyed gynaecology and general surgery she did more or less what she fancied. She worked very hard, though in a slightly scatty way, spending much of her life in transit between the ward, her out-patient office and the theatre. I would trail after her and was always losing her so that the patients, fascinated by my antics would call out, 'Have you lost your mummy, dear?'

It was with Margarita that I was forced to start speaking Spanish. She spoke a little English, having worked for a year in America, but she was only prepared to use it in emergencies. Painfully, therefore, I began to stammer out a few phrases and would write the progress notes as we did our ward round. When a new patient arrived I would sometimes be deputed to take the history; this was agony so they usually only gave me people who had something very simple. Even so I would get into trouble: there is a story for which I became famous in the hospital and which loses its charm when told in English; while interrogating a middle-aged lady to ask her if her varicose ulcer itched I asked her instead if she had a penis! She went very red and so did I and then the whole ward of fifty ladies who had been listening spellbound to my performance collapsed with laughter.

After a month of working with Margarita I spent a night working at the emergency hospital with Consuelo. I was delayed for my work at the San Borja by the fact that I had stuffed my nightgown into my handbag and then got it irrevocably caught up in the zip. I carried it into breakfast and the entire team involved itself in my plight; artery clips were sent for and after about half an hour of concerted effort the nightgown was freed, though at the expense of the zip. (I could perhaps mention that the zip 'injury' is a common feature of casualty departments in countries where zips have replaced buttons and my friends were delighted to employ their skill to save damage to an uncomplaining nightdress rather than a mortified and hysterical patient!)

So it was that, that day when I arrived breathless at the San Borja, Margarita told me, 'Thank God you've come. I've lent you to Professor U., my old chief, for a month. You're to go at once to the INDISA.

The Clinica INDISA is a tall, modern, black building built alongside the Hotel Sheraton in the rich residential area of Santiago. Its name means Diagnostic Institute and it is a highly efficient complex of doctors' offices and facilities for diagnosis such as x-ray units and laboratories of all kinds. It is here and in other similar clinics that the rich and the upper middle class of Chile receive their medical

care. Probably the most famous of the clinics is the Santa
Maria which runs an in-patient service, a twenty-four hour
emergency service for domiciliary medicine, and boasts
such refinements as a coronary care unit for those with
myocardial infraction (heart attack). These clinics had a
very different clientele from the San Borja. Tall, well-
dressed men and women would wait in carpeted lounges on
soft chairs of leather and chrome, while in San Borja there
was always a milling throng of short, darker-skinned people,
either standing or sitting on hard, narrow benches. Small
wonder, really, that many doctors preferred their well paid
afternoons of dealing in a leisurely way with articulate,
cultured people to the hectic mornings with an endless
stream of the 'broken ones'.

Margarita's order to go to the INDISA put me into a
state of acute panic; I slammed the door of my locker with
coat, keys and money inside it and then raced frantically
about looking for someone to lend me the bus fare. Eventually I arrived panting at the clinic and was shown up to see
the great man. I was overwhelmed at the warmth of his
greeting and believed that I had found a new friend. He was
a highly skilled professor in plastic surgery who had retired
from hospital work and now did only cosmetic surgery in
the mornings. I worked as his assistant for five weeks and in
the first halcyon days I luxuriated in his good favour and
hospitality. The first weekend I was invited by his family
to their country house and had my second taste of gracious
Chilean living. Like many good plastic surgeons he was a
true artist and his house, an old colonial one the restoration
of which he had personally supervised, was quite lovely.
There were endless spacious rooms with wide stone fire-
places and beamed ceilings; the colours were a dream, the
natural beams being highlighted by a deep blue-green roof.

For a weekend we lived the grand life. Three course
meals were served by white-coated servants and in the day
time we went riding on fine horses which were brought, im-
peccably groomed and saddled, to the door to await our
convenience. In the evening the professor liked to play
bridge or chess but as my knowledge of and aptitude for

both was distinctly limited I was not an asset. The whole family spoke English, but though we conversed amicably I never felt totally at home and was happy to return to my rather primitive establishment in Santiago. Although I was invited again the following weekend I declined and as the weeks progressed my relations with the professor broke down. Like the passing of an Indian summer into autumn and then into winter his manner to me changed; I suppose he wearied of me, or found that he had been misinformed as to my importance. Whatever the cause, he became first cool and then openly unpleasant. I shall never forget the day when, scrubbing alongside him prior to operating he said, 'Is it not the custom all over the world that the assistant scrubs before the chief and awaits him in the theatre?' As I had been standing by to learn and assist while he prepared the patient's hair I found this hard but from then on I made sure that I arrived well before him and was standing silently in a corner when he entered the operating theatre. (Incidentally this type of servile behaviour has long since ceased in England.)

The more intimidated I became the earlier I arrived and one day a waiting patient started to tell me that she thought she was allergic to local anaesthetic. I was listening to her story when suddenly I heard a cry of rage from the great man, 'How dare you talk to one of my patients?' After that my life became a nightmare. Terrified of his wrath I became more and more stupid and he berated me daily up to the point of rapping my knuckles with instruments when he found my assistance inadequate. Finally, after a particularly humiliating morning when I had fainted in the operating room, he gave me the sack as his regular assistant was returning from America. I have never been dismissed from a position before or since but that was one of the happiest days of my life!

I returned to the San Borja to work with Margarita and we became firm friends. She took a great personal interest in me and worried about my health as I was repeatedly ill with gastro-enteritis and was losing weight at an alarming rate. At first I was rather pleased to get slim but after a while it ceased to be a joke; my bones stuck out so that they hurt and I was forced to seek medical aid. At first I was found to be suffering from amoebas and was treated, but I continued to get thinner and thinner and was sent from specialist to specialist. For the two years that followed I was subjected to a battery of tests many of which were both painful and undignified. Everyone was exasperated by the fact that I neither died nor got better. Eventually in 1974 I began to gain weight and recovered completely. Although many diagnoses were put forward even I never really knew what had ailed me.

By June 1972 I was still working, unpaid, with Margarita and my prospects of paid employment seemed very distant. I was eventually forced to acknowledge the fact (which incidentally had been made abundantly clear to me in London) that one could not work as a doctor in Chile without a Chilean medical degree. With the help of a kind doctor I began negotiations to 'revalidate my title'. I had had the wit to bring my Oxford diploma and my various certificates with me to produce evidence of my medical training begun some fifteen years earlier. All my certificates from the earliest days at the University of Sydney were required to be translated and the signatures legalized. This curious process of the legalization of signatures was something quite foreign to me though in a country chained by its own bureaucracy it is common practice.

Eventually, after about six weeks of to-ing and fro-ing, my papers were in order. I was then advised not to place my application for consideration as the law governing the length of time foreign doctors had to study before their titles were recognized was about to be changed and those in the know were sure that the time period was to be shortened. Week followed week. Every Thursday I awaited the decision of the committee but either something prevented them from meeting or they would fail to consider the matter. I grew more and more desperate and impatient and by August I demanded that my papers be presented.

Just how the Latin American way of life has led to a system of *mañana* in which days drift into weeks and weeks into months is hard enough to explain now but it was quite impossible in 1972 to explain truthfully to my father the manner in which I was frittering away my time. How could I tell him that after nearly a year I was still not earning enough to keep myself, that I weighed seven stone and was working as an intern in general medicine? Worse still was the impossibility of explaining that though I was working and living under conditions far lower than anything I had experienced before, I was falling in love with Chile and had no intention of returning home.

For my first six months in Chile, although everyone around me talked and argued politics non-stop, I was too busy fighting my own private battle for survival to take any interest. Consuelo had explained to me that Allende's government was trying to bring about in five years the sort of socialism which we had gained in England after a hundred years, and as I was fully in agreement with socialized medicine, education and all forms of social security I was all for it. It never occurred to me, however, to read the papers or try to understand what was happening politically in the country. As most of the people I mixed with were either poor people or belonged to the intellectual left I got the impression that everyone was united in building the new Chile.

Half way through 1972, however, came the first big anti-government strike, and to my amazement more than half the doctors at the hospital simply left their patients and went home. Never in the fifteen years since I had entered medical school had any doctor of my acquaintance considered going on strike and I could not believe what I saw. Quite unconcerned with the reasons for the strike I joined those doctors and students who banded together to keep the medical services going. I found that the medical care in my part of the city was being organized by a group of final year medical students. I offered myself to them to help in whatever way I could and was sent to run a surgical out-patient clinic in a nearby hospital. Driven there by jeep because there were no buses I found my way to the clinic but there was already someone there so I was deployed to run the orthopaedic clinic. My knowledge of orthopaedics is limited but I have many years of experience in accident work so working entirely on physical signs and with x-rays I treated the patients who came my way. I forget now how long I worked at this but it was nearly three weeks before the strike ended. The doctors returned, relaxed from their rest, and life went on more or less as before. I marvelled at the maintenance of good relations between men who had worked themselves to exhaustion and others who had calmly sat by doing nothing.

6

Life under Allende,
September 1972–1973

'To create a new society in which men can satisfy their
material and spiritual needs, without causing the ex-
ploitation of others.'

Salvador Allende
'The Purpose of Our Victory' —
Inaugural address in the National
Stadium, Santiago, 5th November 1970

This book does not pretend to be a political treatise and
those wishing to understand in depth the circumstances
which led to the overthrow of Allende's government have
ample books at their disposal. What I relate is simply what
I saw, what I heard and how it seemed to me; and for all my
ignorance of politics and general naiveté – I was there. I
lived in Santiago, in an ordinary middle class area and
worked in a state hospital for the two years before the coup
and the two years after it until I was thrown out. My view
therefore is not the coldly analytical one of the unbiased
professional political historian, studying dispassionately why
the first democratically elected marxist government in
history failed; neither is it the passionate view of the left-
wing Chilean revolutionary who can only write in the
politically loaded terms of 'the class struggle', 'the bour-
geoisie' and 'the proletariat'. It is simply the eyewitness
account of an English woman doctor who lived there.

I cannot of course present the whole story either; this is,
as it were, a series of Instamatic colour photographs of *my*
Chile.

As 1972 progressed, day-to-day life became more
difficult. There were already shortages of certain goods
when I arrived but these shortages did not affect us greatly
and because we understood why they happened, we toler-

ated them good-humouredly. There was for example, a shortage of pine. Chile is rich in pine and it is a very cheap wood. During the time of the Allende government it was always in short supply because more people were building houses; this meant that I couldn't afford to build myself a bookcase: but what was my bookcase against a man's house? Likewise, beef was hard to come by. It is said that the farmers in the south of Chile, when Allende came into power, knowing that prices would be controlled and farms expropriated, moved their cattle over the border into Argentina and sold them. I cannot vouch for the truth of this, but I know that meat prices were pegged and beef was therefore within the reach of the poor people and supplies rapidly ran low.

Middle class Chileans are accustomed to eating beef every day and they did not take kindly to this shortage. It was because of this scarcity that the famous saucepan marches began: middle class housewives banded together and marched through the streets banging their empty saucepans in protest because they had nothing to put in them. The fact that they could have filled their saucepans with chicken, mutton or any one of a dozen varieties of fish was immaterial. They wanted beef and did not care that if there was no beef for them it was because other Chileans were buying it! Chileans who for generations had eaten so badly that they were shorter in stature and lower in intelligence than their richer brothers. Statistics and tables are tedious enough for doctors and unintelligible to laymen; it its however well documented that the heights and weights of the children of the upper class residential area of Santiago are the same age for age as those of children in North America. The heights and weights of children of corresponding ages in the peripheral areas of Santiago fall progressively away from the average as the areas become poorer. This, put in simple terms, means that children who are undernourished are shorter and weigh less than their luckier brothers and if this undernourishment is prolonged and severe they also grow up stupid. A simple but significant observation that I made in Chile was that my back ached when I worked in the kitchen; all the sinks and working surfaces on sale in Chile are lower built than in Europe because the people who work in the kitchens – the maids – are lower in stature than Europeans. Maids, as a class, are women of short stature because they come from an underprivileged, undernourished society.

It is hard for those who have never been to a third world country to imagine the degree of poverty in which human beings can live and love and laugh and have their being. We can read about it and we can see photographs but it is not until we see with our own eyes that it becomes credible. This dawning knowledge is a terrible thing and I believe that it drives men to madness: either to the madness of saying that it is not true or the madness which drives them to atonement and total giving of leisure and even of life.

It is not the sight of a house with a dirt floor which is home to a family of eight that drives the truth like a knife deep into the heart; it is the sudden dawning realization that the people who live there are not members of some strange tribe or race from another world, but that they are people who feel hunger and cold and weariness just as we do.

These are strong words, perhaps a little melodramatic; but how else are we to explain the co-existence, cheek by jowl, of comfortable living with abject poverty? I remember that a friend, a young lawyer who is a good man and a practising Christian, said to me, when we were discussing my proposed trip home to see my father, 'Go to Miami and Bermuda, it's so beautiful, but don't go to Peru, the poverty is so depressing.'

I know another Chilean lawyer, son of a rich family, who when he graduated worked free for more than a year giving legal aid to women who could not get their husbands to support the children. Each day he cleared his desk of cases and each morning there was a similar pile, so after a year he looked for ways to treat the root of their problems rather than the problems themselves. Those Chileans who have vision speak harshly of the '*parche*', the patch upon the old garment, and are determined to re-shape their land so that men shall have equal opportunity.

So it is that Chile is a divided land; a land of those who are happy with the status quo as it has been for three hundred years and those who see hunger and malnutrition, illiteracy and subhuman housing as a sore upon the face of their land that must be healed or cut out.

Chile is a country rich in natural resources and should be able to look forward to a future in which all its people can live and work in conditions fitting to human beings. The greatest natural resource is copper and Chile is one of the world's most important suppliers of this metal. The copper mines of Chile were owned by American companies until they were nationalized under the government of Salvador Allende. This nationalization of the nation's major source of wealth was a momentous step and one which not only was unanimously accepted by Congress but which has not been rescinded by the present government. This was the year of copper and Chile 'put on long trousers' as the posters told us. It was to be the beginning of freedom; the freedom to own their own natural resources and either work them or sell them at a fair price.

America, however, was not happy. I do not feel competent to discuss in detail the extent of the involvement of the CIA in the downfall of the Allende Government but it would not be right in this context to omit mention of the ITT documents. In 1972 documents were made available to the press: these were photocopies of letters and memos of high level interchange in the United States discussing what could be done to prevent Allende's victory in the elections and, in the case of his victory, how his fall could be achieved. But in 1972 in Chile I knew nothing about multinational corporations and the problem of developed nations owning the natural resources in developing countries, buying the products cheaply and then working them to sell at an immense profit. The Chile I saw was a vibrant country, alive with hope and the challenge of building a new land, and of bridging the centuries-old gulf between rich and poor. There was a whole art in the Popular Unity Government; the battered brick walls of Santiago's buildings were covered with brilliant posters – posters which spoke of union between all men who toiled: between doctors and farmers, miners, school teachers, women, house builders, artists and soldiers. The posters were a radiant expression of the hope which swept the country and allowed people to eat fish when they preferred meat and put honey or saccharine in their coffee because there was no sugar. There were the songs too – young folk composers, especially Angel Parra, son of one of Chile's most famous folk singers, and Victor Jara, son of a peasant farmer, were leaders in the new art. The popular music of Chile was written for its people by its people and the words were rich in meaning and hope. *Venceremos* remains for me one of the most powerful of the songs of this epoch.

> *Desde el hondo crisol de la patria*
> *Se levanta el clamor popular.*
> *Se anuncia la nueva alborada,*
> *Todo Chile comienza a cantar.*

> From the deep crucible of our country
> There rises the cry of her people.
> The new dawn is announced
> All of Chile begins to sing.

> *Venceremos, venceremos!*
> *Mil cadenas habrá que romper.*
> *Venceremos, venceremos!*
> *La miseria sabemos vencer.*

> We shall overcome!
> There are a thousand chains to break,
> But we shall overcome.
> We know how to conquer our wretchedness.

Pablo Neruda, one of Chile's two Nobel prize winners in poetry, wrote verse for this historic moment in his country's history; an older man, who had seen and suffered much, and who knew perhaps better than the younger writers that the road would not be an easy one, wrote three months before the coup:

I do not want my country to be divided,

I do not want it bloodstained by seven daggers,
I want the leafy light of Chile to shine
On the new house that we have put together.
I do not want my country to be divided,
I do not want it bloodstained by seven daggers.

I do not want my country to be divided.
There is room for all of us in this land of mine,
And let those who feel themselves to be prisoners
Take that old melody and go far away.
The rich were always foreigners amongst us,
Let them go off to Miami with their aunts.
I do not want my country to be divided,
Take that old melody and go far away.

I do not want my country to be divided.
There is room for all of us in this land of mine.
I am staying here to sing along with the workers
In this new history and geography.
I am staying here to sing along with the workers
In this new history and geography.

These words were set to music and sung by Victor Jara,
Chile's leading folk singer who was battered to death in the
Santiago football stadium two days after the coup. The
record of his voice singing it is a poignant reminder of the
spirit of Allende's Chile.

I think what most moved me when I arrived in Chile was
the spirit and the art of the university students. Outside all
the faculty buildings and on many of the grey walls of the
city were painted the slogans of the day. This sounds offensive but it was not so. Painted with love and care by young
artists in a multitude of brilliant colours were murals: words
and pictures of hope for Chile. Through the centre of
Santiago there runs the Mapocho river; once a mighty
torrent with massive stone walls built by the Spaniards to
contain it, the flow is now small after an earthquake which
changed the course of the river. The brick walls, built by the
Conquistadores centuries before and presenting a blank un-
lovely face, were transformed with immense and beautiful

murals by a youth afire with a passion not for their own pleasure but for the building of justice in their country.

This was the bloodless revolution of a doctor who had captured the hearts of so many of his people, rich and 'poor, young and old. This was the year of construction: the building of houses, schools, clinics, roads, and of peace. The effort was to be a united one and school children and professors spent their weekends in the shanty towns teaching the illiterate to read or their holidays in camps building houses. I remember vividly how moved I was by the account of something which happened before my arrival: in the winter of 1971 there was a rare event in the city of Santiago. It snowed. This may not seem very dramatic, but in a country where thousands of people live in unheated, windowless houses made of planks of wood or even cardboard, it was a national disaster. Allende closed the schools a month early and the children of Santiago went out to help their brothers save and rebuild their shattered houses.

By September 1972, I was working officially in the Hospital San Borja, as intern in charge of the small ward where private patients were cared for. After six years of surgery I had returned to work in internal medicine and was very happy. This was part of the process of retraining to enable me to get the Chilean medical degree and therefore work on equal terms with Chilean doctors. They were exhausting, hilarious days. When my British-style dedication to duty (partly natural and partly born of the determination to make good) became known the little ward which had been a place of convalescence turned into an acute medical unit. I worked from 8 a.m. to 10 p.m. and found the days short; the change from working in my own tongue, in a branch of medicine with which I was familiar, to running a ward full of gravely ill patients whom I could barely understand was taxing to say the least. The simple task of history taking, the eliciting of the relevant medical information, which would normally have taken me ten to fifteen minutes, now took up to four hours as my patients and I laboured to understand each other. They were wonderful: trusting and endlessly tolerant and compassionate as I sat by their beds asking questions in my laboured Spanish. Never once did they laugh at me; it is true that we laughed together about many things but they treated me with respect and affection and made my baptism into Chilean medicine a pleasure. It was not until several months later, when I thought I had mastered medical Spanish, that I realized that I was speaking a frightful mixture of coloquial Chilean, a good deal of which had been acquired from my workmen.

And so it was that as the weeks turned into months I became used to the Chilean way of life, or rather, my version of it. For the country as a whole things became gradually more difficult. The shortages of vital consumer goods and spare parts for machinery were beginning to hurt everyone. By the end of 1972 nearly everything that was essential to life was in short supply. Meat was a luxury rarely seen, for although small quantities did arrive in the shops the queues were immense and it did not seem worth while. Queueing became a way of life; I became accustomed to spending up to four hours queueing for half a litre of oil or a packet of detergent. The entire car park of the supermarket would be filled with people waiting patiently in line, and they overflowed into the street and around the block so often it would take a while to find where the queue began.

In the different urban areas people banded together to try to stop black market trading and ensure that goods were fairly distributed. Each zone of the city and suburbs was divided into areas. The people who lived in a given area were entitled to enrol and then, as goods became available, they were distributed according to the size and composition of the family group. This work required long hours of packaging and distribution of food but professional and working class men and women worked hard to ensure fair distribution of food and essential commodities.

Slowly my struggle to get the Chilean medical title was being won. In April and May I worked in the obstetric unit of the San Borja and was very happy to refresh my knowledge of midwifery. The standard of treatment was high and I learned much from the doctors and midwives. As in all medicine in Chile, however, there was the existence side by side of the old world and the new. Attending a special 'high risk' ante-natal clinic I listened for the first time to the foetal heart magnified by an electronic stethoscope, a magic sound like a galloping horse. In another part of the hospital, however, there was the ward for the treatment of septic abortions, for in a country with the most up-to-date equipment there are still uneducated women who died from blood poisoning because they try to abort themselves with sticks of parsley.

In March 1973 there was a general election and Allende retained his power, but as the year unfolded life became progressively more difficult because of the ever increasing scarcity of consumer goods and the growing unrest among a large sector of the middle class.

Every night at ten o'clock a group of well dressed women gathered to protest at the food shortages, making strident the night air with the clatter of saucepan lid upon saucepan. At home we marvelled at the selfishness of people who could not understand that it was better for all to eat meat one or two days a week than for a small group to have it every day while others had none. Little did we realize that these women were so convinced of their right to a privileged position that they were prepared to defend it at all costs.

7

The Beginning of the End

I do not want my country to be divided,
I do not want it bloodstained by seven daggers.
                                   Pablo Neruda, 1973

By July 1973, eighteen months after my arrival in Chile, I seemed well on the way to getting the Chilean medical title. I had completed four months as a resident in internal medicine, four months in surgery, two months in obstetrics and had only to complete two months in paediatrics before I would be free to return to my training in general and plastic surgery. The future seemed bright and I could see myself working in the plastic surgery unit of one of the big Santiago teaching hospitals.

Although the later course of events was to deflect me from this ambition I am still fascinated by plastic surgery and find it one of the most exciting and satisfying of the many branches of surgery. Plastic and reconstructive surgery is not confined, as so many people believe, to cosmetic work. It is a highly skilled speciality which requires a combination of great manual dexterity, immense patience and an ability to improvise and design to a degree rarely demanded in more routine general surgery. The difficulty of plastic surgery is at the same time its challenge and its fascination. The reconstruction of a face after an accident or the removal of a facial cancer is an artistic feat requiring the joint skills of carpenter, sculptor and seamstress combined with the vision of a painter.

Although I had always been attracted by the challenge of rebuilding the broken and the burned and visualized my future working in facial reconstruction and in hand surgery, I enjoyed the cosmetic side of plastic surgery also. People, women in particular, want so much to present a pleasant

face to the world, so that if by an hour's or two hours' work
one can transform an ugly woman into a beautiful one, as
for example by reducing to normal the size of an abnormally
large nose or breasts, then this is immensely worthwhile.
Likewise the face lift, a relatively easy operation, can make
a woman look ten years younger, and the joy and morale
boost that she gets is worth more than a hundred hair dos or
new dresses. After all, in medicine we are concerned with
the whole person, and the interdependence of health and
happiness are well known. It is also, I think, good for the
surgeon, who spends much of his time with people so
deformed that he can only turn monsters into ugly people,
to have the satisfaction and the privilege of adding as it were
the final touches to the production of a masterpiece.

So much for plastic surgery. Ten years after receiving my
Oxford degree I was back at school, and instead of brushing
up subjects at which I had always been reasonably good and
with which I had never totally lost touch, I now had to
return to a branch of medicine which I had always disliked
and never been good at and which I had thankfully abandoned eleven years before.

Paediatrics, the study of the diseases of children, is traditionally a field of medicine in which women prosper. Most
girl medical students fall with delight upon the sick babies
and dandle them on their knees, and coo to them expertly
and are rewarded by smiles and gurgles. I, however, had no
such reaction. The youngest child of an eccentric mother
who openly preferred dogs to babies, I had never so much
as changed a nappy and was always terrified of dropping the
offspring which my proud friends laid so lovingly in my
arms. Not only was I as bad or worse than a man in feeling
acutely ill at ease with small children, but I have always
been very bad indeed at mental arithmetic and, curious as
it may seem, the care of children requires endless multiplica-
tion and division either on the back of envelopes or prefer-
ably in the head. Because they are so small, babies and
children up to the age of two are fed, watered and dosed
according to weight and therefore everything has to be
calculated in grammes or millilitres per pound or kilo of

baby. For someone with a mathematical weakness the calculation of the amount of sodium required for a dehydrated baby and then the deciding what sort of salt solution and how much it needs and how quickly to give it, seems to me a feat for professors of higher mathematics. Couple with this the interrogation of a patient who screams without ceasing, won't answer your simplest question, requires two strong women to hold him down, is constantly wet or dirty and who has veins so minute that they seem to require the eyesight and patience and dexterity of a Chinese embroidress to find them, and you will have my vision of the horrors entailed in the management of sick babies.

To do my paediatric studies I had to journey to a hospital some forty minutes' distance from my house. Instead of walking in a leisurely way to the San Borja, I had to catch one bus to the centre of Santiago and another for several miles to the other side of the city in order to reach the small but well organized hospital for children. The change in my life when I began work in this hospital was much greater than I had anticipated. The bus journey alone added a whole new dimension to my life.

Difficult as it may be to believe, I had never travelled much by bus before going to Chile. As a schoolgirl in Australia I rode my father's old bike to the station. When I qualified as a doctor I bought my father's old car and for the next eight years of my life it served me as a sort of travelling home, suitcase and overcoat. I had little pride in it as a possession but valued it greatly as the symbol and means of my emancipation. In Chile, however, a car was out of the question. The multiple demands of driving on the wrong side of the road in four-lane traffic in an eighteen-year-old Ford (Consuelo's father's car) was too much for me. Yet it was over a year before I had the courage to go alone on a bus.

Not only did these bus journeys to the hospital teach me how different is the way of life of the car owner from that of the man in the street but I went daily through one of the poor suburbs of Santiago and saw much of the city and its people. Perhaps the walk to the hospital was the most enlightening. I still have stamped on my heart the memory of

a young couple, both in tears, walking slowly away from
the hospital carrying just a white shawl. In Chile many
children die in the first two years of life, of diarrhoea,
bronchitis and malnutrition.

It was while working in this hospital that I was first
forced, like Thomas, to put my finger into the wound of
Chile's poverty and thus come, like him, to believe. My first
month was spent in the ward for children with infectious
diseases. There were fifty beds and the children were all
desperately ill; here I saw the diseases which I had never
seen in England where they are now rare because of the
vaccination programme.

Initially, however, what I found most shattering was the
attitude of the other doctors. At the San Borja I had been
treated in a courteous and friendly manner by doctors and
nursing staff alike and I had come to regard all the world
as my friend. In this hospital, however, the atmosphere was
very different. I found the attitude of the older doctors cold
and hard and the younger ones were often openly aggressive. It was a while before I came to realize that my casual
way of dress and behaviour marked me for them as a 'leftist'
and I was therefore suspected of being a political activist. I
remember one pompous young doctor several years my
junior telling me that to sit without my sandals on while I
drank a lemonade in the sun was not in keeping with the
dignity of the profession. I suffered a good deal in my
months at this hospital from the unfriendly attitude and the
way in which I was humiliated for my ignorance of Chilean
paediatrics. They were hard days and I was not very happy.

This was, however, a very important time for me in
understanding more about Chile. When a new patient was
admitted it was my duty to interrogate the mother. At first
I was embarrassed to ask these women whether their house
was stone or wood, whether the floor was cement or earth
and how many people slept in each room and in each bed.
I soon learned that the vast majority of my patients lived in
wooden plank houses with earth floors, no running water
and a simple hole-in-the-ground lavatory. Shattering also
was the interrogation about the other children. There was

scarcely a mother who had not lost one or more children from diarrhoea or bronchitis. Later in the year when I worked in the ward for the under two-year-olds I saw cases of gross malnourishment – babies of a year who still did not sit up and who looked like little old men; babies with big, dark, sad, sunken eyes and wrinkled skin who looked blankly into space and never smiled. These were not the fat gurgling babies that I was used to, but a race apart; little creatures who looked like men from another planet. In the developed world paediatricians are concerned with the problems of the bed wetter or the obese child and with the multitudinous congenital defects that afflict the human race. Child medicine in the third world deals with children who are dying from malnutrition or from diarrhoea caused by un-hygienic practises by ignorant parents in an area with poor sanitation. There are other problems common to poor people; burns for example. When I worked in Leicester we usually had at any given moment half a dozen toddlers with scalds from upset kettles or saucepans, whereas in one hospital in Santiago the entire emergency ward was full of severe flame burns from overturned paraffin stoves and those children who survived were transferred to a 50-bed burns unit for further care. In summer the children died from gastroenteritis from infected milk and in winter from bronchitis and pneumonia because the house was unheated or from burns when the toddler upset the paraffin stove.

Little by little I came into touch, albeit from afar, with a Chile in which people lived in one-roomed houses and there were two beds between six people and the babies were fed on tea instead of milk. I believe that working in paedi-atrics in Chile has a profound effect upon its doctors. The situation is so appalling that either they have to take stock of the social situation of their country or else develop a sort of shell and immerse themselves in the study of the rare conditions that are the concern of their colleagues abroad. They treat adequately the children who arrive at the hospital but give no thought to why they come or where they go when they are discharged. It is in this way that some of the young paediatricians grow into smart young men with private consulting rooms' where they practise European-style medicine on well fed children from the middle class while others, differently affected by what they see, go into public health and perhaps later into politics. It is not without significance that Salvador Allende was a doctor, as also were Bautista van Shauwen, the head of the MIR at the time of the coup (he was tortured until he became an imbecile); Miguel Enriquez, another doctor from a well-to-do professional family, died in 1974 as head of the MIR, the Chilean resistance force.

It is estimated that over a thousand doctors had to leave Chile after the coup. Over 300 of them had been in prison camps, and at least 50 died. Allende's personal physician, Danilo Bartolin, spent nine months in Chacabuco, a detention camp in the desert, before he was released and allowed to leave Chile to go into exile. He comes from one of the richest families in the south of Chile and was never a member of any political party.

In August 1973, there began the second big general strike which was to lead to the division of Chile. The aggression that I sensed towards myself purely because of my informal way of behaving was symptomatic of the rising level of discord between Chileans who were in sympathy with Allende's road to socialism and those who were not. The friendly arguments of a year ago had been replaced by distrust and dislike which was to flower suddenly into hatred and violence on 11 September. In the strike of October 1972, I had worked to help maintain the medical services and now, nearly a year later, I again saw doctors leave their patients in an effort to bring down the government. This time it was more unpleasant, for whereas in the San Borja there had been sufficient pro-Allende doctors to maintain essential services, it was not so in the Gonzales Cortez. The children's hospital was situated in a densely populated poor area and the vast majority of its doctors were opposed to Allende's government. Wards which had hitherto required ten doctors were left without medical supervision and only the emergency team, already grossly overworked, was available in case of urgent need.

In the first two weeks I worked with another girl, also revalidating her title. She knew little more about paediatrics than I did but between us we tried to treat some of the children. I remember vividly a baby which arrived very ill and was dying, and though we rang for help it did not come until too late. I gave mouth-to-mouth respiration to try to save it and when the doctor arrived some time after the baby died he made me gargle with 100 per cent alcohol because I was in danger of catching whatever the child had died of.

Eventually, it was decided by the Medical College (the equivalent of our BMA) that the work done by the foreign doctors was impeding the effectiveness of the strike so we were prohibited from entering the hospital. The assistant chief came every day and sat in his office and made sure that we didn't work.

Thus it was that I spent the month before the coup at home. Living only a mile from the centre of the city we were barely aware of the trouble brewing. We heard of the minor confrontations in the city centre and the police used water carts and tear gas to break up demonstrations from aggressive schoolchildren and university students. I do not recall ever hearing gunfire or seeing violence. Gradually, however, the strike began to wreak havoc with daily living. The transport workers' strike meant that the transport of fruit and vegetables from the south of the country ceased, as did the supply of fish from the ports. By the end of August there was no sugar, coffee, rice, oil, meat, fish, detergent, toothpaste, soap or toilet paper. Because of the strike of the flour mills supplies of bread were strictly limited and when spaghetti, the last available carbohydrate in the shops, became scarce, I began to be afraid for the future. The queues for bread were immense and often people would spend a whole morning queueing for one loaf.

Thus it was that the strike broke the morale of the country – without tooth-paste and soap it is difficult to remain clean and without bread a man is hungry. It was a beautifully planned exercise in demoralization and it worked. It is not without reason that I say this because it became evident after the coup that the shortages had been due not only to failure of transport but also to deliberate hiding of goods. Forty-eight hours after the fall of Allende's government, the shops were full of all the goods that had been in short supply for over a year. Within three days, however, this same food began to go rotten because the prices were suddenly raised and many people were unable to buy.

The night before the coup was curious. I had befriended an elderly neighbour, the sister of an old and senile colonel who lived in genteel poverty and a certain amount of squalor on the other side of the street. This lady was a lover of cats and owned about sixteen; not only did this make her house very unattractive to visit but when the fish supply dried up she was not able to feed them. Finally, in tears, she asked me to help get them put to sleep and I solemnly took pussy after pussy to the vet. Eventually she ran out of money so Consuelo and I went to her assistance with some ether but we found that it is not for nothing that cats are said to have nine lives. Eventually we managed to dispose of one, and very sick and scratched came home and then, feeling in need of comfort, set out in search of a drink. Now Santiago used to be a city with a busy night life, but that night we noticed to our surprise that all the shops and restaurants were closed; the shopkeepers knew that tomorrow was D-day. Thus it was that the following morning, 11 September, many children were kept home from school and husbands stayed in the house listening to the radio and waiting for the storm to break, while those not in the know went to their work as usual, little dreaming that the day had come when Chilean would turn upon Chilean and the armed forces, traditionally the loyal supporters of the government, would in the space of a few hours put an end to over one hundred years of democracy. On 11 September 1973, there came, as *Time* magazine put it, 'the bloody end to the marxist dream.'

8

The Coup – 11 September 1973

Treacherous generals
see my dead house, look at broken Chile
from every house burning metal flows
instead of flowers
come and see the blood in the streets
come and see
the blood in the streets

On the morning of 11 September I opened the shutters of my room which overlooked the Calle Bilbao, one of the main streets of Santiago, and stepped out on to the balcony to see what the day promised. Although the streets were quiet, this did not strike me, but what I found peculiar was the way in which the woman in the block of flats opposite waved joyfully at me. This was curious. She was a middle class lady who lived alone in a smart flat and we were not friends. I thought no more about it and after making breakfast went out to buy the milk. As I stood in the milk queue I noticed idly that there seemed to be more men in the queue than usual and that they were conversing in excited undertones; I could not understand what they said but caught the mention several times of Valparaiso, the big port north of Santiago. It was just after eleven when I got home and I was met by an ashen-faced Consuelo who said, 'There's been a take over by the army.' She had been listening to the radio when suddenly the music stopped and a harsh voice said, 'This is the Military Junta . . .' I listened with her to the voice of the new rulers of Chile, already issuing orders to the people: Every station carried the same voice: free speech had ended.

Always practical, my immediate thoughts were the feeding of my household and dogs so I set off at speed for the local open air fish and vegetable market. Already there was chaos, the people were hastily packing up their stalls and many abandoned their wares and set off in horse and cart for home. I bought what I could, fish and eggs, and picked up a large quantity of celery which had been discarded by a fleeing vendor. As I filled my basket I could hear the sound of gunfire from the centre of the city only a mile away. I returned home and found Consuelo still glued to the radio and she told me with horrified unbelief, 'They're going to bomb the Moneda.' The Moneda was the traditional House of Government. One of Santiago's most famous monuments, it stood right in the middle of the city's densely populated shopping centre, opposite the Hotel Sheraton Carrera. We were informed by radio that Allende had been ordered to leave the seat of government but that he had refused. At eleven o'clock he made his last speech to the nation via Radio Magellanes, a small radio station which was the last to fall to the military. I did not hear his speech at the time but months after the coup I was given a tape recording of it. Much has been said of Allende: that he was a hero – that he was a traitor; that he was a strong man – that he was a weak man; that he died for his country– that he betrayed it. The military did not wish to make a martyr of him but he refused all offers of safe conduct and died alone in the house of government. I believe that his last words are testimony enough that he was a man of integrity who lived and died for the people he loved, the underprivileged citizens of Chile, and 'Greater love hath no man than he who lays down his life for his friends.'

Compatriots,
This is certainly the last time I shall speak to you. . . . Having an historic choice to make, I shall sacrifice my life in loyalty to my people and I can assure you of my certainty that the seeds planted by us in the noble consciences of thousands and thousands of Chileans will not be prevented from growing forever.
They are strong, they can enslave the people, but it is neither by crime nor by force that such social processes can be held. History is ours. It is the people who make it.

Workers of my country,

I want to thank you for the loyalty that you have always shown, for the trust you have placed in a man who has only been the mouthpiece of the great aspirations of justice, who gave his word to respect the constitution and the law and who was faithful to this promise. . . .

I am speaking above all to the humble women of our land, to the peasant woman who believed in us, to the working woman who was making that extra effort, to the mother who knew that we cared about her children.

I am speaking to the members of professions, those patriots who a few days ago were continuing to struggle against the revolt led by the professional unions. . . .

I am speaking to the young people, to those who sang, to those who gave their joy and their spirit of struggle.

I am speaking to the man of Chile, to the worker, to the peasant, to the intellectual, to those who will be persecuted because fascism has already been in existence in our country for many hours. . . .

Workers of my country,

I have faith in Chile and its destiny. Other Chileans will come. In these dark and bitter moments, where treachery claims to impose itself, you must know that sooner or later, there will again open up broad ways along which worthy men will pass to build a new society.

Long live Chile!

Long live the people!

Long live the workers!

These are my last words. I am certain that my sacrifice will not be in vain. I am certain it will be a moral lesson which will punish treachery, cowardice and treason.

True to their threats, the new government of Chile dropped bombs in the centre of the city. Consuelo and I watched from the balcony of our house while Hawker Hunter jets precision bombed the House of Government and a little later they bombed the presidential residence in the highly populated residential area of Calle Tomas Moro.

It is difficult to convey in words the significance of these acts. The armed forces had combined and had surrounded both the Moneda and the President's home; the President was in his office and his wife was at her home. The people of Chile were unarmed save for the President's bodyguards: and yet it was found necessary to bomb the centre of the city and Allende's house. It is as though the armed forces took over control of England and then bombed Westminster and 10 Downing Street to give the world the impression that they were quelling a massive armed uprising.

By the early afternoon it was a *fait accompli*. Allende was dead, his ministers prisoners and the whole of Chile under military control. From the radio there came a continuous stream of orders: workers were to abandon their factories and walk home; anyone found in the streets after six o'clock would be shot dead, anyone found conversing in the street would be arrested. A Chile long used to total freedom of speech and action suddenly found itself a prisoner within its own walls.

All day we sat in the house listening to the radio and watching the factory workers hurrying home on foot because the buses had stopped running. All day we heard gunfire from different parts of the city and the smoke from the burning Palacio de la Moneda filled the sky with a great black cloud. No one came to the house and for a while the telephone was dead. We knew nothing of our friends, only that we were now under martial law. Order after order was given and the first ones repeated. Chile was in a state of emergency; the frontiers were closed: we were cut off from the rest of the world. Then orders began to be given for people to present themselves to the authorities: long lists of names of government ministers, doctors, lawyers, university lecturers. Like the Lord High Executioner in *The Mikado*, the Junta had a 'little list' of those whom it considered its enemies.

The day wore on. I moved my bed so that I could see the street because I wearied of standing endlessly at the window. After the workers had plodded home the street became busy with military traffic: lorries full of soldiers, tanks and fast sleek cars with high ranking military officials. We knew nothing but what we could see and hear – the smoke from the Moneda, the constant sound of gunfire, the mobilizing of troops, and the monotonous voice of the radio announcer who gave only orders, not news.

So this was a military coup: in less than a day the vision of the new Chile was destroyed along with the man who had believed that he could bring about a redistribution of wealth in his country without the spilling of blood. Allende's had not been the violent way of Fidel Castro or Che Guevara: he had believed that he could achieve a bloodless revolution but he had not reckoned with the CIA's investment of eight million dollars to bring down his government nor with the triumph of the latent fascism in a certain sector of the Chilean middle class. He had believed with Pablo Neruda that 'there is room for all of us in this land of mine'.

9

The Days that Followed

How much humanity
exposed to hunger, cold, panic, pain
moral pressures, terror and insanity?
Victor Jara
Written in the National Stadium,
12 September 1973

I slept fitfully during the night of 11 September, disturbed
by gunfire and the endless passing of military vehicles. The
next day the street was deserted and the radio told us that
there was to be a curfew for the whole of the day and that
anyone found in the streets would be shot. Further lists of
people required to present themselves to the military
authorities were given and it was also announced that all
foreigners in an 'irregular position', i.e. without their documents in order, were to go to the nearest police station.
Having been unable to face the endless red tape required to
renew my visa I had allowed it to lapse, and I now found
that not only was the visa nine months out of date but my
passport had expired a year before. I was extremely unnerved and wondered if I should report to the authorities
but Consuelo told me firmly not to be stupid so I lay low
and said nothing. It was as well that I did so because I later
learned of an Englishman whose documents were out of
date who spent two days in detention in the stadium after
innocently presenting himself.

We spent the day watching the steady passage of army
lorries and tanks along the main street that only two days
before had been a busy normal thoroughfare. The only light
relief of the day was when the old lady whose cats I had
helped to their reward rang me to say that she'd baked me
some bread and would I fetch it. Torn between upsetting

her and committing an act of great folly I chose a moment when the street was deserted and dashed across and returned unscathed with my loaf.

That night the helicopter made its appearance. Flying without lights so that it could not be shot down by resistance fighters it circled over the city like some giant bat searching for prey. We learned later that in those early days attacks were made on shanty towns and men, women and children were killed and hundreds of people taken prisoner.

Although I only came to know about it much later thousands of Chileans, adults, students and schoolchildren were taken prisoner during the first few days of the coup. So great were the numbers of detainees that they were housed in the two big sports stadiums of Santiago: the Estadio de Chile and the Estadio Nacional. Raids were made on factories and universities and anyone suspected of having been pro-Allende was taken in. In the National Stadium alone there were between five and seven thousand prisoners, held in groups in the underground changing rooms and allowed out for an hour a day. These prisoners were interrogated and many of them were tortured and killed. Women were raped and both men and women were subjected to beating and electrical torture. Bored soldiers amused themselves with multiple violations of women and played Russian roulette with pistols in which some of the chambers were loaded and others empty.

A well known and tragic case from those early days is the death of Victor Jara. He was one of the best known and best loved folk singers of Chile; during the Allende regime he wrote, composed and sang songs for the emergent nation: tender songs and songs of protest. His was a voice of freedom and justice known throughout the land and on 11 September he had been invited to sing at a festival at the Technical University. Thus it was that he was detained along with hundreds of students and professors when the university was raided. They were taken to the Chile Stadium and it was there in the last three days of his life that he wrote the following poem:

There are five thousand of us here
in this little part of the city.
We are five thousand.
I wonder how many we are in all
in the cities and in the whole country?
Here alone
are ten thousand hands which plant seeds
and make the factories run.
How much humanity
exposed to hunger, cold, panic, pain,
moral pressures, terror and insanity?
Six of us were lost
as if into starry space.
One dead, another beaten as I could never have believed
a human being could be beaten.
The other four wanted to end their terror
one jumping into nothingness,
another beating his head against a wall,
but all with the fixed look of death.
What horror the face of fascism creates!
They carry out their plans with knife-like precision.
Nothing matters to them.
For them blood equals medals,
slaughter is an act of heroism.
O God, is this the world that you created?
For this your seven days of wonder and work?
Within these four walls only a number exists
which does not progress.
Which slowly will wish more and more for death.
But suddenly my conscience awakes
and I see this tide with no heart beat,
only the pulse of machines
and the military showing their midwives' faces
full of sweetness.
Let Mexico, Cuba and the world
cry out against this atrocity!
We are ten thousand hands which can produce nothing.
How many of us in the whole country?
The blood of our Compañero President

Will strike with more strength than bombs or machine guns!
How hard it is to sing
When I must sing of horror.
Horror which I am living.
Horror which I am dying.
To see myself among so much
and so many moments of infinity
in which silence and screams
are the end of my song.
What I see I have never seen before.
What I have felt and what I feel
will give birth to the moment . . .

On 16 September, five days after the coup, Joan Jara the British wife of Victor Jara was visited by a friend and told that he was dead and that his body was in the city mortuary. The following is her account of what happened:

> They entered the morgue by a side door and saw what Mrs Jara describes as heaps of bodies filling the whole of a large room.
> The space normally reserved for corpses was full and so was the space normally used for handling bodies. Mrs Jara had to go upstairs to the space normally used for administration before she found her husband's body which, they told her, had been there for three days.
> His clothes, Mrs Jara says, were torn and some had been torn off him. The bones of his hands had been broken and his back, she believed, was broken too. In addition, he had received many bullet wounds.
> Joan Jara. As related to Mark Arnold-Forster.
> *Manchester Guardian*, 23 October 1973

I did not know Victor Jara in Chile and I never heard his records until after the coup, but I remember that the British consul was helping Joan and the children to leave Chile when I went to enquire about my passport and visa in October. Hers is one of the important eye-witness accounts of the events in Chile in the first days after the coup.

Joan Jara is witness .to some of the deaths in the immediate post-coup days. In Amnesty International's report
on Chile they publish the testimony of a group of Brazilian
prisoners held in the Chile Stadium. This testimony was
handed to the Amnesty Delegation during their stay in
Santiago:

The Amnesty report says of those early days:

> Immediately after the coup, general conditions were
> appalling. This was before any foreign observers were
> able to enter the country. The junta, announcing that no
> visits would be permitted to places of detention before
> the International Committee of the Red Cross (ICRC)
> had made inspections, kept the ICRC waiting on the
> Argentine-Chile borders for a full week before the bor-
> ders were opened. During this period the Chile Stadium
> (not to be confused with the National Stadium which is
> also in Santiago) was in use.
>
> The first, and probably most notorious, of the ad hoc
> detention centers used was the Chile Stadium, a small
> stadium built for basketball and similar pastimes. The
> majority of prisoners were detained in very crowded
> conditions for five days in the first few days after 11
> September. Many report having received no food and
> drink during that period. Detainees there alleged that
> they had witnessed executions and had heard prolonged
> machine-gun fire which could have indicated either the
> death of their comrades or simulated executions.

the report continues

> From the Chile Stadium, prisoners were transferred
> to the National Stadium of Santiago, which was even-
> tually vacated after the first week of November 1973. In
> the National Stadium there was at least some degree of
> protection. Officials of the ICRC and the United Nations
> High Commission of Refugees (UNHCR), as well as
> foreign diplomats whose nationals were detained there,
> were enabled to pay frequent visits. By mid-November,
> the UNHCR had procured the release and expulsion
> from Chile of almost all foreigners.

For Chileans, however, there were no such guarantees. Although the authorities gave statistics for the number of detainees, their refusal to give lists of prisoners made many prisoners fear for their lives. It was significant that one Chilean ex-senator detained there handed over a roughly scrawled list to the Amnesty International representatives who visited the stadium on 7 November, urging that these names should be published abroad in order to protect the prisoners' lives. The AI representatives also heard two pronounced bursts of machine-gun fire within the stadium on 7 November, the day on which many of the prisoners were transferred.

In retrospect it appears that the number of simulated executions was far greater than the number of actual executions, and few of the continual bursts of machine-gun fire were directed against prisoners; yet the death of some Chileans in or near the National Stadium has been documented. Moreover, in an interview with a foreign journalist, National Stadium Commander Jorge Espinoza once claimed that approximately 60 people had been killed by left-wing extremists after their release from the stadium. How many of these had died inside?

Immeasurably larger than the Chile Stadium, the National Stadium is a vast football stadium with a capacity for up to 80,000 people. Again, we reproduce a report written by a group of foreigners describing the overall physical conditions in which they were detained. It was given to the AI delegation in Santiago:

The National Stadium is a sporting arena in which the football and athletics stadiums are situated in an ample space of 25 to 30 hectares surrounded by walls of more than two metres in height, with a capacity for 80,000 people; there is also the velodrome (cycle-track) with capacity for over 1,000 spectators.

Prisoners were transported to the stadium from the prisons or police stations in buses. On arrival they were handed over to the soldiers who acted as their guards. After their entry had been registered, prisoners –

whatever their state of health – were led to the changing-rooms or hatchways which had been transformed into cells. In some cases the prisoners had to remain in the corridors, waiting to be allocated one of the cells when they were full.

The small changing-rooms were 70 square metres in size, including the baths and showers. The useable area, for living and sleeping, was about 45 square metres. In these cells about 90–100 people were massed together (about half a square metre or less for each person). The larger rooms were of about 70 useable square metres, plus the baths and showers in an adjoining room; in these rooms there were between 120 and 160 persons. On some days both the small and large rooms could be more or less full than this, given the persistent transfers. The so-called hatchways, also used as cells, were the corridors which were the entrances to the rows of seats to the north and south of the vast cement building. In each hatchway there were between 120–200 people, who for sleeping purposes had to use parts of the bathrooms and the flights of the adjacent staircases (the hatchways were about 15 metres in length by 3 in width). The door leading to the outside was shut by a large iron grille which permitted the wind and dust to enter. In other words it is a building of which the very interior construction and character could have been made for an immense and organized prison.

During the first week's functioning of the concentration camp, prisoners passed the 24 hours of the day locked in the changing-rooms and hatchways. Each one was given a blanket, and for food he was given a cup of coffee with milk and a small piece of bread in the morning, and a similar ration in the evening. Nothing else. After the first week, the bread ration increased . . . from the tenth day onwards, the prisoner had his ration improved with soup, lentils, peas or beans. One slept on the flagstones, half the blanket below and half above. In the course of time some prisoners succeeded in obtaining a second blanket. The cells are cold and very humid, given the proximity of the showers and the lack of sunlight. From the second week onwards, prisoners were taken to the public platforms, from the hours of 10.00–14.00, and 16.00–19.00. This began when both Chilean and foreign journalists were taken to the stadium in order to 'prove' the 'good treatment' that the prisoners were given.

Thousands of relatives of prisoners and disappeared persons came every day, up to the grilles of the sporting center that had been transformed into a political prison, seeking news of their relatives or some fact that would confirm their presence in the place, or to bring them food and clothing. Except for exceptional cases, not a single thing or message was conveyed to the prisoners from outside, nor could they say a single word to their relatives. Of the packets – the distribution of which was under the control of the Chilean Red Cross – only one out of every two reached their destination; all parcels were carefully inspected, and neither biscuits, chocolate, fruit or cigarettes were handed on to the prisoners.

For all prisoners, the most frightening prospect was that of interrogation. Junta spokesmen have said much about the speed of interrogation, but suitably little about the methods. Between 200 and 300 prisoners were interrogated daily, either on the third floor of the stadium or in the velodrome. On the third floor interrogations took place in a large hall occupied by military prosecutors seated at separate tables, or in small rooms situated behind these tables where more 'intensive' interrogations were conducted.

During interrogation, we estimate that about 50 per cent of all prisoners were severely maltreated, usually through prolonged beating of a primitive type, although (as can be seen below), more selective torture techniques were used in specified cases. In the velodrome, where most interrogations occurred, about 200 prisoners were taken daily under the escort of a heavily armed guard. They were then handed over to one of the interrogation teams (the teams came from each sector of the armed forces, also from the National Police and 'the investigative police'). It was in this building, some 300 metres from the main part of the stadium that the most systematic beating took place.

Depending on the type of general accusation facing the prisoner he might be treated with comparative leniency, or beaten and kicked for several hours. There are also cited cases of prisoners being tortured with electricity, of having water forced up the nose or mouth, or being confronted with simulated execution. After the interrogation, prisoners were classified as either 'conditional liberty', meaning he could expect to be released within a few days; 'suspect', meaning he had to await a second interrogation while his charge-sheet and the results of the first interrogation were examined by military intelligence; or 'dangerous suspect', meaning he had little hope of release, and could anticipate torture and repeated interrogation.

This report of atrocities committed is corroborated by Amnesty International which sent a delegation to Chile in November 1973 and by many of the prisoners who were released from the stadium and who were brave enough to talk in Chile or felt free to give evidence once outside of the country.

For us, in Bilbao there was no possibility of knowing what was happening in other parts of Santiago until 13 September. When the curfew was lifted between 12 and 3 p.m. we crept out of the house to buy provisions from local shopkeepers. Suddenly in the afternoon the doorbell rang and there was Consuelo's sister Claudia with two other girls. Trying to appear casual I greeted them at the gate and, smiling and chattering happily for the benefit of the watching neighbours, I led them in.

Unlike Consuelo, Claudia had been politically active,

working with the Socialist Party and had worked as supervisor and co-ordinator in some of the factories which had
been taken over by the workers. On 11 September she had
been visiting Luccetti, Santiago's biggest spaghetti factory.
After the coup she had stayed to accompany the workers
and she told us how the factory had been raided by the
police. They had come in and ordered all the women to lie
face down on the floor while the men were marshalled outside prior to being taken away. A Brazilian student had
been shot dead in front of her and she herself had escaped
detention because it was thought she was just another
factory hand.

After spending the nights of the 11th and 12th in the
factory she had left with the other women when the curfew
was lifted and walked through the side streets the four miles
to Consuelo's house. With her was another girl whose husband had been at the Technical University and a third who
had seven children stranded since the 11th the other side of
Santiago.

With the arrival of Claudia and her friends I realized
that although this was not my war I could not remain uninvolved because Consuelo had to give shelter to her sister.
It was as simple as that for Consuelo: you risked your life for
friend and family (although Claudia's ex-husband obviously felt differently as he refused to allow her near his
house). With little more than an hour till the time of the
curfew Consuelo took her car and drove the third girl
across Santiago so that she would get home to her children
who had had no food for two days. I sat at the window with
my heart in my mouth wondering if she would ever return.
There was, however, no problem and when she returned she
and Claudia began to telephone to try and find out about
other members of the family.

At first there was no news but the next day rumours began
to filter in that the husband of her other sister, her niece and
the girl's lover were all dead. They were grey, tense days. I
spent most of my time trying to make meals for the increased household and various visitors who came to discuss
Claudia's future. I understood little of what was said but

recall having a furious row with Claudia, who I thought was trying to organize a centre of resistance from our house. I told her that I was not prepared to die for a lost cause – only to be told firmly by Consuelo that this was her house and her sister and her country and if I felt like that I'd better go back to England at once. This shook me and I began to think she was right.

On 15 September I was able to go to the hospital for the first time, the whole area having been cordoned off by the police until that day.

This was a memorable visit: I found my doctor friends grouped in the patio of the hospital discussing the events of the preceding days. After I had greeted them I went to my ward to see how my patients were and told a couple of friends about my expired visa and passport. After half an hour I wandered outside again and found the group had gone; looking for them I returned to the ward only to learn that some twenty doctors had been arrested and taken away in a bus and that the hospital was closed and nobody could leave without police authority. My friends, however, were well informed and more concerned for me than I was myself. They told me I must get out immediately and that the door to the maternity section was still unguarded. Luckily I knew my way around the rabbit warren of the hospital and I slipped out unnoticed into the street.

As I walked home I passed a record shop and on impulse entered and asked for a Chilean record that I had only heard once – the cantata *Santa Maria de Iquique*, a very beautiful modern work which tells of the days when the saltpetre workers of Iquique in the north of Chile were exploited by the British and Chilean lords of Iquique. At first the man denied having it and then sold me his last, damaged copy. Thus it was that I purchased my first Chilean protest music, from which I was to learn much of what this war was about.

After five days Claudia was smuggled into an embassy with her two children. Never will I forget the tension of those days when she hid with us. Typical of thousands of Chileans, she was suddenly faced with the fact that she was wanted by the police and that they would probably kill her if they found her. There was one nightmare morning when a bus load of soldiers actually stopped outside the house and we thought that she had been discovered but after a few minutes they went away.

She was torn at having to leave for a country she didn't know and without knowing whether her lover was dead or alive. There was an added drama when she refused to go without her child who was with his father; eventually he relented and she disappeared from our lives, taking with her a sad little package of a dress, a pair of sandals and a book.

10

The New Way of Life

No hay ni que hablar, amigo, es peligroso.

You must not even speak, my friend, it is dangerous.
Luis Advis
Santa Maria de Iquique

Little by little life took on a new pattern. Consuelo returned to work and was faced with the problem of trying to
hold her tongue in the presence of colleagues who were
jubilant about the new regime. Physically unwell, she was
even more sick at heart. Gone was the hope of the new Chile;
democracy was dead and the country which she loved so
much was in the hands of violent and brutal men whose
aim was to destroy without trace all the changes of which
she had been so proud. Her two sisters and their families
were forced to seek exile and her only other relative, her
stepmother, was passionately pro-Junta.

Chile was now totally divided and hatred and fear ruled.
The face of the city changed dramatically. One of the first
public acts of the new government, and one which was to be
symbolic of its future policy, was to whitewash the walls to
obliterate all the slogans, a task willingly performed by
students from the Fatherland and Freedom extreme right
wing movement. Street vendors, always a prominent feature
in Latin American towns, were banned from the streets and
Santiago truly became a whited sepulchre as the Junta prepared to open its frontiers to inspection by delegates from an
outraged world.

The most sinister part of life was the night. The curfew
was fixed at eight o'clock for some weeks and in the minutes
before frantic workers raced for their homes. Almost on the
stroke of eight the firing began. Prisoners in our houses, we
never knew if this was due to soldiers firing in the air to

maintain the atmosphere of terror or if houses were being raided and people killed. Within minutes of the curfew the military vehicles would appear: long fast cars racing towards the centre of the city with important looking officers and lorries full of soldiers or tanks. The helicopter surveyed the city each night and bus-loads of steel-helmeted soldiers would speed away to assignments searching for 'terrorists'.

Area after area was searched and friends told of the aggressiveness of the military and of the blatant way in which they robbed private citizens of jewels or money. We were never searched but I lived in constant fear that the dogs would be mown down by trigger-happy soldiers at the gate. There was one night when shortly before the curfew a friend of Consuelo's arrived and told her that she had her car full of bandages and medicines to treat casualties and had realized that she had to pass a group of soldiers searching all cars. She left her booty with us and I spent until three o'clock in the morning hiding the bandages and penicillin in packets of spaghetti or Rinso in case the house was searched in the night.

Of all the traffic that streamed past our house I did not see one ambulance in the first three days of the coup. Instead there were covered lorries and we wondered who or what was in them. After a few days bodies began to appear in the Mapocho, the river that runs through the city, and certain prisoners were said to have been shot 'while trying to escape'. According to the Amnesty International report, 'the Chicago Commission of Inquiry, after its visit to Chile in February 1974 asserted that 410 prisoners had been listed as "shot while trying to escape" in 42 separate newspaper reports up to 12 December 1973.'

It will probably never be known accurately how many people died during the coup. Estimates vary between 5000 and 30,000. Official government figures in March 1974 were around 3500 but as early as October 1973 John Barnes, the Santiago correspondent of the American magazine *Newsweek*, reported that his own careful investigations had revealed a total of 2796 corpses processed in the Santiago morgue in the first two weeks after 11 September. An

unofficial report of the US State Department in March 1974
indicated that the total number of dead was in the region of
10,800 by the end of December 1973.

It is important to see these figures against the background
of a completely tranquil city. The coup took place on the
morning of 11 September. By six o'clock that night all
Chileans were confined to their houses by the curfew. This
was not a civil war with prolonged fighting in the streets
and the lobbing of hand grenades, but the overthrow of a
president and his bodyguards with jet bombers and then
the cold-blooded killing night after night, under cover of
curfew and darkness, of thousands of unarmed citizens. The
military coup was not a war but a massacre.

These words from *Santa Maria de Iquique*, written in 1970,
spoke of the killing a hundred years before of a group of over
2000 miners from the saltpetre works who had dared to protest for better conditions, but they could have been prophetic for September 1973:

> *A los hombres de la pampa*
> *que quisieron protestar*
> *los mataron como perros*
> *porque había que matar.*

> *No hay que ser pobre, amigo,*
> *es peligroso,*
> *No hay ni que hablar, amigo*
> *es peligroso.*

> *Las mujeres de la pampa*
> *se pusieron a llorar*
> *y tambien las matarían*
> *porque había que matar.*

> The men of the prairie
> wished to protest
> and they killed them like dogs
> because they had to be killed.

> you must not be poor, my friend,
> it's dangerous,

You must not even speak, friend,
it's dangerous.

The women of the prairie
began to weep
and they also were killed
because they had to be killed.

Indeed – the final song of the cantata warned that the tragedy of Iquique could be repeated

*Quizas, mañana o pasado
o bien, en un tiempo más,
la historia que han escuchado
de nuevo sucederá.*

Who knows, tomorrow or the next day
or perhaps in a little while,
the history which you have heard
may be repeated.

Perhaps the hardest thing to bear, for us who had not personally been bereaved, was the rejoicing of right wing colleagues. The division between Chileans cut clean as a knife: one section rejoiced in the restoration of law and order at the expense of justice and the other wept behind closed doors for the death of loved ones and of freedom.

One of the most remarkable changes in my daily living happened in the shops. During the weeks preceding the coup there had been an almost total absence of all household necessities but three days after, when the supermarket opened again, the shelves were stacked with the coffee, sugar, soap and tooth-paste that we had not seen for months. They had been in short supply because they had been hidden in an effort to provoke economic chaos and so turn Chile against Allende.

There was, however, a difference: the prices rose immediately and continued to rise. Never will I forget the sight or smell of chickens rotting in the refrigerated compartment at the supermarket because the shoppers hadn't the money to buy them. The price of milk rose so that instead of having to queue for it, it was brought to the door:

but I had to be careful to make sure it wasn't sour because
what the vendors did not sell one day they would try to sell
the next.

Days dragged into weeks and we became accustomed to
life under military rule. There was an intense propaganda
effort to win support for the military and to destroy the
image of the previous government. We were told repeatedly
from posters that in every soldier there is a Chilean and in
every Chilean a soldier. Allende was 'exposed' as being a
corrupt man who had lived in luxury while proclaiming
equality for Chileans. Those who wanted to believe were
jubilant to have been saved by their brave army; the newspapers told of the discovery of plans for the killing of hundreds of Chileans on 18 September. 'Plan Z' was invented to
justify the coup and it became a crime to have been a member of Allende's government. The ministers who did not
give themselves up were hunted and caught and exiled to the
near-antarctic conditions of Dawson Island 500 miles away
in Chile's extreme south, so that they could not have access
to family, friends or legal aid. Meanwhile, in the north of
Chile, the ruins of the old saltpetre mine of Chacabuco were
rebuilt to form a detention centre in the desert.

Even in the midst of fear and oppression the Chilean
sense of humour could not be squashed and macabre little
jokes would be told among friends.

'Have you heard of the new bus route?'

'No, where does it run?'

'From the Stadium to the cemetery.'

Anti-Junta jokes have now become a part of the Chilean
way of life; the nicest one I've heard is this. 'General Pinochet went to the movies disguised as an old lady so that he
could see how many people applauded him when he
appeared on the screen. He sat entranced as people clapped
his image until his neighbour nudged him and said, "Clap,
you silly old fool, or they'll shoot you".'

It was not long before anti-Junta slogans began to appear
on the back of the bus seats and now every bus in Santiago
carried the warning: 'Persons found writing anything
against the government will be immediately detained.'

After the initial weeks of 'clean up' of the city, with most of its principal enemies either dead or detained, the Junta confirmed its now openly declared policy of obliterating every trace of Marxism from Chile. Confident that their military training fitted them for all types of work, members of the armed forces replaced the heads of all government departments, hospitals and universities.

In the hospital and university worlds where I had many friends all doctors or lecturers who had been pro-Allende were suspended from duty. Those few who were not suspended were demoted and their work supervised to a humiliating extent. In the San Borja Hospital there had existed an extremely high-powered and united cardiology department with teams of cardiologists, radiologists and surgeons who worked together in the diagnosis and treatment of the valvular heart disease which is very common in Chile. Overnight this unit, which has been doing such esoteric surgery as valve changes and the insertion of cardiac pacemakers, was disbanded. Some of the doctors were imprisoned and the others either dismissed or suspended. In its place there was formed the new department of cardio-respiratory (heart and lung) disease headed by two right-wing doctors who, though capable physicians, were nothing approaching the calibre of the previous men, most of whom had many years' training in specialist units in world famous departments abroad.

The suspended doctors were not militant political figures – indeed political militancy is a full-time occupation and is not compatible with an eight-to-ten-hour day's work in medicine – but doctors who believed in Allende's road to socialism. Their 'crimes' had been the holding of political beliefs different from the new government and the manifesting of those beliefs by participation in work in shanty town clinics outside the hospital or by working during the medical strike.

I was suspended along with all foreign doctors, but after investigation of my 'case' for some weeks I was allowed to return to work and a month later I did the paediatric exams and scraped a pass.

Christmas was upon us. We felt little cause for celebration and the festive week passed almost unnoticed. On
New Year's Eve we stood at the window, champagne glasses
in hand, and looked out into the silent and empty streets.
Suddenly as the old year died there came the mournful
notes of the Last Post played on the trumpet. Again and
again the poignant music sounded and we waited holding
our breath to see if the block of flats from which it came
would be searched, but there was not a screech of sirens and
eventually the lone player wearied or was silenced by more
prudent friends.

January, always a quiet hot month when most professional people take their holiday, was for us uneventful.
Towards the middle of February, however, Consuelo, who
had not been well for some time, suddenly became acutely
ill and was admitted to the emergency hospital near our
home.

After a week she seemed better but the day before she
was due to be discharged her condition worsened and in the
week that followed she lost ground daily. It was a bitter
time. Always optimistic, and with my medical judgment
blinded I never dreamed that she would die. Mary Jane and
I passed hours with her, for she hated to be alone, and the
two nights before she died I spent at the hospital. Either
because of her illness or because of fear of death she could
not sleep and was desperate for company. I, who had been
witness to death so often in my patients, stood impotently
by while other doctors fought for the life of my closest
friend. On the morning of 5 March 1974, Consuelo died
from acute hepatic and renal failure. She remained conscious until an hour before her death and maintained the
dignity and consideration for others which were so charac-
teristic of her until the last. We never spoke of death: I did
not feel able and perhaps she did not want to. I cannot even
claim that I helped her to die but at least I was there, and
in the last hours of darkness when she was so afraid I was
able to keep watch with her and my hand was there to hold
when she wanted to do so. Her parents being dead and her
sisters in exile, her only relatives were a cousin and her step-

mother, and as she wished to see no one Mary Jane and I were the only visitors during her last two weeks.

After she died we were helped with the arrangements for her funeral by her cousin and a doctor friend. After a requiem mass she was buried in the beautiful Santiago general cemetery where she had loved to study as a medical student. There I saw, through a haze of tears, the inscription over the gate of the cemetery which she had quoted to me many times:

Ancha es la puerta,
pasajero avanza, y mire como guardan el sueño de la muerte, la fe,
la caridad y la esperanza.

Wide is the gate
advance ye who pass by and see how the sleep of the dead
is guarded by faith, charity and hope.

Life is never the same after the death of someone you love. Consuelo's death was indeed a turning point in my life. Sad and lonely I sought refuge at the feet of the God to whom I had given little thought for many years and quietly and naturally returned to my undergraduate practice of daily attendance at mass and communion.

Suddenly, after years of tepid practice of my faith, I again felt as it were the hand of God on my shoulder. After a lapse of ten years I felt incredulously a return of the call to the religious life.

I was 36 years old, emerging out of the grief of loss to see the brave new world which seemed there for the conquering. I saw myself as making a new life in Chile, staying loyal to the people I had grown to love and who now needed so much the care and support that they had given me when I was lonely and bewildered. But now, nearly twenty years later, the Hound of Heaven had caught up with me again:

I fled Him, down the nights and down the days;
I fled Him, down the arches of the years;
I fled Him, down the labyrinthine ways
    Of my own mind; and in the mist of tears
I hid from Him, and under running laughter.

Up vistaed hopes I sped;
And shot, precipitated,
Adown Titanic glooms of chasmed fears,
From those strong Feet that followed, followed after.
But with unhurrying chase,
And unperturbed pace,
Deliberate speed, majestic instancy,
They beat – and a Voice beat
More instant than the Feet –
'All things betray thee, who betrayest Me.'

Francis Thompson
The Hound of Heaven

At eighteen I had felt called to renounce the career that lay before me. Now at 36 that career was a reality and I loved it. Not only was I free to work as a doctor in three continents but I had a house, a maid and three dogs. At first I thought that I or God had made a mistake, but the weeks turned into months and I knew that there was no mistake, and once again I was afraid and distressed.

For, though I knew His love Who followed,
Yet was I sore adread
Lest, having Him, I must have naught beside.

New Friends

I love you because you
Are helping me to make
Of the lumber of my life
Not a tavern
But a temple;
Out of works
Of my every day
Not a reproach
But a song.

Roy Croft

After the first sad weeks that followed Consuelo's death my life began to take on a new shape. Teresa, a childhood friend of Consuelo's who was married with three children, befriended us and after months of hardly going anywhere because of Consuelo's ill health I began to be invited out to other people's houses and to have them to the house in return. It was as if I was emerging from a long, dark tunnel into a brilliant new world. So great had been the change in my life when I left England that a part of me had become quite dormant and I had forgotten that it existed.

During Consuelo's last year she had been chronically unwell and though she had continued working it had been an uphill struggle and most of her time at home had been spent asleep or just quietly reading. As a result she had few friends to the house and as her health deteriorated I saw less and less of other people apart from those with whom I worked. My spare time was spent reading and luckily I had Consuelo's library of nearly a thousand paperbacks to help me in my loneliness.

In retrospect I find it curious that I did not seek comfort in religion. The Spirit, however, is famous for breathing where it will, and though I lived less than five minutes' walk from the church I did not feel moved to go there and with

time hanging heavily on my hands I neither opened the
Bible nor prayed. Deep in a slough of loneliness and despond
I lay on my bed and read novel after novel and found com-
panionship only in my dog.

Just how desperately unhappy I was during those two
years I only realized after Consuelo died. So it was, that
after her death I began to live again. Teresa was marvellous.
She would come and visit us and invite us regularly to her
house, so that what might have been a bitterly lonely time
became increasingly filled with friendship and joy. Born
into an aristocratic Chilean family Teresa had the charm
and poise and education of her class but with the outlook of
those who had opted for the building of the new Chile. She
was small and slim and very elegant and tried hard to
smarten us up as both Mary Jane and I in our depressed
state had ceased to care about our appearance, dejectedly
swapping jeans and shirts as she grew fatter and I grew
thinner.

When she realized that I was a Catholic Teresa brought
one of her friends, a Dutch priest, to tea. For the first time in
two and a half years I realized that there were English-
speaking priests in Chile. It took me a further six months to
discover that not only were there hundreds of foreign missionary priests and nuns but that one group, the Columban
Fathers, had their headquarters in the street next to my
house. During those two desperately lonely years I had been
living practically next door to a house of English-speaking
missionaries who were later to become my close friends.

Teresa's friend, Father Jan, was a short fair-haired man
who had been many years in Chile. He lived in a far distant
shanty town and it was through him that I first began to
extend my vision of the country. It was with his help too that
I started the first steps towards living the Christianity that I
professed. The day after he came to tea I rang him up and
then visited him at his office and went to confession for the
first time since I had arrived in Chile. I told him of the
absurd return of the feeling that I was called to the religious
life and he listened patiently as I related how this feeling
had come and gone ever since I had been at school. He

advised me to pray and read a little of the Bible and some theology and that I should 'listen' carefully to what God was saying to me as it seemed clear that he was saying something.

I continued to see him from time to time and once or twice I was invited to visit the house where he lived with three other priests. The first time I went I could hardly believe my eyes. The cultured Father Jan lived in a tiny wooden house in the middle of a row of similar houses in a shanty town. I had of course seen these houses from the bus, but I had never been inside one and it had never occurred to me that educated Europeans could choose to live in this way.

Until one has seen the houses that the poorest people of Chile call home it is difficult to realize the conditions under which millions of its citizens live. Perhaps the nearest equivalent in England is an old-fashioned chicken house built of planks, with one window and with an earth floor. These houses are patched with odd sheets of corrugated iron and polythene and held together as it were by love and chewing gum. There is no running water apart from a tap halfway down the street and often no lavatory at all.

Father Jan's house was also built of wood, but well made and clean with every available space put to full use. He and his fellow priests had installed a cold shower and a lavatory and each man had his own room with its wooden bunk, a few nails upon which to hang his clothes and a bookshelf. Their communal living and dining room served also as a chapel for mass during the week and as an interview room for parishioners.

As I helped him to make lunch and then sat with the three of them afterwards the immense difference between their standard of living and mine gradually came home to me. I had thought myself poor, living with what I deemed the bare necessities of life: cooker, fridge, bed, gramophone and my books and pictures, and I had thought of myself as sharing in the life of the Chileans. In a way I had been, but I was living alongside the middle class Chileans and enjoying their way of life while Jan had cast in his lot with the marginal people, the broken ones.

Perhaps it was this encounter which made real for me the passage in St Luke's gospel where a rich young man says to Christ, 'Good master, what must I do to inherit eternal life?'

The young man is told, 'Keep the commandments', but he protests, 'All this I have done since my youth', at which he receives the absurd, impractical, unexpected, below the belt answer:

'If thou would'st be perfect, go sell what thou hast and give to the poor and come, follow me.'

It is small wonder that, having many possessions, he 'went away sad'.

I went away from Jan's house not so much sad as disconcerted and afraid. Could it be that this was what was being demanded of me?

Little by little, almost without realizing it, I began to part with a few of my things. I could not face the wrench of a violent and massive parting, although in retrospect I think it might have been easier. I began by giving away the clothes I didn't like and those which didn't fit me and I gave a couple of my best sweaters to Jan, who pronounced himself delighted but warned me not to be upset if he gave them away to someone else.

In June, just over two months after Consuelo's death, Teresa and her family came to share the house in Bilbao. Mary Jane was going home and I planned to go to England to visit my father before getting a long term job, and anyway the house was far too big for me. So it was that Mary Jane and I squeezed ourselves into the two downstairs rooms and Teresa and her family moved their entire household, furniture and all, into the first floor. Suddenly the house which had been so quiet became alive as Teresa, her husband, their children and their nanny settled themselves into half the space they were used to. Pedro, Teresa's four-year-old son, was no respecter of boundaries; he was a beautiful and naughty little boy and he knew himself to be the prince of the house and acted accordingly. Luckily he adored the dogs, and the chows, although not always good with adults, were completely trustworthy with children. He would fling himself upon them and was often to be found curled up on the floor with his head resting on the patient Jericho who regarded him as a somewhat overgrown and fractious puppy.

In July Mary Jane went back to England for good. She had come to Chile to study and had worked many hours, mainly at night, in preparation for a higher medical exam. Now she returned to seek work in England and I was left with the maid Margarita, Teresa and her family and the three dogs.

The month before my own return to England was a busy one spent doing the seemingly endless paperwork required before I could qualify for the Chilean medical degree. After weeks of journeying from office to office I eventually had my papers in order and in early July I was the proud possessor of the degree in Medicine from the University of Chile.

On 11 August I said goodbye to Teresa's family, and promising to be back in six weeks I took the plane to Buenos Aires. I stayed with friends of a medical colleague and was fascinated by the rich and cosmopolitan city. After eleven months of curfew it was incredible to walk about the streets late at night and see people sitting happily in cafés drinking or having an after-theatre dinner party. I had forgotten that this sort of life existed. Speaking to an economist, however, I was told that Argentina was not as calm as it appeared and that a coup was likely before many months passed.

After three days, I set off for Rio de Janeiro, taking with me a new pair of shoes from *Los Angelitos*, Buenos Aires' most famous shoe shop where the shoes are so soft that they need no breaking in. I carried, too, half a dozen records of Chilean protest music which I had never bothered to listen to in Allende's time and which now was strictly banned in Chile. I was to spend many hours listening to these records in Devon: songs of protest for the freedom of Latin America and simple, beautiful music of the *altiplano*, the high mountain country between Chile, Peru and Bolivia where Indian peasants forget their hunger by chewing cocoa

leaves and play simple wind instruments to produce a music
so sweet and so pure that it seems to come from another
world. The young musicians of Allende's time had made
much use of the *cena* and its music was so evocative of the
time of the Popular Unity Government that even the sale
of the music without words was prohibited.

I found Rio breathtakingly lovely. The long white beach
set against a brilliant blue sky and the two mountains, the
Sugar Loaf and the Cristo, rising out of the city is a sight
which I shall always treasure. I arrived on the night of 14
August, the eve of the feast of the Assumption of Our Lady
and was fascinated to find the beach lit with candles. After
supper I walked along the waterfront and counted more than
fifty small shrines. As I sat and watched, well-dressed people
came up and after scooping out a hollow in the sand planted
a candle and lit it and then, throwing a few flowers into the
sea, went on their way. I came across one shrine with a
champagne glass full of wine and a bowl of pudding placed
beside the candles. I asked a group of lads and later the
hotel manager what it meant and was told that this was
Macumba. It seems to be a mingling of Christianity with the
African influence in Brazil. On the feast of the Virgin the
people were making offerings for their dead loved ones, and
perhaps also to the god of the sea. The following morning I
walked along the beach and collected as many candles as I
could carry. I still have a couple now but they no longer
burn.

I had little conversation with the engineer who was
pleasant but uncommunicative but he told me that the one
thing to buy in Rio was semi-precious stones as there was a
ready sale for them in England at five times the price. I am
not by nature a business-woman but this seemed money for
jam and without giving undue thought to the ethics of the
matter I set out to purchase the stones. The hotel sent me to
a small back street jeweller where I spent the best part of
two hours and nearly £50 on amethysts and topaz of all
shapes and sizes. Shopping is by far my favourite sport and
I felt like a cross between an Eastern princess, an American
movie star and a high powered smuggler as I studied the

gems against a background of black velvet and saw them weighed carat by carat on a special balance.

The jeweller added the final touch to my private drama by putting the stones into individual little leather bags, just like those I'd seen on the films, and I walked out into the street, a very excited and satisfied customer. Later in my room, still happily filled with the sense of drama, I put the stones one by one into a jar of face cream and threw away all but one of my little bags. I was now the complete smuggler. In retrospect, of course, this does not seem quite right but nearly three years in Latin America where rules are made to be broken and dollars are changed on the black market almost as a matter of routine, had somewhat blunted my conscience in these matters and I did not feel in the least guilty.

The final laugh, of course, was on me as I had paid nearly ten times their value! This I learned first from my family who instead of being shocked and thrilled said, 'Oh, how pretty, they're just like those in Gallery Gems.' I didn't know what they meant until I went into our local seaside town and found that do-it-yourself jewellery had become the rage in England since I went away.

After a day and two nights in Rio I caught the British Caledonian flight for London. The plane was filled with a group of middle-aged British ladies loudly complaining about the lack of a decent cup of tea and a clean lavatory in South America. I sat there, silently despising them for their insularity.

Although I was on British soil (or should it be metal?) I had not yet left Latin America and I found to my delight that the passenger in the seat next to me was not one of the touring British ladies but a handsome black-bearded Brazilian. He was in a state of great rage having just lost 200 dollars while changing some money in Rio and was on his way to a European demography conference. I told him firmly that he was wasting his anger and that he should have a drink and forget it and by the time we arrived in Recife, the capital of the poor north-east of Brazil, we were firm friends.

Next morning, stiff, dishevelled and not nearly so cheerful we arrived at Gatwick. My new friend helped me with my luggage and we travelled together to Victoria where we had a meal of baked beans and chips off a dirty table which left me in no doubt that I was back in Britain. As we sat surrounded by our luggage eating this somewhat unglamorous lunch, he asked me to marry him!

Eventually we parted and he went in search of his hotel before flying off the next day to wherever the conference was, while I took a taxi to Paddington and made my way to my home in Devon.

12

Interlude in England

I am hungry and thirsty,
And the whole world cannot satisfy me.
Michel Quoist
Prayers of Life

In August of 1974 I returned to England to see my father. He was an old man and in failing health, and I knew that if I was to see him again I must not delay many months.

My fears were justified, for the day after my arrival in England he became acutely ill, and for the next four months he was in and out of hospital until on 8 December he died quietly in his sleep.

For me his passing meant the end of an era and the beginning of a new life. Although I was 37 years old and a qualified doctor, he had always regarded me as his baby and had never ceased to feel responsible for my successes or failures. He had never understood why I preferred to work in Chile and had written endlessly to me trying to persuade me to re-enter the career race in England. I in my turn, although knowing that I was free to do as I pleased, always felt guilty about him and hated to think that I was making him unhappy. So it was that when he died, in the midst of sadness, I felt a freedom that I had never known before and I knew that I could go where I pleased and work as I chose and that I was answerable only to God.

During the long months of his illness I was deeply troubled by an increasing sense of the call to the religious life. I rose early in the morning to pray. I did not feel like telling my family what was troubling me, and when they enquired what I was doing I told them simply that I liked an early morning walk by the river. They must have found this peculiar as I have never been either an early riser or a walker, but they did not comment. In fact I would walk just out of sight and sit down on the muddy river bank on my anorak and read the psalms of the day from an old breviary and pray quietly for an hour. Morning after morning I dragged myself out of bed and watched the sun come up on the river and prayed to know what I should do. It is not easy to explain to those who have not felt it just how powerful and mysterious and devastating is the call of religious vocation:

I am afraid of saying 'yes', Lord.
Where will you take me?
I am afraid of drawing the longer straw,
I am afraid of signing my name to an unread agreement,
I am afraid of the 'yes' that entails other 'yeses'.
And yet I am not at peace.
You pursue me, Lord, you besiege me.
I run after noise for fear of hearing you, but in a moment of
    silence you slip through.
I turn from the road, for I have caught sight of you but at the
    end of the path you are there awaiting me.
Where shall I hide? I meet you everywhere.
Is it then impossible to escape you?

I am hungry and thirsty,
And the whole world cannot satisfy me.
And yet I loved you, Lord; what have I done to you?
I worked for you; I gave myself for you.
O great and terrible God,
What more do you want?

                                        Michel Quoist

I could have screamed 'WHAT MORE DO YOU WANT?', for even while wanting to do what God asked of me I still could not see myself as a nun. My childhood conception of the nun as a docile black-habited creature seemed so alien to me that I wept at the stupidity of it all.

Far from my friends, I found that, paradoxically, I knew more about what was happening in Chile than if I had been there. For the first time since the coup I had access to an uncensored press. By a curious coincidence I was in England

1. Winston and myself on the S.S. *Brandestein* in Dover.

2. In the patio of the Hospital San Francisco Borja, 1972.

at the time of the dramatic exposition of the United States government's role in the destabilization of the Chilean government.

On 10 September 1974 *The Guardian* reported that Congressman Michael Harrington had 'leaked' a secret testimony made a year previously by the director of the CIA, William Colby, in which it was revealed that the CIA had been authorized by the US government to spend eight million dollars in the overthrow of the Allende government. For nearly two weeks the newspapers contained reports of the battles in Washington as senators demanded that an enquiry be made into the covert action of the CIA in Chile, and government spokesmen hedged and denied the accusations.

The results of the investigation which followed these disclosures were published in 1975 in a report entitled 'Covert Action in Chile'. Known more familiarly as the Church Report, after Senator Frank Church who headed the enquiry committee, the report is 'based on an extensive review of documents of the Central Intelligence Agency, the Departments of State and Defence, and the National Security Council; and on testimony by officials and former officials.' (Church Report.) The report reveals a long history of US interest and investment in Chilean political parties, for at the time of the 1964 presidential elections nearly four million dollars were spent on covert projects whose aim was to prevent the election of a Socialist or Communist candidate. (Church Report, p. 14.)

US intervention reached its height in 1970 when Salvador Allende won the presidential election, beating the National Party candidate Jorge Alessandri and the Christian Democrat Radomiro Tomic. There was an interval of six weeks before Allende's election was to be ratified by the Chilean Congress and a major endeavour was made in this time to prevent his coming to power.

On 8 September there was a meeting of the Forty Committee, a sub-cabinet level body of the executive branch whose mandate is to review proposed major covert activities. Headed by the President's Assistant for National Security Affairs (Henry Kissinger), the Committee includes

the Under Secretary of State for Political Affairs, the
Deputy Secretary of Defence, the Chairman of the Joint
Chiefs of Staff and the Director of the CIA. The Committee
approved the sum of $250,000 for the use of US Ambassador
Edward Korry to influence the Congressional vote on 24
October. (This plan was later found to be unworkable and
the money was not spent.) (Church Report, p. 58).

More incredible even than the bribe plan is the statement that 'on 15 September President Nixon informed CIA
director Richard Helms that an Allende regime in Chile
would be unacceptable to the United States and instructed
the CIA to play a direct role in organizing a military coup
d'état in Chile to prevent Allende's accession to the Presi-
dence'. (Church Report, p. 23.) As a result of these instructions there were two 'tracks' of effort to prevent Allende's
election: one headed by the Forty Committee and one
directly controlled by President Nixon, without the knowledge of the State Department or the Defence Department
and without informing the US Ambassador. The CIA
established contact with several groups among the Chilean
Military that were plotting Allende's defeat and gave them
arms and ammunition. It appears that there were several
plans which involved the abduction of General René
Schneider, the Chief of Staff of the Chilean Army, who was
shot and killed on 22 October. The testimonies concerning
this are conflicting but the report states categorically: 'there
is no doubt that the US government sought a military coup
in Chile.' (Church Report, p. 11.)

The scope of CIA involvement in the media during this
period is interesting: 'On 14 September the Forty Committee agreed that a propaganda campaign should be undertaken by the CIA to focus on the damage that would befall
Chile under an Allende government.' (Church Report, p.
24.) During the six weeks that followed '726 articles, broad-
casts, editorials and similar items directly resulted from
Agency activity'. Articles predicting economic collapse
under Allende were 'generated' in the European and Latin
American newspapers and when Allende criticized the
Santiago newspaper *El Mercurio* for such articles the CIA

'orchestrated' cables of support and protest from foreign newspapers, a protest statement from an International Press association and world-wide coverage of this protest. At least 18 of the pressmen who travelled to Chile to cover the Congressional voting were CIA agents, and 'special briefing' of other journalists by intelligence agents influenced their reporting. (Church Report, p. 24.)

On 24 October 1970, Chilean Congress confirmed Salvador Allende as President of Chile with an over-whelming majority. Ten days after his inauguration as president the Forty Committee made the first of a long series of payments to support his opponents, the Christian Democrat party. In January 1971 the Committee approved '$1,240,000 for the purchase of radio stations and newspapers and to support municipal candidates and other political activities of anti-Allende parties'. (Church Report, p. 59.) 'Between January and July of 1971 the Committee gave nearly half a million dollars to the Christian Democrat party but a request for a loan of $21,000,000 to buy three Boeing planes for LAN, the Chilean National airline, was turned down by the Export-Import bank.' (Church Report, p. 59.)

The refusal of this loan was in keeping with the avowed policy of the US government for (according to Geoffrey Hodgson and William Shawcross, *Sunday Times*, 27 October 1974) John Connally, then Secretary of the US Treasury, had ordered US representatives on international financial institutions to oppose all loans and aid to Chile. This order involved two important institutions, the Inter American Development Bank and the World Bank. Both of these institutions, formerly generous in their loans to Chile, re-fused loans to the Allende government.

On 11 July 1971, after a unanimous decision in the Chilean Congress, Allende nationalized the country's copper mines which had hitherto been worked by American interests. In September he nationalized the Chilean Tele-phone company, 70% of whose shares were held by the ITT Company. It was because of fear of loss of these major financial interests that the multinational corporations had, like the CIA, worked to prevent Allende coming to power.

(Church Report, p. 11.) The ITT documents, a series of confidential memos between high-ranking members of the company, disclose that they plotted to provoke a military coup and that they offered money and ideas for the destabilization of the Allende government to Mr Kissinger and the CIA. One of the most damning statements was made by William Merriman, ITT's Vice President in charge of the Washington office who, on 9 October 1970 wrote to John McCone, ex-CIA director and board member of ITT: 'Approaches continue to be made to select members of the Armed Forces in an attempt to have them lead some sort of uprising, but no success to date.' (The ITT Corporation Subversion in Chile, p. 52.)

In 1970, just after 36% of the Chilean people had voted Salvador Allende to be their President, the combined efforts of the President of the United States, the CIA and the multinational corporations could not bring about a military coup. During the next three years the US government invested 8 million dollars to destabilize the Allende government. (Church Report.) They poured money into support of right wing political groups and paid for demonstrations and strikes. Taking advantage of the freedom of the press they kept up a continual stream of propaganda designed to make the people equate Allende's regime with a Stalinist type of repression. CIA-inspired editorials in Chile's most influential newspaper, *El Mercurio*, reached all over the country and to business circles abroad. (Church Report, pp. 59–61.)

Thus it was that in September 1973, its economy wrecked and its people completely unsettled, the tinder box that was Chile caught fire and there followed one of the most violent and brutal coups in the history of Latin America. What part, if any, the US played in the actual staging of the coup is not known but there are isolated facts which suggest that it was not just an interested spectator.

One of the major coincidences concerns an American student, Charles Horman, who was stranded in a hotel in the port of Valparaiso at the time of the coup. While he was there he and an American girl called Terry Simon, who was with him, met a high ranking US naval officer who boasted that he had come to Chile for the third time 'to do a job for the navy'. Although the phone was not working he showed detailed knowledge of what was happening and during the course of the next few days he and his colleagues spoke freely about the 'coup of which they approved'. This officer drove them back to Santiago and when stopped at a road block showed a pass which identified him as a member of the Chilean navy. The story is then taken up in a letter written to Senator William Fulbright by Richard Fagen, Professor of Political Studies at Stanford University, and published in IDOC No. 58, December 1973, North American Edition. (IDOC stands for International Documentation on the Contemporary Church.)

Professor Fagen was in Chile for eighteen months from January 1972 to July 1973 as full-time social science consultant to the Ford Foundation and as Visiting Professor to the Latin American Faculty of Social Sciences. During his time in Chile he worked closely with two young American students, David Hathaway and Charles Horman. He also came to know many other young Americans one of whom was Frank Terrugi. In the weeks that followed the coup these three young men were arrested: Charles Horman on 17 September, Hathaway and Terrugi on 20 September. Hathaway and Terrugi were taken to the Stadium and the following day Terrugi was led away; on 26 September Hathaway was released into the custody of the American Consul Frederick Purdy, who told him that he had received reports two days previously that Terrugi's body was in the Santiago morgue. His body was not formally identified and his relatives notified until several days later. Charles Horman was never seen again after his arrest, and his wife reports that the US Embassy was extremely unco-operative in searching for her husband. It seems likely that Horman was killed because he knew too much about the liaison between the US and the Chilean navies. Professor Fagen was also extremely concerned because he had been told by a member of the Embassy staff that Mr Purdy was a member of the CIA. He expressed too his concern for the fact that although the arrest of the three young men was reported to the Embassy immediately the State Department apparently knew nothing about it four days later. (IDOC, No. 58.)

Finally there is the account of an interview with General Carlos Prats, former Commander in Chief of the Chilean army, shortly before he was assassinated at his home in Buenos Aires in October 1974. He told reporter Marlise Simons that 'the real co-ordination and planning for the coup took place in Valparaiso'. It is known that there is a close link between the US and the Chilean navies, and that four US navy ships arrived at Valparaiso for 'Manoeuvres' with the Chilean navy on the day of the coup. According to Hodgson and Shawcross, there was established in 1960 'a special secret communications network linking it with each of the navies of Latin America'. In this way, it is suggested, 'the US and Chilean navies could communicate directly in total secrecy, bypassing Embassies and even the Joint Chiefs of Staff in Washington.' If this was the case then the murder of Commander Arturo Araya, President Allende's Naval ADC, on 26 July could be explained as a manoeuvre to prevent the President knowing what was happening in the crucial pre-coup days.

It was while I was in England that General Carlos Prats was assassinated. His was the first of a series of assassinations of prominent left-wing Chileans in exile, for a year later an attempt was made upon the life of Bernardo Leighton, a Christian Democrat living in Rome. The murder of the former Chilean ambassador to the United States, Orlando Letelier, in Washington in September 1976 reached new heights of audacity for he died when a bomb placed under his car exploded as he was driving only a few blocks away from the Chilean Embassy.

In England in 1974, however, I was only beginning to understand that the tragedy of Chile was not an accident but a situation of chaos and bloodshed cold bloodedly and deliberately provoked by rich men who were determined not to lose their wealth. There was much news of Chile that October, for just a week after the death of General Prats came the news of the death of Miguel Enriquez, the doctor who was leader of Chile's underground left-wing revolution-

ary group the MIR. Arrested at the same time was Enriquez's companion, Carmen Castillo, who was seven
months pregnant. An intensive and world-wide campaign
for her release was successful and she was released and flown
to England in November.

Although tormented by a sense of vocation to the religious
life I longed to return to Chile. I felt a deep sense of belonging and a need to be there to share in the hardship and
suffering of these people who had so taken me to their heart.

Unable to come to any firm decision about entering the
religious life, I determined to return to Chile as soon as
possible, but two days before I was due to fly I received a
cable to telephone Teresa's sister in Australia. My heart
sank and I knew before she spoke to me that there was
trouble. She told me that she had received a cable saying
that Teresa was sick and that I must not return to Chile.
Reading between the lines, it seemed probable that both
Teresa and Juan her husband had been arrested by
the secret police and my heart bled for them and for the
children. Neither Teresa nor Juan had been active in the
resistance movement, but I knew that they had from time to
time hidden people who were on the run so I thought that
they had probably been imprisoned because of this. I longed
to help them but knew that I must possess my soul in
patience because any telephone call to Chile would be
monitored and I might be the cause of someone else being
arrested.

I think it must be one of the hardest things in the world
to do nothing when someone you care for is in trouble. I
wrote a very guarded letter to Margarita and another to a
friend asking her to call at the house. I realize now that I was
wrong even to do that, for once someone has been arrested
their house is watched and any visitors are likely to be
detained and interrogated. It was tempting to fly at once to
Chile, but I knew that this would be madness as my house
must be under surveillance and that even in Santiago there
would be no news for some time.

Since the coup, now more than a year before, the military
had been detaining people suspected of being left-wing

sympathisers. I had learned from Father Jan that the ordinary laws of habeas corpus no longer held for political detainees. People were nearly always detained at night during the hours of curfew and were taken, not to the local police station but to special centres of interrogation, where they were subjected to torture if they did not co-operate with their interrogators. It was hard to believe that such horrors were taking place in Santiago itself, but so many cases had been documented by church and other authorities that I knew it to be true. Because of the torture inflicted on detainees the authorities kept them isolated until their interrogation had been completed, and flatly denied knowledge of any individual person until they were prepared to let them go to join other political prisoners in a detention camp. As a rule people disappeared for from one to two weeks after their arrest, so it seemed that all I could do for Teresa and Juan was wait and pray.

Christmas came and went. It was a sober gathering, but I was glad to be with my family though my thoughts were constantly in Chile.

A few days after Christmas I received the incredible news that Juan and Teresa were in Venezuela. I could not believe it and telephoned a friend in Santiago who told me that they had been deported because Juan had dual Venezuelan and Chilean nationality. I put through a call to Caracas to Juan's family, and after over an hour of hanging on got through to Teresa. They had been in prison for a month and then suddenly a few days before Christmas had been taken to the airport and flown with Pedro, their youngest child, to Caracas. They had no idea why they had been arrested, but they told me that my house had been searched and 250 dollars stolen, and that the secret police had asked many questions about me and had said that I was visiting England to gather money for the resistance movement. Margarita, and Teresa's other children, were still in my house with the three dogs. I was determined to return to Chile, and though Teresa said she thought it unwise she could give no specific reason why, as the police had apparently lost interest in me after the first twenty-four hours of interrogation.

In January therefore I left England for the second time to go to Chile. Now I saw before me a new life in the Bilbao house, living with Margarita and fitting out one room as a smart consulting room so that I could work at the plastic surgery for which I had been trained and also practise a sort of Robin Hood medicine, treating rich private patients so that I would be able to give my services free to the poor. I saw too a life of increasing involvement with the Church, and I looked forward to working with Father Jan and his friends amongst the very underprivileged marginal people. I wondered if perhaps I would be asked to treat someone from the underground, but decided that if this happened, it happened, and that I would neither seek it nor refuse to help if I was asked.

As I left England behind me it seemed like the beginning of a new chapter of my life. This time I spoke Spanish and I had the Chilean medical degree, but I was going back to a Chile in a state of siege. There was no Consuelo with whom I could laugh or cry and share the day's experiences, and Teresa, who had been such a strength and comfort after her friend's death, was in exile. Many of my friends from the hospital had also left Chile and Father Jan, through whose eyes I had come to see the Chile of the broken ones, had been transferred to a mission in Bolivia. I was returning to a house with a maid and my three dogs, but I had no job and almost no friends and I wondered seriously if I was quite mad.

13
Return to Latin America

Across the margent of the world I fled,
And battered the gold gateways of the stars.
Francis Thompson
The Hound of Heaven

When we landed in Panama any doubts I might have had as to the wisdom of my return to Latin America vanished. I stepped out of the plane to meet a blast of hot wet air, and as I heard the excited conversation in Spanish and looked at the haze over the mountains I knew that this was my continent. Just as Christopher Columbus had discovered North America in 1492, I had discovered South America more than four centuries later.

There is, I think, a deep truth in this rather flippant remark, for America was there before Columbus discovered it, just as South America was there before the Conquistadores proudly took it for Spain. It had not existed for them before because they had not known about it, and so it was for me in 1971. I had known vaguely that there was a large continent south of the United States, where the people were small and dark with moustaches and where they spoke Spanish, and that was about the extent of my knowledge. But in 1971, when I made my voyage of discovery on the *Brandenstein* accompanied only by the intrepid Winston, I found an incredible new world. Here was a continent of mountains and lakes of unbelievable natural beauty, and here was a people warm-hearted and friendly and hospitable in a way that I could not believe possible. So it was that when I alighted in Panama I had a great surge of joy for my home-coming to this brave new world.

After refuelling in Panama we flew on to Quito where I was met by some English friends. I had decided to take advantage of the trip to see something of the continent, and after two days in Equador I flew on to Lima. From Lima I went to Macchu Picchu, the famous lost city of the Incas, and from there to the *altiplano* town of Puno, on the edge of Lake Titicaca which lies between Peru and Bolivia.

Feeling very unwell in the high altitude, for Puno is situated at 5000 metres, I went down the next day to Arequipa, the second city of Peru.

Arequipa is a city of wondrous beauty. Built in the colonial style of white volcanic rock it sits at the feet of a great volcano, Mistri. I explored on my own and loved the big plaza which is so typical of the Latin American cities. I went to the cathedral and the following day to another church, and in each there was a tenor singer who sang solo. The sweetness of his voice filled the tall white building during the mass.

The day after I arrived in Arequipa I heard news that there had been an incident between the armed forces in Lima and that there had been much violence and looting in the city centre. A state of emergency was declared and curfew introduced. The next day, however, the trouble seemed to be nearly over and the day after that I flew to Lima.

. Despite evidence of violence in the streets around it, the hotel where I had left my luggage was open and tranquil. If I had not already realized that I was back in Latin America, the curfew brought it home to me and a few minutes after eight o'clock the night was filled with rifle shots. As in Santiago one could not tell if they were shots fired in the air by military or if there was fighting. Safe within my hotel and knowing no one in Lima I fell asleep to a background of gunfire. Next morning the city was quiet but people talked together in undertones and I wondered if there was worse trouble to come.

That afternoon I took the plane for Santiago. My holiday was over and soberly I realized just what my return to Chile might mean. Teresa and Juan had been arrested in my house and the secret police had been very interested in me for a while, thinking me a member of the resistance. I wondered if perhaps my name was on the list and I would be detained at the airport and not allowed to re-enter the country. More unpleasant was the thought of midnight visitors to the house, and I was not a little afraid. Although I knew that to return to Chile so soon after Teresa's arrest was perhaps asking for trouble, I had calculated that if my name was on a list of undesirable aliens it would remain there and that I would never know until I tried to go back. So strong was my urge to return that I told myself firmly that the worst that could happen was that I might be asked to leave, and then I would know where I stood. My mouth, however, was dry and I felt sick and afraid as the plane taxied to a halt at Pudahuel.

The line of people waiting to have their documents checked moved at snail's pace, but no one was called ominously to one side. As we stood waiting for the customs examination one woman told me that the list of names was fed into a computer to see if anyone was on the list of wanted or unwanted citizens. Whether or not that was true I don't know, but it was some time before anyone left the arrival lounge. There were, however, no problems and at last the doors opened and I ran to meet the friends who were waiting for me. After six months which seemed like a lifetime I was back in Chile, and thoughts of the secret police vanished as my luggage was piled into the car and we drove happily towards the city.

14

A Time to Build

For everything there is a season and a time for every matter under heaven:
a time to be born, and a time to die;
a time to plant, and a time to pluck up what is planted;
a time to kill, and a time to heal;
a time to break down, and a time to laugh;
a time to mourn, and a time to dance.

Ecclesiastes 3:1–4

We drove straight from the airport to my house. Here at last was the moment of which I had dreamed ever since I learned of Teresa's imprisonment and realized that perhaps I might not be able to return to Chile. There it was, my home, a funny yellowed house of adobe and brick that had firmly withstood two earthquakes and a military coup. Behind the tall metal railings with which all the houses of the rich and the middle class in Chile are protected were my three dogs. They looked very well despite my prolonged absence and were obedient to Margarita in a way that they had never been to me. The house was spotless but I was a little shaken at how shabby my home was in comparison with the way I had been living in England and I realized just how depressed I had been in those first two years in Chile when I had barely managed to paint a room or hang a curtain. Now however I was well and the mistress of my destiny and I would transform the house in no time.

When my kind friends had gone Margarita and I settled down to talk. I told her of my meeting with Teresa and she recounted to me the grim events that followed the visit of the DINA (the Directorate of National Intelligence). She and the children had been held prisoner by armed guards for three days as the DINA waited to see if they could catch any of Teresa's friends. Luckily no one had called and eventually the men left. The month that followed had been one of great sadness and responsibility for Margarita as she struggled to make ends meet and feed the children and waited desperately for news of Teresa. She had told Pedro that his mother was in hospital and with his nanny had fought to remain calm and cheerful so as not to distress him. At last with the joy of their release from prison came the sadness of parting and the knowledge that they would probably never meet again.

Little by little I told Margarita of my plans, of how I was going to build a new life and that I needed her to help me. I decided to redecorate the front part of the house to make it elegant and install a consulting room where I would see private patients for I felt sure that with my Chilean and British qualifications I would soon have a thriving private practice, and with the money I earned I would be able to treat free of charge people who had no money to pay a doctor. Margarita was delighted and saw herself as the receptionist in a white overall ushering the élite of Santiago into a smart waiting room and giving medical advice over the phone in my absence.

After a few days settling in I set out to look for work. It was with some trepidation that I began my search, as various medical friends had told me that jobs were few and far between and that I would be lucky to find employment. It seemed crazy that in a country which had lost 25 per cent of its doctors there should be a shortage of jobs but the answer was quite simple. There had been a progressive decline in the economy since the coup and although expenditure on arms and money spent on maintenance of the armed forces had risen sharply this had been achieved by a massive cut back in spending on the social services. When I went to the San Borja, the hospital where I was best known, I was greeted warmly but told that the direction of the National Health Service had decreed that no new jobs were to be created and that if anyone resigned or died their post was not to be refilled. I was shaken. Could it be that I would not be able to find work or that I would have to abandon my house and go to some isolated rural area?

As my hopes diminished I became less choosy and went

to the Posta Central, the main hospital of Santiago's emergency service where Consuelo had worked for so many years. I went to the staff office where I knew the secretaries as I had often been in on Consuelo's behalf either to hand in sick notes or to collect her pay cheque. To my delight they greeted me enthusiastically and told me that there was a locum job available at the Posta 4, the quietest of the hospitals, and that I could do it for three weeks. They gave me the necessary papers and I took them home to fill in. As I read them through I began to realize just what it meant to live in a police state, for in addition to the various certificates which are routine in any public service employment I was asked to list six of my relatives with their addresses and six of my personal friends with their addresses. I was angered by this intrusion into my privacy but strove to think of people I could call friend who would not be at risk if anything should happen to me.

Within ten days of my arrival in Chile I was at work and I was very pleased with myself. Admittedly it was only half time but it was work and with luck I would be able to keep myself. I became the second assistant on the *Volante*, the 'flying' shift at the Posta 4 in a middle class area of Santiago and I worked each day for two and a half hours and also every sixth night. The hours of the Posta are arranged so that the doctor can do four hours a day in general surgery or a speciality at another hospital, but as I had no other job I was free for much of the day. The return to medicine after more than a year without working was not easy and I was glad of the free time. The loss, too, of a night's sleep every sixth day left me with the need for an early night, so I was content to use my spare time to play with my house until I found more work.

I had arranged while I was in England that £50 would be sent out to me each month to cover the initial months before I received my salary, so I was financially independent though by no means rich. I could not afford to employ a firm of contractors to do the repairs to the house so with the help of a friend I took on two workmen. This was my first mistake but it is one which I do not regret, for though these workmen settled with delight into my house and spun the work out for over nine months it gave me an unparalleled opportunity of getting to know some of the Chilean *rotos*. My workmen were unemployed and I learned gradually that each of them was a *maestro chasqueo*, a jack of all trades or man who knew how to mix cement, change a tap, paint a wall or do rough carpentry. They were, however, clearly masters of nothing but the gentle art of charming stupid foreigners like me. I had a fair idea that I was being had, but as the weeks went by the devils I knew seemed better than those I didn't and anyway despite all their faults I had become fond of them. Antonio and Ricardo were the first of a long line of out of work Chileans to firmly stake a claim in my house and in my heart. Apart from Antonio who was a very charming thief and by far the best workman, I believe that they all did their best according to their lights and although they took advantage of my generosity in a shameless way they would have made me welcome in their homes any day.

Antonio was a good looking young man in his late twenties who was a carpenter by trade. When he put his mind to a problem he had considerable skill and manual dexterity, but he was very lazy and arrived late nearly every morning despite my threats to sack him. After he had been in my employ for about two months and was arriving later and later I tried to be firm and told him that if he was late once more I would go to the employment agency where better carpenters than he were queuing for work from six o'clock in the morning. The next day he was even later and when he arrived asked for a bag to send his apprentice to buy bread. (Chilean bread is very rough and heavy and does not last well so the buying of fresh bread, hot from the bakery, is a daily ritual.) Fuming, I gave the boy a bag and retired to my room to think up the right words of dismissal while Antonio and Ricardo changed into their work clothes. In ten minutes I came down to find the table laid with my best china and a feast of *almejas*, Chile's 'poor man's oyster', laid out. My rage vanished and when Margarita returned from shopping the four of us were having a mid-morning party and all thoughts of dismissal had gone. Whether Antonio was late because he bought the *almejas* or bought the *almejas* because he was late I still don't know, but I was very happy to be eating raw shellfish and onion with hot fresh bread at eleven o'clock on a Saturday morning.

My friendship with my workmen was unusual to say the least by Chilean standards. Both Margarita and my friends told me that I was hopeless and that I had no idea how to handle workmen. I saw it differently. How could I sit down to a cooked lunch while they ate bread and tea in the garden, when I had had scrambled eggs for my breakfast and they a piece of bread? My instincts for justice forced me to share my meals with them and I never regretted it. Margarita complained endlessly about having to cook their lunch but secretly she enjoyed their company and was proud that her mistress should treat working class men as human beings. It would have been different if I had known that they were going home to a large meal cooked by a loving wife, but I knew well that conditions where my men lived were grim and that what I paid them only just kept body and soul together. I could not afford to pay their social security which was 50 per cent of their salary, so when they were ill they came to me and I treated them and bought such medicines as they needed. Although they were constantly late and needing advances on next week's wages which were never paid back, they were always charming to me and managed to walk the tight-rope between friendship and familiarity so at least I was left with the feeling that they liked and respected me and that I was boss. If this was an illusion I don't really mind because it seems to me that it is better to be had again and again than to risk refusing to help someone in genuine need.

Ricardo was my favourite for a long time. Antonio brought him along to help him mend the balcony when I was ill in bed with bronchitis and he tiptoed into my room, cap in hand, every day to ask how I was. Ricardo was an alcoholic. Admittedly he was only an intermittent drinker, which meant that he spent each weekend drunk and Monday recuperating, but it was tedious that he could only work a five day week and it maddened me that he was always broke on Tuesday. He was, however, a genuinely kind and extremely entertaining man which is probably why his wife put up with him. He left my employ in July and the last I heard was that he had a job in a *botelleria* or shop that sold beer and wine. I feared sadly for his liver.

In February Francisco appeared on the scene. He was the carpenter to a friend of mine and cut his hand very badly with an electric saw, nearly losing half of his thumb. I had worked with hand injuries in Leicester for three years so I felt competent to treat him, especially as the care he was receiving seemed pretty dubious. He came twice a week to see me at the hospital and once at home, and it was two months before the wound healed. During all this time he became a friend and when he arrived at the house in May and said he was out of work it seemed natural that he should fall in with the lads. Thus it was that I came to be employing three workmen, but so long as the money held out I was happy. Francisco was endlessly patient and willing, though not as clever as Antonio, but his devotion paid off because in June I found that Antonio was fiddling the bills for the building materials so he had to go and Francisco settled happily into his place.

In the beginning I had planned only to have the front of the house done up but quickly drove the thin end of the wedge into my resolution by deciding that the dining-room was too dark to be tolerated and needed french windows in place of the window looking on to the back porch. The nice thing about building work in Chile is that in a house made of adobe a wall can be demolished in less than an hour and if it is summer it doesn't matter too much how long it takes to fill the gap so long as it is finished by winter. My sub-conscious got the better of me one day and while Margarita was out I told Ricardo to demolish the wall of the dining-room. The men were not stupid and, always delighted to do anything that would ensure the prolongation of their jobs for another couple of weeks, made me a large hole in my dining-room wall in the twinkling of an eye. Margarita was not pleased and muttered that it would be two months before we had the house clear of workmen. Little did she know how wrong she was because one thing led to another and we were still building when I was arrested in November!

The first two months of my time in Santiago were easy in comparison with what was to follow, but while I was finding my feet I did not have the courage to go to work in one of the *poblaciones* or shanty towns. I wondered very much those first weeks if the DINA would suddenly arrive on my doorstep and I felt it would be unwise to draw attention to myself by working in conditions which were only tolerated by leftist sympathizers or missionaries. In retrospect I see this decision as largely conditioned by my fear of involvement with the poor because I knew that I would be forced to change my way of life. In fairness I just was not ready to leave the comfort of my house and the security of work which bore some resemblance to that which I knew. I admired the people who worked on equal terms with the shanty town dwellers but I did not feel able to join them.

Finding myself with a good deal of spare time I spent much of it in search of God in prayer. I had made friends with an American nun who had been seventeen years a missionary in Chile and she and I spent many happy hours gossiping, exchanging books and going to the pictures. She was the first of many friends among the American missionaries in Santiago who slowly led me towards a different view of Chile and of life itself. Rosemary sent me one Sunday to the Benedictine monastery overlooking Santiago and I was enchanted. It was a big white modern building, simply but cleverly constructed so that the sunlight streamed in from windows high under the roof. The Sunday mass was sung and it was marvellous to hear after so long the Gregorian chant which I had loved in my Oxford days. Unable to tear myself away I lingered outside the church after mass and plucked up courage to ask one of the brothers if I might stay a while to pray. He asked me how long I wished to stay, so I told him 'until I'm too hungry to bear it', at which he replied that they would give me lunch. After the midday office I was served with lunch on a tray in the waiting room and thus fortified spent the rest of the afternoon perched on the low wall outside the church and overlooking the city stretched out below me.

This became a favourite place of pilgrimage and, unable to sleep after I had worked all night, I used to take the little bus which went up into the hills and then walk up the steep dirt road to the monastery. The monks became used to me sitting in my poncho and jeans in the front row of their empty church and one of the novices was always deputed to bring me the book of psalms with the place marked. Thus we prayed together many times, the monks and I, high above Santiago. The presence of contemplatives in an active society is always disturbing. The folly of their life spent in prayer and manual labour is a curious sign of the existence of God in a world so preoccupied with its own affairs. I used to look at these men, the old ones who had wasted their life in this crazy way and the young ones who were freely choosing to do likewise, and wonder what on earth God wanted of me. It was a good place to come to pray and to think because, it being a long way, I had to be very desperate before I decided to go home. Sometimes they gave me lunch and sometimes I took an apple and some bread and cheese and sat on my wall until it was time for vespers. Then, stiff and sunburned, I would walk down the hill into the setting sun and know in some incommunicable way that my day had been well spent.

At the end of March my locum post at the Posta 4 came to an end and for two weeks I was out of work and very nervous. Encouraged by friends in the service I beat importunately upon the doors of the director of the *Asistencia Pública* (the Public Emergency Service) and eventually was rewarded by being given a contract for a year in Santiago's sleaziest hospital, the Posta No. 3 in Chacabuco. This was the hospital where Consuelo had worked and it was famous for being one of the busiest and most ill-equipped hospitals in the city. Beggars, however, cannot be choosers and I was extremely pleased to have regular work so I took the crowded bus every day to work from 1.30 till 4 p.m. in the poorest area of town. It was an area famous for its prostitutes

and alcoholics and I came to practise a medicine very different from that which I had learned at the Radcliffe Infirmary
in Oxford.

> For the wildest dreams of Kew
> Are the facts of Khatmandu
> And the crimes of Clapham meek in Martaband!

15
The Posta 3

Do not be afraid of Him!
He is a woman old and wrinkled and dirty
                              and smelling like wine,
With sneakers and a torn sweater and a
                              handbag cracked and torn
Smoking a just rolled cigarette.
Do not be afraid of his language
or the looks of him
or the smell of him,
He is your God.

Christopher William Jones
Listen Pilgrim

The Posta 3 is an old and down-at-heel emergency hospital
in Santiago's red light area of Chacabuco. It is the only
source of medical aid for the thousands of shanty town
dwellers who have a strong love-hate relationship with it.
There are two big wards and various small ones which
together hold about 60 beds so close to each other that it is
just possible to squeeze between them. Over 300 patients a
day come to the Posta with everything from an ache in their
little toe to a knife in their heart, but they are all seen by a
doctor and receive some degree of comfort. It is rare for one
of the 60 beds to be empty for long and more often than not
patients are admitted on to trolleys and at times on to the
floor, but no one really sick is ever turned away because this
is where the buck stops.

The work at the Posta is despised by many more erudite
physicians, who practice European style medicine in
smoothly running teaching hospitals, where they have the
luxury of choosing whom they will accept and deliberately
remain oblivious to the untreatable but desperately sick
dropout or alcoholic. The nurses at the Posta likewise look
in scorn on doctors who lie about empty beds on a Friday

afternoon or jealously guard their accommodation for interesting cases. The dregs of Chacabuco society come home to die in the Posta 3, in the 'Clínica Santa Maria', the hidden ward for those whose only friends left in the world are the lice that infest them. Two miles away is the real Clínica Santa Maria, Santiago's plushest private clinic where elegant ladies in fur coats wait to see their friends and relations and pay more for a day's treatment than these men would earn in a year.

The Posta doctors are a race apart. At 9 p.m., while Santiago's physicians and surgeons settle down with their evening glass of *pisco*, the night team at the Posta checks in. Punctuality here is the politeness of princes, for the Posta, eternally alert for trouble, must not be left unmanned and no doctor may leave until he has passed his torch to his counterpart in the next shift. The chief and the first assistant, both of them competent surgeons, begin a ward round of all patients who are being observed and decide who needs operating on most urgently, while the juniors begin to do battle with the tide of patients which does not cease until the curfew time and often not then. Never before had I worked so quickly, seeing one patient every two minutes, or a little longer if they required suturing.

I developed a great rapport with nurses, especially the *practicantes* or male nurses and, when I could, chose to work among the male patients because I found them easier to diagnose and cope with than the women. I could put stitches in a drunk's head at three o'clock in the morning when practically unable to stand with exhaustion, whereas the long line of women with abdominal pain who might be suffering from anything from indigestion to an ectopic pregnancy were a nightmare of responsibility. The nurses were a great help, for years of experience working in the Posta had given them considerable diagnostic skill. At times the bolder ones would come with the card and say, 'I removed a piece of grit from a man's eye; just sign here please.' The ambulance men, too, took a pride in diagnosis and Consuelo had told me how they would often rush someone with severe internal bleeding straight to the operating theatre without allowing the surgeon to waste valuable time confirming their diagnosis! It is such caring and rapid team work that saves lives, for when a man arrives with a knife wound in the heart there are not many minutes to spare. I remember one such day when within five minutes of the patient's arrival we were putting stitches through the hole in his heart and the next day he was grumbling peevishly about the pain, quite unaware of how nearly he had died.

Although it had been my intention to seek work in a training hospital to increase my knowledge of plastic surgery I shall never regret my time at the Posta, for I learned to make diagnoses with my ears and eyes and hands instead of relying on x-rays and blood tests and was forced to treat practically every condition known to man with one of a basic half dozen drugs. It was of course maddening and harassing to a degree after years of working with superb equipment in a hospital with a round the clock x-ray service, but it taught me to draw on all my reserves of knowledge and skill. The range of pathology too was quite different from that to which I had become accustomed, for in Chile alcoholism, malnutrition and tuberculosis, diseases of which I had only read in my text books, were rampant. Alcohol is the solace of the lonely, the unemployed and the bereaved and many of my patients drank between three and five litres a day. The road to the public cemetery in Santiago is lined with wine bars which bear the glorious name of *quita pena*, the 'taker away of sorrow'. In Chile now there is no free milk for the children of the unemployed and babies are kept quiet with bottles of tea. It would seem a logical step to tax wine and subsidize milk as was done in the time of Allende, but perhaps this is not convenient for trade.

In the little operating theatre at the back of the Posta the chief and his assistant operated upon whatever emergency presented itself. The chief of a team has to be able to cope with any eventuality and both the glory and nightmare of emergency work is the unexpected. When one operates on a man with a small bullet wound in the belly one does not know if it will be just a matter of cleaning up or if the next five hours must be spent meticulously suturing

holes in the intestines. Despite its almost primitive simplicity, we did more heroic surgery with less fuss in that
theatre than I had seen in many years of working in England.

Although my hours of work at the Posta were short they
left me exhausted. The twelve-hour night, worked every
sixth day, came round all too quickly and my inability to
sleep during the day meant that I always spent the day after
the night on duty feeling like death. It was the night and
weekend work which made the Posta a job which most doctors avoided like the plague. In a six-week cycle we worked
one Friday night, one Saturday night, one Sunday night,
one entire Saturday and one Sunday so that there were only
two weekends out of the six which were not interfered with.
In a country where most doctors like to go to the beach at
weekends this is no mean curtailment of activity. For all
this, however, the team spirit and the constant challenge of
the work makes it worthwhile for those who work for the
love of medicine rather than the money they can earn.

It was here in Chacabuco that I began to work with the
marginal people of Chile and as the weeks passed I grew to
love them. Drunk they may have been, alcoholics, rogues
and prostitutes they certainly were, but they were a warm
people who asked little and accepted gratefully what we
could do for them. Most of them were birds of passage,
quickly examined, comforted if time and strength allowed,
which was not always, and sent on their way with an injection or a prescription or a paper for one of the specialist
departments of the teaching hospital next door. Some of
them, however, came back to have their stitches out or a
particularly complicated wound dressed and these became
firm friends. A few of them brought me gifts, the more moving because they were so poor. Occasionally I became personally involved with them and was made desperate by the
enormity of their problems and my inability to solve them.

Juanita was a girl of 22 who turned up every few weeks
after having had an epileptic fit. One Sunday morning after
I had ordered an injection for her the woman with her said,
'She hasn't eaten for four days.' I looked at her more carefully and, finding her pale and thin, asked her if this was so.

It was. It was Sunday and there were no social services available and as she could hardly stand I admitted her to the ward. As I interrogated her I learned the full tragedy of her story. Hers was not a congenital epilepsy but had come on after she had fallen head first into an empty swimming pool where she had worked as an instructress. She had fractured her skull and broken her neck and had spent many months in hospital and a few months after her discharge had developed severe and frequent fits. A year ago her mother had died and her father went off to live with another woman leaving Juanita to care as best she could for six little brothers and sisters. I tried hard to help her by arranging appointments with the social worker, but she was unable to get the children into care nor was she able to get any kind of compensation from the owner of the swimming pool. The last time I saw her she turned up just before I was due to go off duty and I managed to get her admitted to the neurological hospital where they tried to control her epilepsy better, but there is no happy ending to her story.

Another case which made me desperate was a young woman of 33 who was in the terminal phase of uterine cancer and who had been firmly told by the radium institute that they could do no more to help her. After she had come for the third time for pain-killing injections I wrote a beseeching letter to the gynaecological department of the San Juan de Dios Hospital, our neighbour, and they admitted her to die. She came from the parish where one of my American friends worked and she visited her in hospital and was able to give her some comfort in the last weeks of her life. Many of my patients were sad people and their lives were hard.

As I spent more time in prayer and tried to translate my growing love of God into concrete terms I sought Him more and more in my patients, mindful of Matthew 25: 'I was sick and you visited me.' I tried hard to be more caring and more gentle and much of the time it worked, though when I was tired or hungry or harassed my good intentions and humour left me and I was impatient and unfriendly.

For me, the vision of Christ in man was not one that just

happened, it was one that I looked for and found only from time to time. Long hours of praying on my mountain top brought me to a growing consciousness of God in his creation.

> The world is charged with the grandeur of God
> It will flame out like shining from shook foil;
> > G. M. Hopkins
> > *God's Grandeur*

It was easy to see the image of God in the sun setting behind the Andes or behind the restless tossing of the sea, but the image of Christ in his creatures is a very tarnished one and it is too easy to miss it.

> Where is He today?
> He is black
> and beaten
> to a pulp on a Mississippi street.
> He falls off a toilet seat
> dead
> with needle marks in His arms.
> He stands on a corner, wine soaked.
> He is admitted as an OW
> into a maternity ward in a city hospital.
> He is twenty people living in one tenement room.
> He is ten persons living in an Appalachian shack.
> He is all this and
> more.
> > Christopher William Jones
> > *Listen Pilgrim*

As the weeks turned into months and I persevered with my search and extended my hours of prayer to include the bus journey to work and odd moments when I wasn't busy I found that my patience was rewarded and I came to see Him more and more in the broken ones of Santiago.

16

Easter 1975

Nigh and nigh draws the chase,
With unperturbéd pace,
Deliberate speed, majestic instancy;
And past those noiséd Feet
A Voice comes yet more fleet –
'Lo! naught contents thee, who content'st not Me.'
Francis Thompson
The Hound of Heaven

During Holy Week one of my friends was taken by the
DINA. Jaime was a final year medical student and I had
met him at the San Borja where he had been one of the
students who organized the manning of the outpatient
clinics during the strikes of 1973. I had not seen him for
some time and now to my surprise and sadness I heard that
he had been picked up outside the hospital by the DINA
and that there had been no news of him for a week. I wondered bitterly what would become of him and Marietta
his student wife who was expecting their first child. In the
first week after someone had disappeared there was nothing
to do but hope and pray that at least it would not be too
long before they reached Tres Alamos. Although I knew
little of what happened to political prisoners I was aware
of the pattern of events in most cases: arrest, interrogation
and torture, period of incommunicado and then transfer to
the public detention camp at Tres Alamos. Once the
authorities admitted that a person was detained it seemed
that they were safe, but before that happened there was
reason to be worried.

Determined to join in the spirit of Holy Week I went as
often as I could to the Benedictine monastery and on Holy
Thursday, as I sat on my wall trying to think about Christ's
passion, my thoughts came back again and again to Jaime.

Suddenly I saw for the first time the similarity between what I had been reading in my Bible and what I knew was happening to Jaime: the sudden and violent arrest, the insolent interrogators, the rough hands that tore away his clothes leaving him humiliated and vulnerable; then the blows and the laughter of the tormentors and finally the fixing spread-eagled to the bed for the shocks to break his spirit. I was appalled. Never had the passion of Christ, read and re-read since childhood, moved me to more than a gesture of sadness or an act of contrition, but now I was filled with anguish and nausea. The vision of Christ still living and still being crucified amongst us took on a clarity and meaning that was quite new to me and I wept for Jaime and for Christ, knowing that they were one.

On Easter Sunday I went to mass at the Benedictines, and after the sadness of Holy Week I felt the joy of the Resurrection as the monks' voices filled the church with Alleluias and the morning sunlight came through the windows in long white shafts, piercing the clouds of incense which rose to meet it. I had been invited to lunch at Rosemary's house and we celebrated Easter with an enormous American-style feast. As I made ready to go Rosemary asked me if I wouldn't like to come to the centre house of her congregation to a party that they were having. I was doubtful about meeting a bevy of unknown nuns, but it seemed churlish to refuse so I thanked her but insisted on going home to put on my skirt as I felt sure I would be out of place in my jeans. She laughed and said that it didn't matter, but I was unconvinced so she and I stopped off at my house for me to make myself respectable.

When we reached the convent I was filled with gloom; what on earth would I have to say to all these nuns? I must be mad to have come. Nervously I followed Rosemary into the house, not really knowing what to expect but certainly not prepared to find a group of girls much my own age laughing and talking. Most incredible of all, not one of them wore a habit and several of them were in trousers! Rosemary introduced me to Frances, a cheerful, fair-haired girl later to become one of my closest friends. I discovered that she lived with two other nuns, also in their thirties, in a small house right in the middle of one of the most distant shanty towns. Like Father Jan whom I had met nearly a year before, they saw their mission not only as one of teaching the gospel to the poor but rather of living the message of Christ in their midst. I was to learn from Frances and Anna just how much it cost in terms of anguish and harassment and loss of sleep and privacy to attempt to share the lives of the Chilean *pobladores*; but they taught me also of the joy of giving.

As I talked to these girls I realized how much I had to learn about Chile, about its people and about myself. Safe behind the barrier of my white coat and my position as *La Doctora* I could afford to be charming to the *rotos*. It was easy to be kind and friendly on my own ground, safe in the knowledge that I was doing good work and had no obligation to them once they stepped outside and I said, 'Next please.' Now I knew that my instinct to keep clear of the shanty towns had been born of the desire to remain uninvolved and therefore unhurt. The way of Frances and Anna was becoming the way of the Church in Latin America, a Church that was learning to change its approach, to take literally the words of Isaiah,

> He has sent me to bring good news to the poor,
> to bind up hearts that are broken;
> to proclaim liberty to captives,
> freedom to those in prison.
>
> *Isaiah 61:2*

I went home that night both pleased to have found new friends and unnerved at the prospect of what their friendship might cost me, for I had agreed to go and have lunch with Frances and Anna the following week in their house in the *población*. I think I knew that it was the beginning of the breaking down of my protective wall, but there didn't seem any way to avoid it so I ignored the warning signs and awaited the inevitable.

17

Frances and Anna

> One doesn't just go down to the ghetto and work with
> the Negroes.
> One moves into a certain neighbourhood and gets to
> know Millie and Tommy and Jimmy and Mary.
>
> Christopher William Jones
> *Listen Pilgrim*

The following week I took the bus out to the *población* El Conquistador to have lunch with Frances, Anna and Elizabeth.
Seeing them on their home ground I realized the immense
difference in our way of life. Their house was in the middle
of a row in the centre of the *población* and was only a little
better finished than those which surrounded it. The plank
walls inside were unpapered and unpainted, though gaily
decorated with Chilean folk art and sketches done by Anna.
They had just what they needed for their life and work in
this particular place and no more.

As we ate our lunch they told me about themselves and
their work. Anna was the eldest of the three and had been in
Chile for about fifteen years, arriving in the days when the
sisters wore the full habit. It was difficult to visualize this
tall, well-groomed girl in a veil, but she had worn the habit
for many years until the wind of change that swept through
the Church and the Second Vatican Council led her congregation to discard the habit so that they might relate more
easily to the people with whom they worked. She spoke
with great humour of the rather grim early days, when as a
young nun she had come to the south of Chile and struggled
to learn Spanish in a class with small children (the language
school for missionaries in Cochabamba, Bolivia, had not yet
been opened). Now she worked as a catechist in the programme organized by the Chilean hierarchy, teaching the

mothers so that they in turn might instruct their children in the faith.

Frances, at 37, was my own age and had entered the convent much later. She too had run from the Hound of Heaven until she wearied but now was deeply happy and fulfilled. Like Anna she worked with the adults in instruction and also helped to supervise the women in the *Comedor Infantil*, the children's dining-room, where the children of the unemployed were given one meal a day in an effort to prevent the malnutrition that was becoming increasingly common since the coup. The women got food for their children by begging from shopkeepers in the *población* and from the stall-holders in the market. Frances told me how she would go every Friday with a group of women to the *Vega*, the big fruit and vegetable market in the centre of Santiago, and do a round of the stalls asking for food.

The most important part of their work, however, was the simple fact of their presence in the *población*. Of their own volition three American women were sharing the day-to-day living conditions of poor Chileans. These were not pious foreign missionaries coming in to preach a message of brotherly love and then returning to their comfortable American-style house, but educated young women who lived in a little wooden house like they did, who travelled on foot and by bus as they did and who shared their bread and their friendship and their talents with those who asked. This indeed was a mystery and it spoke more powerfully of the love of God than a thousand sermons.

In the three years that they had lived in El Conquistador Frances and Anna and Elizabeth had made many friends among the *pobladores*. At first the people had been afraid to invite nuns into their homes, but when they found that the *madres* could sit on the bed and drink a glass of wine in company with their other friends they lost their inhibitions and relaxed.

Now, after more than three years, the girls were quite accepted in the *población*. The coup had been a great proving time, for the nuns had stayed in their home and their house had been searched along with those of their neighbours.

Sub-human living.
3. (*above*) A Santiago Poblacion. Photograph : Marcelo Montecino

4. (*left*) Poblacion child in his home. Photograph : courtesy of Maryknoll Magazine

5. (*above*) Joyful workers marching in support of Allende on September 4th 1973, the anniversary of the election of the Popular Unity Government. Each wears a badge bearing the words 'I work for Chile'. Photograph : Cristian Montecino

6. (*right*) Victor Jara, the folk singer who was killed in the stadium a few days after the coup. 'Ever since I was born I have seen injustice, poverty and social misery in my country. I believe it is for this reason that I felt the need to sing for the people.'

7. Poster encouraging students to participate in voluntary work building houses for the homeless.

8. Poster of the Popular Unity Government illustrating the union between all classes of workers in Chile. The verse is by Pablo Neruda : Copper of Chile – you are country, prairie and people ; sand, clay, school, house, resurrection, fist, offensive order, procession, attack, wheat fight, grandeur, resistance.

a trabaja

TRABAJO VOLUNTARIO VERAN

COBRE CHILENO

tu eres la patria, pampa y pueblo,
arena, arcilla, escuela, casa
resurrección, puño ofensiva
orden, desfile, ataque, trigo
lucha, grandeza, resistencia.

They had shared the terror of the *pobladores* when the *población* had been surrounded and the tanks had driven between the little houses and over some of them, and they had stood numbly by as armed men searched their clothes for arms and their bookshelf for Marxist literature. Now, in the days of steadily increasing hardship, they shared their bread and more important, for it is easy to give what you have, they shared the desperate impotence of watching children die because they had nothing more to give. It is this standing by helpless that is so difficult and yet so important, the simple being there to share in the suffering of birth, of living and of death. It is when we have nothing left to give that we are forced to open our hearts to share in the grief of the other. What can you tell a mother whose son has just been shot or whose baby has died of malnutrition, or a woman with no bread in her house when you have none either? It would be so much easier to go away and do something constructive which would make one feel warm inside, but it is in the silent sharing of pain that love is shown.

This living among the people and sharing their way of life, their sorrows and their joys, is rapidly becoming the way of the Church in Latin America precisely because the message of the gospel only has validity if it is lived by the bearer.

I spent the afternoon and evening talking to Anna and Frances, and when it was time for me to go we were firm friends. As I sat in the bus on the way home I thought it strange that I should feel so at ease with these nuns. They were so happy. Tired and harassed they might be, overworked they certainly were, but they had a deep joy and peace that I envied. I wondered where this new friendship would lead me, and I began to feel desperate and trapped. Could it really be that after all these years I must really give up my freedom, with all that it meant to me? It seemed complete madness: there I was, a professional with my future before me and my home established, and yet I could not rid myself of the feeling that I was being asked to give it all up. Again it was Christ's reply to the rich young man which haunted me, 'If you would be perfect, go sell what you have and give it to the poor and come, follow me.' Then the hard truth began to come home to me that the words of Christ were to be taken literally, and that I was going to have to lose my life before I found it again.

18

Naught Shelters Thee

Still with unhurrying chase,
And unperturbèd pace,
Deliberate speed, majestic instancy,
Came on the following Feet,
And a Voice above their beat –
'Naught shelters thee, who wilt not shelter Me.'
Francis Thompson
The Hound of Heaven

The weeks went by and my friendship with the nuns deepened. They introduced me to many of the other missionaries who worked in the shanty towns with them and little by little I became incorporated into the community of foreign priests and nuns working in Santiago. The Columban Fathers were my neighbours and I turned naturally to them for help, for I missed the support of my family and needed friends who spoke English and to whom I could turn in trouble. In return I was able to help them medically, and from time to time I would go out to a *población* to see a missionary who was suspected of having hepatitis or typhoid. The risks of infection to those foreigners living in the marginal areas is very real, for they do not have the natural resistance of many of the Chileans to the various diseases which are endemic in underdeveloped countries. Usually the greatest problem was persuading the patient to abandon his home amongst the *pobladores* and return to the 'centre house' of the congregation so that he or she could be properly looked after; for those who choose to live amongst the underprivileged resent being made to return to the privileged status which they have abandoned.

Although I became completely accepted among my new friends, I was acutely conscious of the difference between us, for though we shared our weariness, our hopes and our moments of joy they had a freedom which I did not know.

They had sold all they had and gone to follow Christ, whereas I still carried all my possessions with me, for as yet

> ... was I sore adread
> Lest, having Him, I must have naught beside.

Still troubled by indecision, I determined once more to seek advice and went to call upon a priest recommended to me by one of my friends.

The logical behaviour when going to meet someone for the first time is to telephone to see if they are at home, but I have always found that my logical behaviour deserts me in matters of the heart and of the soul. It required more premeditation and courage than I possessed to ring this man up and, as I hardly knew myself what my business was, how could I state it? Conscious of the stupidity of my behaviour I preferred to call unannounced and take pot luck, knowing that the man I sought would probably be out or, if he was in, he would be sure to be busy. I had not counted, however, on certain priests knowing very well that people troubled in the spirit turn up at all hours of the day unannounced and that if they are out or busy that person may never come back again. It was just because of this knowledge that they are available to casual callers whenever possible. Thus it was that when I diffidently enquired at San Ignacio the porter pressed a bell and before I could change my mind and run away I found myself saying good morning to a tall, smiling Jesuit. He invited me in and, though it was by this time a quarter to one, gave no indications that he was hungry or in a hurry and asked me how he could help. Stumbling a good deal, for I had no very clear notion why I had come other than feeling that I needed to talk to someone, I told him I wanted to talk about prayer. If he was surprised he gave no indication but invited me to continue. Little by little I told him about myself and how the feeling of being called to the religious life had recurred like malaria for so many years, filling me with an anguish and revulsion that I could not understand. Patiently he sat and listened, questioning carefully if something was not clear, until he had the whole story of my flight from God over the past twenty years. It must have been four o'clock when I stumbled out into the street, feeling as if he had unknitted me like an old sock and with his words ringing in my ears, 'I'm afraid I'm not at all sure that you don't have a genuine old-fashioned vocation to be a nun.'

19

Surrender

Naked I wait Thy love's uplifted stroke!
My harness piece by piece Thou hast hewn from me,
    And smitten me to my knee;
    I am defenceless utterly.

                    Francis Thompson
                    The Hound of Heaven

In the weeks that followed I went frequently to talk to the
priest at San Ignacio. Endlessly patient, he listened while I
repeated that I couldn't possibly become a nun and then in
the next breath told him that I was sure God was calling me
to give up everything I had. After a while he surprised me
by saying, 'I can do nothing more for you until you make a
retreat.' It seemed a peculiar idea to take time off from work
to go away and pray, and I couldn't see where it would get
me, but I had sufficient faith in his judgment to accede to
the request.

I had made retreats years ago, when I was at school and
once as a medical student, and had spent the time listening
to talks given by the priest conducting the retreat, praying
and, when I got bored, reading the life of some interesting
saint. These retreats were never more than three days and
always made in a group of twenty or so other people, so there
was always company even if there was no talking. It was
with some trepidation, therefore, that I considered making a
retreat of eight days on my own, but I was told that I must
leave my home and work so as to be completely alone with
God.

Accordingly, in the last week of May I packed a bag with
some books and sweaters and went by bus to a retreat house
in a village about an hour's distance from Santiago. It was
winter and I had the large retreat house completely to myself except for the three nuns who ran it. The priest came

each day to visit me. Although I did not know it at the time, a directed retreat such as I was making is a privilege granted to certain people at crucial times in their lives, expecially when the making of an important decision is involved. I found the whole business rather awe-inspiring, and it gave me a very uncomfortable sense of the importance of my own soul.

The retreat was 'structured' according to the 'Spiritual Exercises' of Saint Ignatius of Loyola, the founder of the Jesuits. Ignatius was a Basque nobleman, born at Loyola towards the end of the fifteenth century. He became a soldier and seems to have led an extremely gay life, fond of wine, women and song, until he was wounded in battle at Pamplona. He was taken to recuperate in the family castle where, in the boredom of convalescence, he was reduced to reading the lives of the saints because there was no more entertaining literature. I have always enjoyed this part of the story; it is so easy to visualize the young gallant, bored and restless with his leg on a stool, demanding something to read. His response to the sisters or aunts who could only provide him with pious literature must have been worth putting on record. But we are told only that Ignatius was so moved by what he read that his world turned upside down, and when his leg was mended he embarked upon a life of service to God, with all the enthusiasm and vigour which he had hitherto spent upon amusing himself.

The Ignatius described to me was a very practical man, a soldier and man of the world who had been bowled over by his encounter with Christ and who, consumed with love for his new king, devoted his whole life to trying to inflame those he met with that same love. Ignatius spent much of his time in Paris and would persuade those who were interested in the service of God to spend a few days on their own in prayer and reflection. He would visit them each day in their houses or the room where they had gone to be alone, and carrying with him a grubby exercise book of his notes he would guide them through their days of retreat. This exercise book, battered and much corrected but still with the writer's spelling mistakes, became known as the Exercises

of St Ignatius and they are still used over four centuries later
when men go to a place apart to be with their God.

Ignatius' fundamental premise is that 'Man has been
created to praise, reverence and serve Our Lord God and
thereby save his soul, all the other things on the face of the
earth have been created for man to help him achieve the
end for which he was created.'

Of course there is nothing new in this observation. Hadn't
I known since I was a child at school the truth 'What doth
it profit a man if he gain the whole world and suffer the loss
of his own soul?' It is difficult to know why one presentation
of an old truth should strike home on one particular day,
but that is how it is. It was as though I had put on a new
pair of spectacles and things which had been blurred or
distorted now fell into perspective. It was all so obvious.
Values which had loomed larger than life scuttled back into
line like naughty children. There they stood, health, success,
fame, achievement, in a silent row, reduced to their proper
place among all the other things on the face of the earth, to
be used or discarded in the measure in which they assisted
or impeded the pursuit of the will of God.

My day was largely spent in prayer and I spoke to no one
except my guide, who came in the afternoon to see how I
was progressing. Much of the time I spent in the garden
praying on top of a pile of fallen leaves. It made an excellent couch, being soft and dry, and the leaves lying on the
ground around me made a loud noise if anyone walked on
them so I had no fear of being surprised in this undignified
position. I ate my meals alone and in silence, and my life
at the hospital and at home seemed a thousand miles away
as I faced myself and my maker in the quiet of the retreat
house garden. With no one to talk to and no novels to read
there was no escaping, and I ceased running and tried to
listen to what God had to say to me.

After five days of prayer and reflection I was asked to
read and meditate upon a passage from the third chapter of
the book of Samuel. I read that the Lord called Samuel
three times and that the boy did not understand who was
calling until he was told by his master to go and lie down and

wait and, if the Lord called, he was to say, 'Speak, Lord, for your servant hears.' So it was that on a winter morning in 1975 I lay face down on a pile of leaves at the bottom of the garden in a Chilean retreat house and made those words of Samuel my own. As in the days of my childhood twenty years before I heard no voices and I saw no visions, but gradually it became clear to me that God was calling. I knew beyond any reasonable doubt that I was being asked to follow Him, for better or for worse, for richer or for poorer, in sickness or in health, for the rest of my life.

How can one convey the agony and the ecstasy of being called by God? At one moment one is overawed by the immensity of the honour, the incredible fact of having been chosen, and in the same breath one screams, 'No! No! Please, not me, I can't take it!' That which seconds ago was a privilege becomes an outrageously unfair demand. Why should I be the one asked to give up marriage and career? Why me? Why may I not lie with a man I love and bear his children? I have only one life; how can you ask me to sign it away as if it meant nothing to me?

> Ah! is Thy love indeed
> A weed, albeit an amaranthine weed,
> Suffering no flowers except its own to mount?
> Ah! must –
> Designer infinite! –
> Ah! must Thou char the wood ere Thou canst limn with it?
>
> Francis Thompson
> *The Hound of Heaven*

As I lay there in tears, my ears and my hair full of autumn leaves, I knew that this was the end of the chase. I had chosen to come to this place and I had invited God to speak and he had. Of course I was quite free to say, 'No, I don't want to', But this would be a clear and deliberate refusal. I thought about it, and I knew that I did not want to say No and that, however much it hurt, I could only humbly accept. So, as hundreds of men and women had done before me, I said my '*Fiat*'.

20

The Committee for Peace

He has sent me to bring good news to the poor,
to bind up hearts that are broken;
to proclaim liberty to captives,
freedom to those in prison.

Isaiah 61 : 1–2

My decision to become a nun did not mean that I packed my bags at once to go home. It was explained to me that I must live with the decision for a while to see how I felt. If the decision was a right one I would grow daily in peace and joy, but if I had made a mistake it would become apparent by making me unsettled and unhappy. For a while, therefore, I was to continue living and working as before and see what happened.

On my return home I was immediately caught up in the day-to-day problems of life in Chile. As the economic situation of the country deteriorated, construction was grossly reduced, factories were closed and more and more people lost their jobs. Inflation soared and the situation became desperate. The government, in an effort to right its balance of payments, made further cuts in spending on social services, and the hospitals which had for years given free treatment to the indigent population now began to charge for attention and treatment. Those whose social security payments were not up to date became ineligible for free medical attention, and the prices charged by the hospitals were far outside their reach. In an effort to alleviate in some small way the desperation caused by this non-availability of medical aid, the Church implemented a plan for small clinics in the shanty towns, and in June I was asked to work in the new clinic in the *población* El Salto.

This was for me a moment of truth. Although my friendship with the Americans and other missionaries was growing daily and I deeply admired their life of solidarity with the poor, I had never seriously thought to go and work in a shanty town. I had always worked in hospital medicine and greatly enjoyed the life with its combination of excitement, companionship and prestige. In particular I enjoyed surgery and had arranged to receive further training at a well-equipped hospital near my home.

At first it seemed madness to go so far away to do non-specialist work when I could be furthering my training in a good, well-organized hospital, but sadly I realized that the one hospital was overstaffed with people wanting to be hand surgeons while in the same city there was an empty clinic with no doctor. I knew then that this was a crucial moment. If I opted to keep my wealth of satisfying work in good conditions when there were people in desperate need of a doctor I could not say in truth that I was committed to the service of the under-privileged. It was true enough that I was wasting my specialist training, but it was also true that there were enough doctors in this specialized field and a great shortage of those prepared to practise simple general medicine amongst the poor. So it was that with the same bad grace that I had accepted the calling to the religious life I now accepted the bishop's invitation to work in the clinic. In the months to come I developed 'a love-hate relationship with the people of El Salto, hating the work and yet knowing that it was right that I should be there.

> Simon of Cyrene did not want to carry
> Jesus' cross on the way to Golgotha,
> but he did it anyway. . . .
> If we are pushed
> by conscience or by
> other people
> we may end up carrying it for a while.
> Christopher William Jones
> *Listen Pilgrim*

The clinic was one of four which had been set up by the *Comité pro Paz*: the Committee for Co-operation for Peace in

Chile. *El Comité*, as it was familiarly known, was founded in December 1973 by the Catholic, Lutheran and Jewish churches in Chile. It began as a response to the appeal to the churches by desperate people who had nowhere else to turn for help when their loved ones disappeared or were imprisoned. The scope of the work expanded rapidly to meet the needs of the thousands of imprisoned and unemployed and of the growing numbers of hungry children and adults in the marginal areas. In December 1975 it was closed by the Cardinal after a personal request by President Pinochet, but in the two short years of its existence it became a legend, an example of the way in which, in times of hardship and persecution, people can lay aside their differences and work towards a common goal.

In the early days the work of the Comité was primarily with the families of the political prisoners and the *desaparecidos*: those who had disappeared. The names of the detainees were registered and requests made to the authorities that families should be informed of their whereabouts. A number of lawyers gave their services free, or at greatly reduced fees, to defend those detainees who came to trial. By 1976 the Comité had given legal aid to over 28,000 prisoners. Details of all cases helped by the Comité were carefully recorded, and as the months passed the statistics showed a frightening pattern of arbitrary detention, institutionalized torture and disappearance without trace.

In 1974, concerned because of growing unemployment and resultant hunger in the shanty towns, the churches extended their work to include the founding of the *comedores infantiles*, the children's dining-rooms, in many of the shanty towns. In the 1974 Christmas letter, Bishop Fernando Ariztia, Vicar of the West Zone of the diocese of Santiago and co-founder of the Comité, spoke of young children unable to sleep because of hunger, and said that in his section of the archdiocese one third of all children under the age of seven years were in a state of malnutrition. 'The fact that children are hungry is a sin that cries out to heaven. If our meals are assured every day, that sin is ours.'

By 1975 there were *comedores infantiles* in virtually every shanty town in Santiago. Priests, nuns and lay people, Chileans and foreign missionaries devoted hours of their time and energy to organizing and assisting the women of the *poblaciones* to give their children the one meal a day which would keep them alive.

Conscious that the providing of free meals for the children of the unemployed is at best a 'patch', a partial response to an emergency situation, the Comité extended its work to the formation of work projects in an effort to provide employment so that men might support their children rather than accept charity. This increasing commitment of the Catholic Church to the underprivileged is a reflection of the change of vision of the Latin American Church arising out of an Episcopal Conference held at Medellín in Colombia in 1968. The conclusions arrived at in this conference have changed the orientation of the Catholic Church in Latin America. Since that time there has been a growing body of clergy who have altered their lives in response to the call of Medellin:

> We have seen that our most urgent commitment must be to purify ourselves and all the members and institutions of the Catholic Church, in the spirit of the gospel. It is necessary to end the separation between faith and life. . . . This commitment requires us to live a true scriptural poverty expressed in authentic manifestations that may be clear signs for our peoples.
> (*The Church in the Present-day Transformation of Latin America in the light of the Council Conclusions.*)

Perhaps the most famous of these bishops is Dom Helder Cámara, the Archbishop of Olinda and Recife in Brazil's impoverished north-east who, like Bishop Ariztia, was sent away from the capital because his radical Christianity had become an embarrassment to the establishment. The indomitable Helder Cámara in his shabby black soutane and wooden cross has become a prophet of the third world and is able to speak so powerfully precisely because he lives what he says:

> ... first get free
> of that excess
> of goods
> which cram
> your whole body
> leaving no room
> for you and even less
> for God.
>   Helder Càmara
>   *The Desert is Fertile*

Had the Comité confined its work to feeding the hungry
and tending the sick it would have received little opposition
from the government, but the bishops at Medellín declared
'The firm denunciation of those realities in Latin America
which constitute an affront to the spirit of the gospel also
forms part of our mission.' In August 1975 such a denunciation became necessary. Under the headlines '*Miristas* ex-
terminated like rats' two Santiago newspapers published
lists of 119 Chileans said to have died in guerilla activities
outside of Chile.

The brazen nature of this plot may be seen by the fact
that all of the 119 names in question had long been on the
list of disappeared political prisoners compiled by several
international human rights organizations, and that writs of
habeas corpus had been presented by the Peace Committee,
Amnesty International or relatives and friends on behalf
of 115 of the 119 missing persons. Furthermore, 77 of these
persons had been detained in the presence of their families
or identified by fellow prisoners in different Chilean gaols.

The distress of the families concerned was appalling, and
the Comité issued a statement of protest the following day.

On 5 July the bishop who had replaced Fernando Ariztia
celebrated mass for the *desaparecidos* which was attended by
several thousand people.

In September the antipathy of the government to the
Peace Committee took a new turn. One of the secretaries,
Georgina Ocaranza, was arrested. She was six months preg-
nant and was detained until after the birth of her baby. The

following month the co-founder of the Peace Committee, the Lutheran Bishop Helmut Frenz, was refused permission to re-enter Chile after he had been to the meeting of the World Council of Churches in Geneva. This was only the beginning of the period of open aggression, another worker, Betty Walker, being arrested soon after. In November two girls of the staff, Loreto Pelissier and Aura Hermosilla, were arrested with the Catholic chaplain to the women's prison, Father Patricio Gajardo. Both of these girls were tortured.

In November 1975 General Pinochet sent a letter to Cardinal Silva requesting the closure of the Peace Committee, accusing it of being 'a means used by Marxist Leninists to create problems which disturb the civil peace'. The Cardinal found it advisable to accede to the President's request but stated that it was his frank opinion that 'the Committee for Peace has under very difficult circumstances been carrying out a social task of a clearly evangelical nature within the framework of existing laws.'

The Peace Committee was disbanded on 31 December 1975, and on 1 January there was created a new division in the Archdiocese of Santiago, the Vicariate of Solidarity, to replace it. The persecution of those who work for the political prisoners has not ended. José Zalaquett, the lawyer who was head of the legal department and who was imprisoned along with other Comité workers in November 1975, was expelled from Chile in April 1976 after he had given information about prisoners to a visiting congressional delegation from the United States. Hernán Montealegre, the lawyer who was head of the legal department in the Vicaria de Solidaridad, was arrested in May 1976 and detained for over six months.

The Church of Chile, far from being the opium of the people, continues to fulfil its prophetic role and, refusing to be silenced, is the voice for those who have no voice.

21

The Clinic in El Salto

I would have stayed unsullied in my ivory tower.
But, Lord, you have discovered a breach in my defences,
You have forced me to open my door,
Like a squall of rain in the face, the cry of men has
    awakened me.

Michel Quoist
Prayers of Life

In June 1975 I began to work in El Salto, in a tiny clinic
built of wooden planks by unemployed workmen. Everything had been carefully and lovingly prepared by the
nursing staff, many of whom had been out of work for several
months, and there was an atmosphere of hope and of joy in
service that was not present in the Posta. El Salto is in Con-
chali, one of the poorest marginal areas of Santiago, and the
clinic provided the only free medical treatment for over
100,000 people. The patients arrived at the clinic at seven
in the morning to queue in the hope of getting a number
which would authorize them to see the doctor.

In the beginning I tried to see twenty patients in three
hours and it was a while before I realized how different was
to be my practice of medicine here. My patients were nearly
all women and when they came into the consulting room,
they sank on to the chair and waited for me to speak. When
I asked them what the trouble was they would launch into a
description of pain or strange sensations that as often as not
seemed to bear little resemblance to any known disease.
('My knees are so cold, Doctor.') It was quite impossible to
convince them that there was nothing serious amiss without
performing a full general examination and after a while I
developed a routine of stripping and examining them from
head to toe. This was no mean task as it was winter and they
wore layer upon layer of clothes, most of which were either

sewn on or fastened with safety pins as the clasps had long since been lost. It was very difficult to wait patiently while they undressed and dressed knowing that there was a long queue outside. After a careful explanation that blood pressure heart and lungs were normal and that there were no signs of cancer or other problems I would ask the question which acted like a sluice gate releasing a tide ˙of anguish which nearly drowned me. The answer to 'How are things at home?' provided the reason for their presence in my consulting room whether or not they knew it.

All of them were unemployed and the majority were hungry.˙ I discovered that on average they were eating one meal every other day and that this was usually soup and bread or spaghetti. If they were lucky their children received lunch at a soup kitchen but although this was enough to prevent gross malnutrition it did not prevent hunger and crying, irritable children.

Although hunger was common to all, their problems were legion. There was the woman whose son had gone to Argentina and she did not know if he was alive or dead. What could I say except give words of comfort and hope that perhaps were false? Was no news good news? Who could say? Another woman, after a fifteen-minute recital of pains in her head and her chest and her legs, suddenly burst into tears and told me that she could not send her five children to school because they had no shoes. Sometimes common sense was all that was needed: I well remember a woman who had severe pains in her shoulders because she was carrying two heavy buckets of water half a mile to her house. I told her to make two journeys with half the quantity.

Little by little I evolved a technique whereby each patient was questioned, examined and then asked about her home situation. While they told me their problems I tried to think of a solution or at least some words of consolation. After sympathizing with their very real troubles I looked for something positive in their lives to make them count their few blessings. In many cases this worked well as people were brought to realize how lucky they were to have a husband who was kind and faithful or who did not drink or children who had enough to eat. I tried hard to instil some community spirit into them, suggesting that those who were able should visit the elderly or those who were housebound. Finally, in desperation, I told them to thank God that the winter was nearly over and I told them to pray. I realized that I was practising a mixture of general medicine, counselling, black magic and religion but more often than not there was nothing wrong with them except a situational neurosis or anguish born of unemployment, hunger and loss of hope. I found that there was little to be gained by dismissing them with a few pills, as they returned in a week saying they were no better or with the pain in a different place.

The stress of this type of work was enormous. To listen hour after hour to people who had had no breakfast and who were going to have no lunch when I was eating three full meals a day did a violence to my soul that I cannot describe, and I usually walked out on the verge of tears. Had there been anyone else prepared to do the work I would have left but it seemed that there was no one.

This immediate contact with the under-privileged produced a change in my whole way of thinking. I soon realized that the majority of my patients' ills stemmed from their lack of work and that all I was doing was sewing a very small patch on the threadbare garment of their existence. I set myself therefore to think of ways in which they could earn money. Gone were the peaceful days of idle daydreaming and I sat in the bus and examined idea after idea until my head ached with a confusion of plans.

I had many schemes but lacked the time and strength to implement them and I think, in retrospect, that I accomplished little because of lack of organization and ability to follow through.

After a couple of months it became apparent to the staff at the clinic that a large part of our work with the adults was a very simple and primitive form of supportive psychotherapy. I analysed the way I spent my time and decided that only twenty per cent of it was spent in examining and the rest was spent in questioning or advising them. As we had an extremely competent nursing staff it seemed logical that they should help in the questioning and the counselling. We had a meeting to discuss it and I elaborated a plan whereby a patient would see the nurse first and talk to her, and then come to me for further questioning and examination; she would then return to the nurse's office for such comforting and advice as was necessary. I calculated that I would be able to see many more patients in this way as I would not have to wait while they dressed and undressed nor spend so much time listening to their domestic problems.

Although the plan found favour with my colleagues it was difficult to implement for lack of space and while awaiting the building of an extension to the clinic we coped as best we could.

One of the biggest problems that we encountered was that of getting specialist treatment for the chronically ill who after years of follow-up in a state hospital were now turned away because they could not pay. As each new problem arrived I wrote to some doctor that I knew in the appropriate department of the hospital, or if I did not know anyone I would write an impassioned letter and tell the patient not to take no for an answer. Often we had to send a strongminded relative or neighbour to the hospital with them to insist on seeing the doctor and not allow the clerks to send them away. The struggle to get a patient seen made the work harassing and exhausting and often just before I was due to go home to lunch someone would arrive back from the hospital saying they could not be seen.

One case I will never forget is that of the daughter of Señora Beatriz, a young girl of about fifteen who came to see me complaining that she would suddenly pass out without warning. I thought that she must be suffering from some form of epilepsy until I asked the mother about their diet. At once it became clear: this child sometimes went a whole day without eating anything and when she didn't eat she fainted. It was as simple as that.

I knew that this could happen as a couple of months previously I had just come out of the bank and was walking along one of the main streets in the centre of Santiago when a youth of sixteen passed out at my feet. I took his pulse and found that this was a true faint and one of the people clustered around said, 'He hasn't eaten for days.' When he got up I propelled him into the nearest restaurant and bought him a meal. He told me that he was from Arica in the far north of Chile and that he had come to Santiago to arrange the funeral of his mother who had died in a Santiago hospital. He had not eaten because he was saving money for his fare back to Arica to take care of his small sister. I had no proof of his story but boys of sixteen do not faint without good reason, and I paid for his ticket home.

I discovered that Señora Beatriz had six children and that though her husband had work he did not earn enough to keep his family. His wife went out to work as a washer-woman but times were hard and she only had a few hours' work a week. I could see no solution to her problem and in desperation I told her that she could come to me twice a week to do the washing. Before long she drove me quite mad by her endless tales of distress and by bringing a different sick child to work with her every week. The worst part was that I was quite sure that her tales of woe were true and her underfed children picked up every passing cold or bronchitis germ. The girl who had fainted became very ill with a urinary infection and I had to borrow money for drugs from the Columban fathers as the hospital gave her a prescription without giving any thought to the fact that she had no money with which to buy it.

Her thirteen-year-old brother also joined the ranks of the workers and spent a happy morning spreading red paint about on my chairs and himself. I tried to teach him to work carefully and honestly, realizing that one of the basic problems of the poor was the careless and shoddy character of their work. The conditions of long hours and low wages give men no incentive to work carefully.

After she had established herself in my life, Señora Beatriz became quite shameless in her requests for help. One week she came to me and asked for an advance on her salary to buy a food parcel from a co-operative in her *población*. This seemed a reasonable enough request and I gave her two weeks' salary. She was effusive in her gratitude but the next week she arrived in tears and said that her money had been stolen on the bus. I did not have the strength to harden my heart and tell her that that was her bad luck because I knew perfectly well that if it was true it meant that the children wouldn't eat. The next week she arrived with a beautiful stainless steel lamp saying that her husband had got it cheap at work and would I like to buy it? It was a fine lamp and very cheap so I bought it happily but the next week she arrived with a very ugly lamp, twice the price, and begged me to buy it as they had nothing to eat. I obliged but told her firmly that she was to bring nothing more and that I couldn't afford to go on lending her money.

Mercifully not all my patients were like Señora Beatriz. One that I came to be very fond of was an alcoholic whom I helped to go dry and another was an old man who recovered from a severe depression on small doses of anti-depressant pills. He became my most vociferous champion and admirer and I saw him regularly to keep both of our morales up! Most of all I grew to love the very old and infirm. Dressed in layer upon layer of petticoats and knitted under-garments it took ages to unwrap them. Often they were extremely dirty but I could not blame them as it was bitterly cold and I too would have thought twice about washing in the freezing water. Somehow the grubbier they were the more I loved them and they were pathetically grateful for my caring. Their visit to 'the doctor' was the highlight of their week and I tried to make it memorable in terms of love and compassion, but it was a slow business and could only be done at the expense of the other patients.

One of the young men of the parish became a self-appointed social worker and would help the old and infirm to the surgery. I rapidly came to lean on him and gave him lists of people whom I thought should be visited and other lists of bored young women without enough to do who might perhaps forget their own troubles if they went to call on someone worse off than themselves.

As the weeks went by I hated the work more and more but I knew that I must keep on because however inadequate our care we were providing a vital service and were a tangible proof of love in the *población*, a sign that there was reason still to hope.

As I write this account of my work with the people of El Salto I am acutely aware that I treated their symptoms with palliatives and platitudes. Theirs was a totally unjust situation maintained by an oppressive government, a situation of hunger and subhuman living which has been termed the 'primary violence' because such conditions cannot be said to be peaceful only because there is no fighting. These people should be made aware of their rights and motivated to demand them and yet, in practice, it was not quite like that. The people of Chile were aware of their rights but overnight they found themselves living under a regime where not only were these rights denied them, but where to protest put their very lives in danger. They came to me in search of relief and I was faced with the task of trying to heal, in one short interview, someone who was sick from hunger, anguish and desperation. It was impossible, and all I could do was choose to comfort or not to comfort. Feeling myself unequipped for the work of changing society, I left it to others and tried only to heal the sick and comfort the desolate. If this was a giving of opium to the people, may God forgive me.

22

The Dieciocho

No passing bells for those who die as cattle.
Only the monstrous anger of the guns.
                                        Wilfred Owen

September the eighteenth, the '*dieciocho*', is the anniversary
of Chile's independence and is traditionally a day of great
rejoicing and celebration. It is a night dreaded by *posta*
doctors, for as at New Year, hundreds of people get drunk
and the incidence of car accidents and fights is greatly increased. Not only are those on duty missing their own family
celebrations but they know that they will be worked to the
point of exhaustion patching up drunken motorists and
those friends who, in their cups, have taken offence at what
was said to them and lashed out with the nearest thing at
hand: anything from a broken bottle to a carving knife.

Although the night of 18 September in the Posta 3 ended
in tragedy it began like any other night. At two o'clock all
seemed quiet so I went to bed for a couple of hours, leaving
a colleague to hold the fort. At 4 a.m. I was awakened by
the nurse to do my shift which, if there were not too many
patients, would end at 6 a.m. when I would be able to go
back to bed for another couple of hours before we were all
relieved at 8 a.m.

As I walked towards the examination room I heard loud
hysterical weeping and I entered to find a group of Air
Force men standing around a young soldier who was lying
on an examination couch sobbing, 'I killed someone! I
killed someone!' Just as I was about to ask what had
happened the other doctor on duty called me. I went to
where he was standing behind a curtain and found him
examining the body of a boy of about seventeen who had
been shot dead by the soldier.

I have been engaged in casualty work for many years and

death is no stranger to me. The destruction of the human person caused by fire or by road accidents is a terrible thing but I have learned to keep the distress and grief caused by the sight of such deaths at a distance from the vulnerable parts of my soul, for such deaths are wished for by no one and those not personally touched must remain strong and calm to deal with the sick and comfort the living. I was not prepared, however, for the sight of this boy, his flesh ripped by machine gun bullets so that I could put my hand into the wound. There were seven bullet wounds. Seven. This was no terrorist, no violent guerilla, but a lad of seventeen who had made the mistake of being out a few minutes after the curfew on the night of his country's national holiday. His was the mistake of being poor, a marginal person in a marginal development where lorry loads of soldiers cruised about looking for trouble. What mattered the death of a *poblador*? His mother would be told that he was a Marxist who deserved to die, or that she had made a mistake in thinking he had been shot because he had run away to join the 'subversives' fighting in Argentina, or perhaps simply that she had counted her children wrong and that she had never had a son called Alejandro. The song makes no mistake when it says

> *No hay que ser pobre, amigo,*
> *Es peligroso ser pobre, amigo.*
> You mustn't be poor, my friend,
> It's dangerous to be poor, my friend.
> Luis Advis
> *Santa Maria de Iquique*

In the main streets and the suburbs of Santiago a man caught out after curfew will be taken to the police station and after spending the night there will be fined and allowed to go, but in the *poblaciones* the story is different. Because the people live in dwellings like those for animals they are treated as such and, voiceless, they have no redress.

I was sickened and enraged. The soldiers, it seemed, had been drunk and they had said to the young recruit, 'Shoot', and when he hesitated they told him again, 'Shoot! If you

don't, we will.' So he had shot and now the faceless figure
in the dark, the unknown enemy, had the face of a boy of
seventeen, a boy who would never become a man.

After the coup the streets of Santiago bore posters de-
claring that

> *En cada soldado hay un Chileno*
> *En cada Chileno hay un soldado*
> In every soldier there is a Chilean
> In every Chilean there is a soldier.

They were advertising for recruits but the slogan spoke a
truth that becomes more tragic every day, for there is indeed a Chilean in every soldier so that Chilean is turned
upon Chilean as dog upon dog.

Eventually the young soldier was taken away, still weeping. What happened to him I do not know except that his
tragedy is greater than that of the boy who died, and that it
is an example of the tragedy of Chile and indeed of the
universal horror of war. At the time I saw only the death of
Alejandro and the grief and impotence of his mother and I
longed that his death should be avenged. 'Vengeance is
mine', says the Lord and indeed, how can WE avenge the
death of an innocent man? How many deaths will pay for
the taking of a young life? Not one, not two, not a thousand
dead soldiers would bring Alejandro back and indeed who
can pass judgement on the guilt of a boy of eighteen who is
allowed to go on duty drunk and with a machine gun in his
hands?

Who shall we arraign in our court of enquiry? The
soldier, of course, who fired the shot. And how shall we
judge him? Is he a murderer or is he a good soldier who
obeyed the order of his commanding officer? But he was
drunk, remember, so do we find him guilty of manslaughter
and put him in prison for ten years? Or do we say he was a
lad who should never have been allowed to go on duty in the
state in which he arrived for work and acquit him on grounds
of diminished responsibility? And what of the years to come?
What of the sleepless nights, the tears, the bitter hours of re-
crimination, the nightmare of estrangement from his family

and friends? How can we recompense him for the loss of his peace of mind and soul? We cannot.

But a man has died, someone must be responsible, so who next shall we call upon to answer for this crime? The officer who let him go on duty drunk? Certainly, but perhaps he didn't look drunk as he stood on parade. And what of his bosses who decided that a shanty town must be patrolled by men armed with machine guns when they knew that the inhabitants were unarmed? And the machine guns: where did they come from? They weren't made in Chile. Why were they sold to the Junta when it was known that they would be used as they are? The answer is simple: they were sold because business is business and the selling of armaments is very good business indeed.

When the soldier had gone I went to speak to the mother of the dead boy and tried to comfort her. I gave her the address of the Committee for Peace so that she could at least register the fact of her son's death. Perhaps his dying might be more powerful than his living and the atrocious waste of a young life move those in authority to reconsider the wisdom of sending ill-trained youngsters with weapons of war to patrol the *poblaciones*.

This incident was among those which made me more personally aware of the state of injustice in which Chile lives, and it convinces me still further that only in seeing is there full believing. The knowledge of the death of 30,000 men and women during the coup did not touch me as deeply as did the dying of this one boy whose killing moved me to such anger that I risked much in an effort that justice might be done. Slowly I was learning why it had been found necessary to write out such seemingly obvious statements as

Every person has the right of life, liberty and security of person.
Everyone has the right to recognition everywhere as a person before the law.

Articles 3 and 6 of the Universal
Declaration of Human Rights

23

The Christ in Stranger's Guise

I saw a stranger yestreen –
I put food in the eating place,
Drink in the drinking place,
Music in the listening place,
And in the sacred name of the Triune
He blessed me and my house,
My cattle and my dear ones.
And the lark said in her song:
Often, often, often
Goes Christ in stranger's guise.
                    Traditional Gaelic
                    Rune of Hospitality

As 1975 wore on Chile's economic condition deteriorated. Prices rose almost daily and the middle class tightened its belt while the numbers of the poor who were hungry increased at an appalling rate. In the middle class residential areas all the dustbins were methodically searched for food and the feeding of beggars was now a part of daily life. For me this was a new experience for there had been only the occasional down-and-out during my first two years in Chile. Now the door bell rang many times a day and Margarita gave a piece of bread and a cup of tea to those who seemed most in need.

It is so hard to explain, even to myself, what was my communication barrier with these people. A proportion of it was certainly linguistic for they speak a rapid colloquial Spanish in which the ends of many of the words are dropped and they use many slang words and expressions which the foreigner must learn almost as an additional language to the basic Spanish. In hindsight, however, I see my problem as a fear of becoming involved, a fear of the demands which they would make on me and a real terror of having my comfortable life disrupted.

Margarita was a buffer between me and the people who came to the door. She would answer the bell and listen to the tale of woe of whoever was begging and deal with them as she thought fit. Thus she protected me so that not only was I not troubled by having to talk to strangers but I did not have to share in the anguish of those who knocked on my door.

One day, however, while Margarita was out shopping the door bell rang and when I went to the garden gate there was a small boy. He was poorly dressed and very grubby but poised beyond his years; he asked me if I had any bread. I went into the house and came back with a sandwich which, to my surprise, he put into his pocket instead of eating it. I realized then that he was saving it so I asked him if there was anyone with him. He indicated a little way down the street where, pressed against the wall in an attempt to hide, were a very old lady and two more children, a boy and a girl; they were hiding so that I should not be put off by so many people at once. I asked them if they were all hungry and when they nodded I went back and made three more sandwiches and brought them with milk and tea to the gate. Alberto, who was the first visitor, then introduced his granny, his brother and his cousin. Alberto was nine, his brother ten and his cousin thirteen and lived together with their granny, their parents and a younger sister. We chatted amicably while they ate their sandwiches and then, after thanking me profusely, they left. I went back into the house feeling that I had done well and congratulated myself that I had treated these poor people like friends.

Even as I thought it I realized how patronizing had been my attitude and what a mockery of true Christianity my behaviour was. I had generously given fifteen minutes of my time and a little surplus food to three children and an old lady. I had fed them like animals through the bars of my gate and had sent them away without a moment's thought as to who else was hungry in their house and what they themselves were going to eat that night. I felt sick and chastened, caught out again in not being able to live up to what I believed.

It was a salutary moment and although I was to some extent indulging in an orgy of self-reproach it illustrates the gradual awakening of my awareness to the fundamental problems of the third world.

It is patently obvious that neither I nor any individual could, even by selling all that I possessed, feed the hungry of Santiago. Likewise I could not invite them all into my house and share my every meal with them. Of course I could perfectly well sell all my books and my record player and all the rugs and pictures that decorated my home: but by doing so I would feed a small number of people for one day and then, denuded of all the things which gave me joy in my home, I would probably become so depressed that I would no longer be able to do my work in the Posta and the clinic. The other extreme is exemplified by the remark of a doctor friend of mine when he said that he had closed his shutters so that the sight of the people coming to his door to ask for bread would not distress him.

The problem of world hunger, of course, is an immense and complex one and will only be solved by action at international and governmental levels, and perhaps, as it says in the Gospel, the poor will always be with us. The immensity of the problem, however, and our manifest inability to solve it does not answer the question of how we should behave towards a given hungry man, woman or child who asks our help at a given moment of a given day.

I need not have bemoaned the lost opportunity to put into practice my Christian principles because the next day Alberto came again. It was a Saturday and I was once again alone so I went to answer the gate to be greeted by a radiant small boy who was bouncing up and down in the street. With him was his sister, Jaqueline, a fair-haired child of about seven years, and his granny. This time I invited them in and we had tea together on the patio outside the dining room. I made scrambled eggs and the four of us ate and drank and talked happily until Margarita came home. '*La abuela*' (the granny) told us a little of her family. They lived in a *población* the other side of Santiago and were forced to beg because her son was dead and her son-in-law, Jaqueline's father, had recently suffered a severe injury to his back and so was unable to work. She said little about her dead son and I wondered if he was one of the thousands of *pobladores* who had died after the coup. After a very leisurely tea party Margarita gave them a couple of packets of spaghetti and they went off home.

The next afternoon Jaqueline came again and with her was a young woman with a baby. I was frankly irritated and though I greeted her I did not invite her in and went back into the house. After a few moments, however, the door bell went again and looking out of the window I saw Jaqueline on her own; she was not tall enough to reach the bell but managed to touch it by jumping in the air and hitting it with her finger. I went out and she asked me politely but firmly if I could give her mother a cup of tea. Unable to resist I acceded and she called her mother who was standing dejectedly fifty yards further up the street.

Maria was about 23 and was the mother of Alberto, Jaqueline and a seven-month-old baby, Bernadette. She had reason to be dejected, for her husband had fallen into a hole while carrying a load of bricks and fractured his spine. After seven months in hospital he was home again, an invalid. His young wife, untrained for any trade and not particularly intelligent, could barely cope with Jaqueline and the baby, let alone go out to work, even if she had been able to find a job at a time when unemployment was increasing.

Although I was deeply sorry for Maria I could do nothing to help her because such work as there was in my house was already shared between Margarita, Señora Beatriz and Francisco. Jaqueline however had decided to adopt me and little by little staked her claim in my house and in my heart. She let a day go by and then came again with her granny laden with gifts from their garden. *La abuela* had green fingers and brought me a fascinating array of flowers and herbs which she had grown from cuttings and planted in a variety of tins, saucepans and even an old kettle. She and Margarita and I would sit in the shade drinking tea while Jaqueline played with the dogs or the large golden teddy bear which was the only survivor of my childhood toys.

Eventually she threw pretence to the winds and came every day at tea time with Maria and Bernadette. Margarita and I realized we were beaten so she would install Maria and the baby comfortably in the shade and talk to Jaqueline while she got on with her work. After this had gone on for a couple of weeks and I realized that I was almost keeping Maria and her family, I decided that it was bad for her to be living on my charity so I consulted with Margarita to see what work we could find her. Knowing how much Señora Beatriz irritated me, Margarita suggested that we give Maria a trial with the ironing and if she was good enough we could reduce Señora Beatriz's visits to once a week. The next time she came, therefore, the ironing board was set up and she proved herself to be very efficient. She worked most of the afternoon and I paid her accordingly; she and Jaqueline went off happily and I felt she would be happier earning her keep.

That evening, however, Margarita discovered that a packet of cigarettes and a bottle of nail varnish had gone from the shelf in the kitchen and Maria and Jaqueline were the only possible culprits. I was very sad but I felt that I couldn't cope with petty thieving. After that our relationship was never quite the same again and though I gave them tea from time to time they always stayed in the garden.

I did not want to shut my house and my heart to Maria but I could not cope with the knowledge that I couldn't trust her, for I had too many treasures that she might be tempted to steal. Perhaps one day I will achieve the freedom from attachment to my possessions of a priest friend of mine in London whose house is always open and who, though he knows that he is robbed from time to time by the people he is trying to help, just carries on like a fool – like Christ.

Pilgrim,
do not be afraid.
Take it for granted
that this is your brother.
Do not previously judge him
to be the one who is out to get you

or who wants to rob you of all you have.
And even if he does,
so what?
Did not your Master tell you
'If a man takes your cloak, give him your tunic also'?
If a man takes something from you,
do not ask anything in return.
If he takes something from you,
give glory to the God that has allowed you
to be Christ in the world.

Christopher William Jones
Listen Pilgrim

9. (*above*) Mourners at the funeral of Chile's Nobel Prize winning poet, Pablo Neruda. He died of cancer a few days after the coup and was buried without any tribute to his greatness. He was a passionate supporter of the Popular Unity Government and much of his later poetry spoke of Chile's peaceful revolution. Photograph: Marcelo Montecino

(*below*) A soldier during the post-coup days. Photograph: Peter Hellmich

11. (*above*) A white flag during
    the curfew. Photograph
    Peter Hellmich

12. (*centre*) Prisoners and
    guards in the Stadium,
    September 1973.

13. (*left*) Prisoners in the
    Stadium, Santiago.
    September 1973.

(*above*) A street arrest.
Santiago 1973. Note the
smile on the face of the
soldier second from right.

(*centre*) The Stadium. Note
the prisoners kneeling at
gunpoint in centre of
photograph.

(*right*) The Stadium. Naked
prisoners being escorted by
two non-uniformed guards.

17. Prisoners in the National
Stadium. Photograph :
Cristian Montecino

18. A police official and guards
at the National Stadium,
September 1973.
Photograph : Marcelo
Montecino

24

A Thirst Mostly Unquenched

We bless you Father
for the thirst
you put in us,
for the boldness
you inspire,
for the fire
alight in us
that is you in us,
you the just.

Never mind
that our thirst
is mostly unquenched
(pity the satisfied).
Never mind
our bold plots
are mostly unclinched,
wanted not realized.
Who better than you
Knows that success
comes not from us.
You ask us to do
our utmost only,
but willingly.
                        Helder Cámara
                        The Desert is Fertile

As the months passed I became obsessed with the problems of my patients in El Salto. I spent hour upon hour trying to think of a work project, for though I knew well enough that the state of economic recession in Chile was such that there was no market for anything made in the *poblaciones*, the people were unemployed and they had no money and no food so it followed as the night the day that somehow or other work must be found for them: there was a place for realism but not for despair.

The obvious focus of thought was the approaching

Christmas season. Money might be scarce but only those Chileans at starvation level would let Christmas come and go without a single gift being exchanged. It seemed logical therefore to concentrate on the making of gifts, especially toys. I come from a family in which many of the members are 'good with their hands' and over the years had made many different dolls and toys. Now I tried to use this past experience in designing toys for the *pobladores* to make.

I went to visit the workshops organized by some friends in a *población* in another part of Santiago and found that although the women were able seamstresses the design of their handiwork was such that they would have no appeal to the more sophisticated Chileans. There was little point, therefore, in these women wasting precious time and materials on making things that no one would buy, for it was the more educated people who had the money. The problem therefore had many facets: acceptable designs must be found which were within the capabilities of the women and they must be taught to make them. The materials, too, must be as cheap as possible so as to have goods priced low enough to compete with those produced in factories. I decided that the only way to explain to the women what I believed would appeal to rich Chileans was to make some models myself and then teach one or two of the women how to make them.

Full of enthusiasm I went out to buy materials and my house became a toy factory. Margarita, who at first thought I was quite mad, became more interested as things took shape and stopped complaining about the scraps of material and wool that I scattered all over the place. My first effort was a very simple mouse which I had made many times before. Made in brightly coloured material it was a charming and, for Chile, unusual toy. Inspired by the enthusiasm of my friends I became more ambitious and determined to make a doll.

It was years since I had given dolls any thought but I had vague memories of elegant gingham-clad creatures with carefully coiffured wool hair sitting in supercilious rows on the shelves of smart London stores. Striving for a combina-

tion of European style with simple design I made a very
long rag doll and after finding that even foam stuffing was
very expensive filled her with sawdust. Her initial shapeless-
ness was corrected by pulling her waist in with some string
and immediately she took on an Edwardian look. The not
very attractive limbs were covered by a long dress trimmed
with lace and of course a pair of long bloomers. I learned as
I went. The body was easy to make and the sawdust made
excellent stuffing and could be inserted by pouring it down
a funnel. One major problem was that the charm of the doll
lay in its lanky and floppy character and the dress used up
a lot of material which was not cheap. Finally I went to
work on the hair and found that by winding half a skein of
brown wool twice round the head I produced a character
straight out of some Edwardian drawing room.

I was greatly pleased with my endeavours and sat her on
the ancient clavicord which was my only respectable piece
of furniture. Jaqueline came to tea that afternoon and took
my new creation for a walk holding her irreverently by an
arm or leg or even by her hair. Trying not to look nervous
I made rapid mental notes about points for reinforcement!

After the doll came a black corduroy hobby horse with
red-lined ears and a red stick. I had made hobby horses
before and the only problem was painting the broom
handle completely without covering oneself with red paint.
Eventually I suspended it from a tree in the garden and
fretted for it to dry so that I could attach the head.

My models complete I summoned Susie, an American
nun friend who in addition to teaching catechism, running
a children's dining room and many other projects worked
with a group of women making scarves to sell in America.
She was very enthusiastic but doubtful about how we would
find a market. Suddenly it hit me: a Christmas fair. The
Church should organize a fair where all the *pobladores* could
sell their wares and all the churches would appeal to their
parishioners to buy their Christmas presents there. Susie
went off to a meeting of the Peace Committee to put forward
our plan, and that night she rang to say that it had been
accepted and they had already decided on two big churches

in different parts of Santiago where the fair would be held. What was more, they were prepared to advance money for materials to any group of women who wished to join in the project so that no one would be prevented from participating through lack of funds.

The next day, which was a Sunday, Susie brought a group of her ladies to the house and we sat on the floor in my living room while I explained how the toys were made. They borrowed the models for forty-eight hours and then returned them to be sent to another group. We discussed, too, possible projects for the men. Francisco made, under my direction, a coffee table with a wooden frame supporting eight floor tiles. It was easy to make and attractive and the materials were cheap, though the finished product was very heavy.

Excitement for the project ran high. I talked to Rosemary and a friend of hers who was an artist and we looked into the possibility of a workshop in the adjacent parish hall where the work could be supervised by the nuns. Another friend who already had a large group of men and women working, borrowed the toys and it was funny to watch a grown man walk down the street carrying a rag doll and a hobby horse and wonder if this could be the beginning of an enterprise that would bring hope to the hopeless.

In the two months that followed toys were made all over Santiago and a Christmas fair was held, but my life took an unexpected turn and I was not able to participate further in the project.

As I became more interested in the problems of creating work for the people my friends invited me to see what they were doing on similar lines. Sally was one of my American friends who lived in a house in a distant *población*. She was a merry girl, always good natured and cheerful. She ran a washing co-operative in which some young American wives who lived in an upper class residential area collected washing from their friends once a week and brought it by car to a house which Sally had acquired for her ladies. There they washed the clothes and sheets by hand and ironed them ready to be returned the following week. This way the women did not have to travel far from their homes to do washing in people's houses and they both saved the bus fare and enjoyed the companionship of the other women. Sally supervised the work and discussed their problems with the women trying to help them, as we all did, to have faith and hope in better days to come.

I paid a visit too, to the *comedor infantil* run by the mothers of the children under the supervision of one of the priests who worked in the same area as Sally. There were two sittings for lunch and each time over 100 children sat down to bare plank tables and tucked ravenously into a plate of *cochayuyu*, and a glass of milk. *Cochayuyu* is a seaweed that is sold dried in the markets in Chile and, stewed and served with onions and potatoes, makes a tasty dish.

It was an experience to both move and rend the heart. In most cases this was the only meal that these children ate in the day. The spirit of the women who prepared and served the food was wonderful, but what desperation and anguish they must have experienced in their homes, no longer able to feed their children or clothe them decently. The food came from Caritas and other international relief agencies and also from the local vendors who gave what they could to help the children. The dining room was made of rough unpainted planks and there were no windows. The walls were decorated with pictures out of the women's magazines, bright colourful scenes and posters with messages of solidarity and hope in the future. What moved me most was a simple photograph of a plate of food: perhaps it was bacon and eggs or roast beef and carrots, I don't remember, but I know that it was food which most people in England eat and take for granted and which these children had never tasted. More distressing by far than the bare hall and the rows of children who ate once a day six days a week was the knowledge of those children who never came at all because there was no money to buy food for them. A priest in another shanty town had told me that, on average, for every child who eats in a church dining room there are another five who would like to come but cannot because of lack of funds.

My visit to the dining room moved me to begin another

project which, like many others, because of lack of time and my untimely departure from Chile, was never finished. If children were going hungry while others were fed it was vital that the best possible use be made of such money as was available and meals planned so that the requirements of the growing child were met but not exceeded. If by careful and scientific planning this could be worked out perhaps two children might be fed with the money that at the moment was feeding one. This thought is of course simple and obvious and I imagined that such data must be readily available. It seemed, however, that this was not so and no one could refer me to a book where a minimum survival diet had been calculated.

I went therefore with a friend to visit the professor of paediatrics at one of the big children's hospitals in Santiago. It was an afternoon to remember, the meeting of men of good will from different worlds in the same city. We sat there, a burly American priest in anorak, jeans and boots muddy from his *población*, the professor in his well creased suit, immaculate white coat and well polished shoes and myself, as always, in sweater and jeans. I explained to the professor that we wanted to work out the minimum diet to maintain health in a child of between two and six years old who was being fed one meal a day.

At first he didn't understand what I meant and as I explained in more detail and my companion spoke of babies who were fed on tea he smiled and said, 'But what about their milk allowance?' Slowly I explained to him that if a man's social security payments had lapsed so had his right to free milk for his children, as indeed had his right to free medical treatment.

The doctor shook his head in a mixture of sadness and disbelief and asked his secretary to call the dietician. She arrived promptly, a smart girl in the crisp white uniform and mauve belt of the Santiago hospital dieticians. These girls, like the nurses and midwives, are highly trained at university and are extremely knowledgeable in their field. We explained our problem once more and she promised to work us out a diet.

True to her word, a week later, the dietician rang me and I went to see her. She had indeed worked hard and I had a beautifully typed diet sheet for a child of four years. There it all was: so many grams of meat, of fish, of cheese, half an egg, half a litre of milk and so on, carefully apportioned into the three meals of breakfast, lunch and supper! We had explained we wanted the cheapest possible diet in order that a child might eat to live and grow normally and that this must be worked out on the basis of one meal a day because our children only ate once a day. This was beyond her comprehension. She could not believe that there were children in Santiago who never saw meat or fish or cheese and who lived on beans and potatoes, bread and spaghetti and seaweed.

The absurd thing about the whole situation was that there had been many Chilean doctors with intimate knowledge of the problems of the *poblaciones*. The public health physicians especially had worked extensively on the problems of vaccination, hygiene, parasite control and alimentation amongst the people in the marginal developments; but these doctors were now either in exile or dared not reveal their left-wing sympathies, and some of them were dead.

Another constant problem in my day-to-day working life was the providing of drugs for my patients in the Posta. In the little clinic in El Salto there was no problem, for the other doctors and I had worked out the minimum of drugs with which we could treat most conditions and the Committee for Peace gave us money to buy them. By an absurd and tragic paradox the state-run Posta had virtually no antibiotics other than the injections of penicillin or chloramphenicol which were given to the in-patients or to those who came with some urgent condition. The significance of this in terms of community health is immense for inadequately treated infections can smoulder on into chronic ill health. In particular, the appallingly high incidence of valvular heart disease in young people in Chile is a result of just such inadequate primary treatment of streptococcal infections.

These facts are well known and penicillin is an inexpensive drug but still it is not available to those patients who cannot buy it for themselves and these are precisely the poor, undernourished people who live in damp, overcrowded houses and who are most at risk of becoming ill with either rheumatic fever or nephritis.

The Posta aims to provide an emergency service only and patients with conditions requiring follow-up were expected to go to the clinic nearest to their home. There, if their social security payments were up to date, they would see a doctor and receive free medicine. The majority of the patients who attended the Posta 3, however, were unemployed and had no provision. It was easy enough to give them a prescription and tell them to buy the drugs at the local chemist but I found that if I asked them if they had money the answer was nearly always 'No'. It was much easier not to ask, of course, but I could not work in this way and I took the problem to Father Howard, the head of the Columban fathers who lived near my house. He agreed to help me and we went together to one of the drug companies and bought a large stock of essential medicines so that I worked much more happily and was reassured that at least my patients would receive medication.

Every day I became a little more involved in my work for the sick and the hungry. It was as if a lens had moved so that their problems which before had been blurred now came sharply into focus. I was both exhilarated and overwhelmed. My head spun with ideas and I had neither the time nor the strength to implement them. I worked absolutely to capacity but took time off with my friends to see a film or go to an inexpensive restaurant. One friend would introduce me to another and I became an 'honorary' member of the missionary community in Santiago.

Remembering how overwork had driven prayer out of my life once before, I disciplined myself to pray regularly each day however busy I was. I went each day to mass and though the agony of dragging myself out of bed an hour early never became any less acute I was filled with peace and joy as I walked up the street towards the church. Instinctively I knew that this was the fuel that fed the fires of my growing love for the people and my longing to help and serve them. I was weary and harassed and swamped with demands and yet at the same time I felt alive and aglow as never before. On fire with love for all the world and possessed by a peace and joy apparently out of all proportion to the life I was leading I slowly realized what was happening. My blank cheque had been accepted, the die was cast, my 'election' was being confirmed.

25

Confrontation in Malloco

> Each and every one of us will pay on demand, his part of
> sacrifice . . . knowing that all together we are getting
> ever closer to the new man, whose figure is beginning to
> appear.
>
> Ernesto Che Guevara

On the night of 15 October 1975, the leading members of
Chile's outlawed revolutionary leftist party, the MIR were
surprised by security forces in their headquarters in Malloco,
a small and sleepy country town some fifteen kilometres
from Santiago. The security forces attacked at ten o'clock
at night and in the ensuing gun battle which lasted for four
hours one man was killed and another received two bullet
wounds in the leg. Incredibly, in spite of vigilance from
helicopters with spotlights, two men and two girls escaped
with a baby. They handed the baby to a sympathetic neighbour and after spending the night in a ditch managed to
elude the forces which had surrounded the area and disappeared. The gun battle in Malloco and the death of an
important revolutionary was headline news all over Chile.
The papers published photographs of the fugitives and an
intensive search was carried out.

It is difficult to explain how it was that this dramatic
event almost escaped my notice. I had no contact whatsoever with any revolutionaries and the names of Andres
Pascal Allende and Nelson Gutierrez meant nothing to me.
I bought newspapers only occasionally and when I did,
rarely read more than the headlines. So on this occasion I
took in the fact that there had been yet another confrontation
between the military and some resistance workers and,
knowing the lack of freedom of the press, wondered how
much of it was true. Glancing at the newspapers on the
stands I noticed that the faces of two men and two girls

appeared for several days in succession on the front pages, but I certainly did not study them.

Early in the morning of Tuesday 21 October I was visited by a Chilean priest friend who asked me if I was prepared to treat a man with a bullet wound in the leg.

So now it had happened. The moment that I had neither looked forward to nor dreaded had arrived, as I had known that it inevitably would. Without hesitating I said 'Yes', knowing quite well that this might mean the end of my work in Chile. I did not weigh up the pros and cons: a doctor faced with a wounded man does not weigh as on a balance the worth of that man against the worth of other possible patients. In a disaster with multiple casualties, of course, priorities must be assigned, but when faced with one patient who is sick, the doctor treats. On reflection, perhaps this is a Christian ethic rather than a purely medical one: the value of the individual as against the state. Anyway, I had no doubts; it was not my place to judge this man but to treat him.

It is perhaps difficult for anyone without knowledge of life in a repressive police state to realize just how unthinkable it was that this man should present himself at a hospital for treatment. The chances of escaping detection were nil, for not only had his photograph been published in every newspaper in Santiago but all patients in Chile must produce their identity card which bears their photograph. Once detected he would have been transferred to one of the hospitals belonging to the armed forces where he would have been interrogated, tortured and probably killed. Well known for their audacity and bravery, the members of the MIR were especially hated by the DINA.

The attitude of the government to the MIR is revealed in the account of an interview between President Pinochet and the two founders of the Peace Committee, Bishops Frenz and Ariztia.

The President said, 'You are pastors and priests and you have to think and act in that way. If I were in your position I would undoubtedly be acting as you do. But consider that I am the President of Chile. And in this capacity I must say to you that state security is more important than the human rights. The members of the MIR must be tortured as they are insane and mad. Without torture they may not sing.' (To the very letter: *Los miristas tienen que ser torturados porque son locos y enfermos. Sin tortura no cantan.*)

Testimony of Bishop Helmut Frenz
given at Helsinki, February 1976

My friend did not tell me the name of the wounded man but indicated that it was one of the recent fugitives from the Malloco incident. He asked me to go to a certain office in the town where I would meet someone who would take me to the patient. After he had gone I collected my instruments and putting them in my handbag set out for the office.

26

The Fugitives

> I was hungry and you gave me food; I was thirsty and you gave me drink; I was a stranger and you made me welcome; naked and you clothed me, sick and you visited me, in prison and you came to see me. I tell you solemnly, in so far as you did it to the least of these brothers of mine, you did it to me.
>
> *Matthew 25:35–40*

I went by bus to an office in down town Santiago and was asked by the secretary to wait. I sat down beside a girl whose face looked familiar though I could not place her. In a little while we were called in together and it emerged that she was Sister Helen Nelson, a North American sister of Notre Dame whom I had met in the home of one of my friends, and that the wounded man was in her house. We spoke briefly to a priest who worked there and I remember him saying to me as we searched for antiseptic solution, 'I hope to God that Christ goes disguised as a wounded Mirista.'

Helen and I drove to the convent. We walked to the back of the house and were greeted by a young girl in jeans and a shirt. This was Mary Ann Beausire, the companion of Andres Pascal, head of the MIR since Miguel Enriquez' death. She led me into the bedroom where in a room darkened by drawn curtains I met Nelson Gutierrez. We spoke little: there was little to say. He showed me his leg and, finding it swollen and inflamed, I told him I would explore the wound to see if I could find the bullet. I went off to the kitchen with Mary Ann to sterilize my instruments and as we waited for the water to boil we talked. She told me that they had spent the first night in a ditch and that they had escaped through heavy undergrowth. I examined her feet and legs and found them deeply scratched. It was hard to realize that this calm and friendly girl was on the run for her life.

I anaesthetized Nelson's leg but the exploration was still very painful. He made no murmur. He had three wounds: the exit and entry wound of one bullet and the entry wound of the other. I probed the second wound but though my forceps entered over two inches I could not feel the bullet.

Contrary to popular belief, it is not essential to remove a bullet which is not interfering mechanically with the function of a vital organ. Provided there is no infection it is often better to leave well alone as searching can be long and difficult and can lead to the destruction of more tissue. After my attempt to remove the bullet in Nelson's leg, therefore, I decided that it was better to treat him with heavy doses of antibiotics and make him rest. Telling them what drugs to buy and how to dress the wound I left and promised to return in forty-eight hours.

On Thursday the 23rd I went again to the convent. I took a taxi but alighted half a block before we reached the street and walked nervously towards the house. I let myself in and made my way towards the bedroom where Nelson and the girls were hidden. I was met by Mariella, Nelson's wife, who told me that Nelson was feverish and much weaker than he had been. There had been a plan to take him by motor cycle to a place where he could hide with less risk of discovery but he had not been able to stand unaided. I found the plan highly dangerous for in his debilitated condition with an extremely painful leg he would almost certainly have fallen off.

When I examined Nelson I found him pale and sweaty and restless and the leg was more swollen and painful than it had been. I explored again for the bullet without success. Looking for metallic 'foreign bodies' is notoriously difficult and is normally never undertaken without the aid of x-rays to localize the object. Searching for a small bullet in the swollen calf of a stocky young man without x-rays and without adequate lighting was sheer folly and yet after two days' treatment with high doses of antibiotics he was worse and bordering on a state of septicaemia. Medically, there were two things which could happen if the bullet were not removed: either the infection would settle with an increase in antibotic therapy or he would deteriorate and become delirious and might even develop gangrene of the wounded leg. It was considered too risky to hide him in the convent any longer and he was to be taken to a place of hiding where he would not receive medical attention.

I bandaged his leg slowly as I tried to decide what to do and what to say to him. I explained that I thought that the only course open to him was to seek asylum for he needed hospital treatment. If he insisted on remaining in hiding he was endangering the lives of the nuns and priests who were helping him and if he became delirious he might well betray himself and his companions. I left him to discuss the prospect with his friends and went to wash my instruments.

I knew that the members of the MIR were forbidden to leave the country without the permission of their party and that they reckoned to die in action rather than take asylum. After a while I was joined by Mary Ann who told me that Nelson and Mariella would accept asylum. From this I realized that she would not and I marvelled at the courage of this slim girl many years younger than myself.

I returned to speak to Nelson who thanked me for my help and told me that he would accept asylum if it could be arranged. It was then that I learned about the child, for Mariella suddenly burst out 'I won't go without my baby!' She told me that when they ran away from the farmhouse in Malloco a woman had stepped forward and offered to care for the child. Running desperately for her life she passed the nine-month-old baby to the woman and it was only as she stumbled after Nelson and Mary Ann that she realized that she did not know the name of the woman or where she lived. Now eight days had passed and there was no news and it seemed likely that she would leave the country without being reunited with her child. Her desperation can be imagined for no one could go and look for the child without risk of detention by the police who were probably anxious to take the baby as a hostage. I had no words of comfort for her: what can one say to a mother who has lost her child except that one hopes and prays that it will be found safe and well?

Helen returned and we went together to tell the priests about the deterioration in Nelson's condition and the need for asylum. They were both incredulous and thankful to learn that at least two of their dangerous young 'guests' were prepared to go into asylum. One of them went to explore the possibilities of a place in an embassy and the other to tell Nelson that he must hand over his arms if he wished to be taken to safety. It was only then that I realized that my patient still had his machine gun in bed with him!

Having explained that as soon as he was under the protection of an embassy Nelson must be taken to a hospital I went back to my house thinking that this was my last connection with the case. The next day, however, I was summoned to yet another meeting and explained once more that medically speaking there was no possibility of Nelson returning to his life in '*la clandestinidad*' and that if he did not receive adequate treatment for his leg he would very likely die. I was then told that in view of the gravity of his condition and of the threat to his life, he would be granted asylum with his wife in the house of the Papal Nuncio (Apostolic Delegate), the Vatican's diplomatic representative in Chile. There was, however, no question of his being able to be admitted to a clinic because the moment he went outside the grounds of the Nunciatura he would be arrested. Any treatment, surgical or otherwise, would have to be carried out inside the Nuncio's house and they asked me to continue caring for him. My heart sank, but I told them that I would come the following morning.

All that night I thought about Nelson. In a well equipped operating theatre with good lights and a qualified assistant, removal of the bullet would have been a difficult task, but on a bed or table with at best an anglepoise light and no one with any previous surgical experience to assist me, the prospect was formidable. The difficulties of surgery were so great that the obvious course was to leave the bullet where it was but so great had been the deterioration in his general condition while on heavy doses of powerful antibiotics that it seemed at the time essential to try to remove the cause of the infection.

As ill luck would have it my night at the Posta was a heavy one and I had little more than an hour's sleep. I went home to breakfast with that mixture of weariness and nausea that are part of extreme fatigue and as I sat over my coffee I wondered if I would have difficulty getting into the Nunciatura. We had decided the day before that for the sake of security I had better give a false name so I was to present myself as a missionary nun, Madre Isabel. We thought that the only way in which a foreign woman could enter the Nunciatura without arousing suspicion was to pose as a nun and the name Isabel was chosen for me by one of the priests because Isabel is Spanish for Elizabeth, the name of Britain's queen! I had to give due thought to my appearance and dressed in a navy blue suit normally reserved for weddings and interviews for jobs. Accustomed to wearing my blue jeans for work, church and leisure I felt completely disguised in a suit! My instruments constituted a problem: Sister Isabel would hardly take a suitcase with her on a visit to pay her respects to the Nuncio and yet I had to take a considerable number of instruments and lotions with me, for I could neither telephone to tell them to buy what I needed nor nip out to the chemist if I had forgotten something. Luckily I had a large black shoulder bag. I filled it full of all that seemed essential and, with my shoulder sagging under the weight, took a taxi to Providencia.

I alighted opposite a smart school and strode purposefully towards its gate until the taxi had disappeared and then walked to the end of the street to the Nunciatura. The Nuncio's residence is next to the French embassy and backs on to the British embassy in a quiet street off Santiago's richest and most elegant highway, Providencia. It is a large house, surrounded by a high wall, and has enormous sheet iron gates. It was guarded by two policemen with machine guns who were conversing with a man who was working on the engine of his motor cycle just outside the main entrance. I felt sure that the latter was keeping an eye on the comings and goings at the Nunciatura but there was no avoiding

him so I walked up to the gate and put my finger on the
bell.

I was immediately accosted by the two policemen who
wanted to know my name and what I wanted. I said that I
was Madre Isabel and that I had an appointment to see the
Nuncio. A voice spoke on the intercom at the gate asking
who was there and again I gave my false name, inwardly
cursing them for the length of time they were taking to let
me in, for any moment now the policeman could ask to see
my identity card. Eventually, after what seemed an eternity,
the gate was opened and I was ushered inside.

My visit, however, proved unnecessary for another doctor
had been summoned and I was politely thanked for my visit
and told that I need not worry about Nelson any more.
With the weight of responsibility lifted from my shoulders I
took my leave and made my way home, congratulating myself that the adventure was over and that I could resume a
normal life.

27

Arrest

Arrest is an instantaneous, shattering thrust, expulsion,
somersault from one state into another.
Alexander Solzhenitsyn
The Gulag Archipelago

The week that followed my treatment of Gutierrez was a busy one and I was much taken up with the care of a new patient. When I went to the Notre Dame Sisters' convent for the second time I met a couple of my American nun friends and they told me that Susie was sick. I was perturbed as she had insisted on going to visit a friend in the south of Chile when she should have been in bed because of a severe cold. It seemed likely therefore that she might be suffering from some complication following the cold and I went off to visit her. My friends had insisted that she move from her own house which was in a very poor area to the centre house of their congregation so that she might be properly cared for. (Her own order had no house in Santiago.)

It emerged that she had been working over fifteen hours a day for several months and was badly in need of rest, so I gave her some sedation and told her that she was to stay in bed. I visited her several times during the week but was not happy with her condition and decided she would be better somewhere quieter. On the Thursday, therefore, I went to Father William Halliden, the head of the missionary priests who lived near my house and asked him if Susie could be looked after in his house for a few days. That evening, before I went off to do my night shift at the Posta, he and I collected Susie and installed her in the sick bay of the house in the Larraín Gandarillas.

She settled in well and with no visitors other than Father Halliden and his assistant was soon much quieter. Enriquetta the maid, tended her lovingly and carried all her meals on a tray so she had nothing to do but rest. On Saturday I was able to spend a good deal of time with her and made frequent visits from my house to hers bringing books and some sewing and my tape recorder so that she might listen to some music to while away the long hours.

It was 31 October, the eve of the feast of All Saints and I went to mass at the Italian church around the corner from my home. As it was the mass of the big feast day it took rather longer than the usual evening mass and it was just on nine o'clock when I got home. I asked Margarita what time supper would be and she told me that it would not be ready till a quarter to ten. I sighed, as I was hungry, but I had long since learned that there was no hurrying Margarita and that there was nothing to be gained in complaining, so I told her that I would go to say goodnight to Susie.

I had promised to call round in the evening as Susie was anxious that we should pray together and this seemed a good moment. I found her in good spirits talking to Father Halliden while she finished her supper and the three of us talked for a while until he said he must go off and write his sermon for the following day. When he had gone I went to the chapel to borrow a candle so that we might give a little atmosphere to the bare sickroom to help us as we prayed. Susie looked at my bare feet and, rummaging in her bag for a pair of socks, told me to put them on because I would be cold.

Like most women I care quite a lot about the clothes I wear and though I dress for preference in jeans and sweaters they are always of a cut and colour that pleases me and which fits in with my private personal view of how I like to look. (The fact that this does not conform with the accepted norms of fashion for 38-year-old lady doctors has no direct relevance.) As it happens I like the sight of my bare feet in their franciscan-style sandals and I would much rather be a little cold than wear socks with sandals. I protested that I wasn't cold, but I could see that my refusal was churlish so I thanked her and put them on, little knowing how I would thank God and her for them later on.

I lit the candle and sitting on the end of her bed was composing myself to pray when the silence was broken by the most appalling scream. It was loud and high and prolonged and had an animal quality that filled me with dread. I put out the candle and, telling Susie to stay where she was, ran towards the stairs. It had been a woman's voice and I had vague thoughts that perhaps Enriquetta had fallen down the stairs; all I knew was that it was unlike anything I had ever heard before and that something terrible must have happened.

Father Halliden and I arrived downstairs at the same moment, entering the living room from opposite ends (for the house had two staircases) and found ourselves confronted by the prone figure of Enriquetta lying in a large pool of her own blood which was still pouring from a gaping wound in her back. I reached her first and as I knelt beside her the firing began, bullets coming through the french windows from the street. Although Father Halliden closed the shutters they splintered like matchwood and bullets sailed over our heads. (We were later to learn that these were specially powerful bullets forbidden by the Geneva Convention.)

My first thoughts were for Enriquetta. Taking her by the arms I dragged her towards the back of the house out of the range of whatever madman was firing at us. I knelt helplessly beside her, feeling for a pulse that I knew must be getting weaker and weaker as her blood ebbed away across the parquet floor. Doctor I might be, but without blood and instruments I was no better then than a first aid worker: perhaps worse, for I knew that she was dying and that there was nothing to be done.

The firing continued and I realized that although we were in a sort of scullery off the kitchen the bullets were still coming close to us. It seemed that whoever was there was firing through all the windows and that sooner or later we should be hit. Still dazed and finding the situation totally unreal I told Father Halliden that Enriquetta was dying and that there was nothing we could do so we should take cover. He disappeared in the direction of the dining room and lying on my stomach I inched my way across the kitchen floor and sat under the table in the corner of the room.

For what seemed an eternity and must have been ten or fifteen minutes I sat there and listened to the firing outside and the crack of the bullets around me. It seemed like a dream, or as if I were watching a bad gangster film, and I had no coherent thoughts other than how very curious it was and that perhaps my life was about to end.

Eventually the shooting stopped and there came the sound of men's voices shouting at us to open the door. It seemed that help had come at last and Father Halliden unbolted the kitchen door to let them in. The moment the bolts were undone the door crashed open and in rushed several men with machine guns. I had expected to see the police and these plain clothes men seemed out of place, but I had little time to think. Two men stayed below. Though we asked them who they were they made no reply. Instead they asked me my name and when I said 'Sheila' they said, 'That's the one we're after', and went upstairs.

Incredibly, we were alone. I went to the telephone, cursing myself that I had not committed the consul's private number to memory but the only number I could remember was my home. A strange voice answered and then I knew that they must have gone to my house first and that they really were looking for me. The voice changed and I spoke to one of the students who was lodging in my house (I had let my three spare rooms to a trio of university students who wanted to live away from home). He spoke hesitantly and I knew without seeing that there was a man behind him with a gun. Not knowing what to say and yet desperate to communicate my situation I told him that I would be late for supper because the maid in the Columban Fathers' house had been shot. There seemed no more to say so I put the phone down and joined Father Halliden beside Enriquetta.

She was weaker but still alive as he held her hand and tried to comfort her for she was moaning and moving restlessly. He told me that he wanted to give her the last rites and, still conscious that any unwise move might be my last, I went to the kitchen in search of the oil. I saw a tin of hand cream on top of the fridge and with that ribaldry that emerges unbidden in moments of tragedy and crisis wondered if that would do! I came to the conclusion that Canon Law probably didn't mention Nivea and cursing it for being stuffy, searched through the cupboards till I found the cooking oil. Kneeling together beside Enriquetta, our clothes soaked in her blood, we prayed for her departing soul and Father Halliden anointed her and gave her the sacrament of the dying.

I heard footsteps on the stairs and there, pale and trans-fixed with fear, was Susie. The man behind her had his machine gun in her back. Furious, I leaped to my feet and berated him for bringing her down to see the dying Enri-quetta. He took no notice of me and returned to aid his friends' search upstairs. We were joined shortly after by the leader of the group and his assistant, again they asked me my name and again, not having the wit to lie, I said 'Sheila'. Once more they said, 'She's the one we're after', and told me to go and find a blanket for Enriquetta.

I searched the bedrooms till I found the blanket cup-board and brought one down, then, as nobody said anything to me, I went upstairs and made my way to the back of the house. I found Susie back in bed again and I told her that these men were looking for me. I remember saying to her, 'I think it's the MIR and they've come to take me to treat someone else.' The absurdity of the idea that the MIR would capture me at gunpoint to treat someone when I'd already treated one of their members voluntarily never dawned on me: it was a crazy thought in a nightmare situation. I remember looking at the window and won-dering vaguely if I could escape, but luckily I made no attempt for I learned later that the house was surrounded and they would certainly have shot me.

Not knowing what was to befall me I went to the bath-room. In the security of the locked room I felt a little safer so I turned out the light and sitting on the floor leaned against the wall by the door so that if they shot through the door it wouldn't hit me. As I sat there I heard them call my name, at first gently and then with increasing urgency and anger. I heard them searching for me, running from room to room until someone tried the door of the bathroom and found it locked. They began to batter on the door and I realized that they would shoot it open so I shouted at them and came out. Roughly they pushed me along the corridor and I went down the stairs with a gun in my back.

Enriquetta's body had gone and I saw two men carrying her on a blanket out into the street. As we walked to the door I saw Father Halliden slumped in a chair and I realized that it was only me that they were taking. He looked at me in a dazed way and as I called to him to inform the consul they pushed me out into the street.

As I slowly walked away, there, sitting on the doorstep in tears with a gun in her ribs, was Margarita. The nightmare quality persisted as I continued down the street to a private car and obeyed their orders to get in. I sat in the rear seat and the man with the gun got in beside me. After he had given an order to the driver we drove away.

As the car left the curb he tied a handkerchief around my eyes and then struck my face with his hand. The force of the blow angered me and I asked him indignantly why he had hit me as I had done nothing to merit such treatment. Perhaps I touched some buried spark of chivalry for he didn't hit me again but said, 'We know you treated Nelson Gutierrez.'

Then I knew. These men were of the DINA and somehow they had found that it was I who had treated Nelson. As the car raced through the darkened streets of Santiago, I sat there and wondered what would happen to me. Although afraid and helpless I was sure that, when I was taken before these men's superiors, things would be very different, for they would discover that they were dealing with a foreign national and the daughter of an Air Vice Marshal to boot. Thus cheered I put my left hand slowly up to my cheek and feigning distress I shielded my face as with one finger I raised the handkershief from over my left eye.

I looked for a landmark to tell me where I was but we were going so fast that I could not read the names of the streets and we turned so many times that I quickly became disorientated. Then I saw a line of trees and some grass and realized that we were in the street called Tobalaba which runs parallel with the canal San Carlos through the residential area of the Barrio Alto, the high class upper zone of Santiago. After a while we turned left over a bridge and on to a bumpy, unpaved road. I remembered that Teresa had told me that she had been detained in an interrogation centre in Peñalolen. This then must be the street José Arrieta which was at right angles to the canal and which ran up the hill to the enormous elegant house of the Arrieta family which had been a hippy commune in the time of Allende. After a couple of hundred yards the car slowed down and turned into a driveway; the driver hooted and as we waited the headlights lit up two huge iron gates set in a wall which surrounded an old house painted the traditional colonial red. This, I later learned, was the Casa Grimaldi, one of the DINA's major centres of interrogation. We drove in and the gates were slammed behind us but as yet I had no inkling of events to come, nor of the experience which was so radically to change my life and have repercussions throughout the world, the full extent of which I shall probably never know.

28

Interrogation

No one shall be subjected to torture or cruel, inhuman
or degrading treatment or punishment.

Article 5
Universal Declaration of Human Rights

It is not easy to decide how best to tell the story of the next
few hours. What happened is so incredible and so appalling
that it is difficult for people without knowledge of interrogation methods used in certain countries to believe. There
is also the fact that the description of what happened is so
unpleasant that it makes distressing reading: it would be
easier to tell and more pleasant to read if I used that British
reserve and the technique of understatement of which, as a
people, we are perhaps rightly proud. If, however, I am to
write anything at all of what happened it must be for a purpose and that purpose is this: that it may be known how
political prisoners are treated in certain countries. What
happened to me is typical of what happens to political prisoners in countries where torture has become institutionalized as an instrument of interrogation and repression.

Deliberately to underplay the horror of what happened
would be as untruthful as to exaggerate it and would be a
betrayal of the thousands of Chileans, Argentinians, Ura-
guayans, Brazilians, Paraguayans, and others, who have
suffered at the hands of the intelligence services of repressive regimes where human rights are deliberately and constantly infringed. So, for a brief moment and by a curious
series of coincidences, I have become the voice of the voiceless and as such I have a strict obligation to speak the truth.

What follows is a factual account of what happened to me
on the night of 31 October 1975. The dialogue is as I remember it: the words may not be exactly what was said but
the general trend of the interchange is accurate. In addition

to telling the story as it happened I have tried to convey something of what I thought and felt at the time and though there are parts of that night which are lost to me there are others which are as clear as if it were yesterday. It is perhaps worth recording that I do not feel, nor have I ever felt, any hatred for the men who interrogated me. I see them as men who are sick in mind or in soul and as products of an evil system in a very sick society.

I was told to get out of the car and was led stumbling across what I think was a courtyard. We paused as metal gates were opened and then slammed shut behind us. I was led into a room and without any further ado was ordered to remove my clothes.

I was incredulous. There must be some mistake. I told them quickly that I was a British doctor and that this would cause an international incident. Then came the reply that brought home to me the appalling truth of the reality of my situation for they said, and I quote

'*Nuestra imagen en el exterior es tan mal que no nos importa.*' – 'Our image in the exterior is so bad that we don't care.'

Again they told me to undress and, searching desperately for something to convince them that they could not do this to me I said, 'My father is an Air Vice Marshal,' but there was no reply.

Frantically I said, 'I'm going to be a nun.' This brought a rapid response, 'You're not one, are you?' to which I replied, 'No.'

Again came the order to undress. Slowly I removed my sweater and could not bring myself to go further. Then I felt a rough hand grab my shirt and one of the buttons came off. Realizing that they meant what they said and wanting to avoid further manhandling I removed the remainder of my clothes. The handkerchief around my eyes was by this time a little loose and I saw that I was in a small room which contained a double metal bunk and a table and chair. On the wall hung a street plan of Santiago and crowded into the room, for it was quite small, were about five men in plain clothes and a woman.

They told me then to lie on the bed and quickly they

secured me to the bottom half of the bunk, tying my wrists and ankles and upper arms and placing a wide band around my chest and abdomen. Then it began. I felt an electric shock pass through me and then another and another.

I made to scream, but found there was a gag in my mouth.

Then the questions began.

'Where did you treat Gutierrez?'

'Who asked you to treat him?'

My brain was very clear and the implications of this question were immediately apparent: if they didn't know where I'd treated Nelson they didn't know of the involve-ment of the priests and nuns and perhaps they never need to know.

My thought processes at this juncture have importance

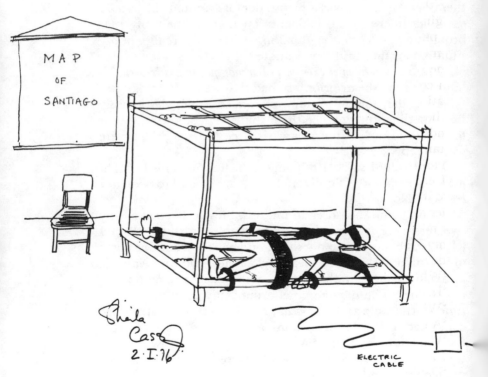

The *parrilla*

for it was at this moment that I made the decision to lie in an effort to save the lives of the Chilean priests involved and, in some way that I couldn't fully articulate to myself, the Chilean church. I knew that the position of the church in Chile vis à vis the Junta was delicate and I thought that the fact that so many priests and nuns had been involved might lead to a breakdown in relations between church and state. The fact that I was mistaken had nothing to do with the decision taken at that moment. I was at that stage quite sure that the treatment could not go on for long, for I believed that every passing minute brought nearer the arrival of the consul and my release.

The hope of release was a very important factor in my initial ability to withstand pain, for it did not occur to me that this could go on for long and it seemed a matter of hanging on till help came. I was taught in medical school that pain had three components: the actual pain experienced, the memory of past pain and the fear of future pain. Thus at the very beginning, with no knowledge of how severe the pain could become, and believing that it would be of short duration, I was able to act more bravely than I did later. At the beginning, too, I believed that the lives of two of my friends depended upon my silence and this is also very important, for resistance to torture is closely related to motivation for not talking.

I embarked, therefore, upon a fabrication which was to have many unexpected repercussions. If it seems that to lie under such circumstances is difficult I can assure you that it was not, for all their questions were direct and their belief in my answers coupled with the repeated painful stimuli made my imagination extremely active.

'Where did you treat Gutierrez?'

'In a private house.'

'Who asked you to treat him?'

'A doctor.'

'What was his name?'

I hesitated and the current came quickly and savagely.

'Dr Perez.' A name, any name so long as it was false.

'What is his christian name?'

'Arturo.'

'Where does he work?'

'The Hospital Salvador.' This was a hospital near my home and the only doctor I knew there was a woman.

'Why did they ask you?' Again I hesitated and again I felt the shocks. Mercifully the answer came: so logical that they were in no doubt.

'He was afraid.'

They changed tack. 'Where did you meet him?' That was more difficult. Where could I have met him and yet not have names to give away? The electricity spurred me on. 'At a party.' That fitted. Now they were on to him and soon they'd have him and with him all his friends.

'Where does he live?'

'I don't know.'

The sharp pain told me they were angry.

'You're lying.' O God, how could I tell them where he lived when he didn't exist? Again the pain, and again.

Frantically: 'He told me he had a beach house in Algarrobo. He invited me there.'

'Where?' They believed me. They could see it all: the soft lights, the music, the invitation for a weekend out of Santiago.

'Where?' Where indeed. I'd never been to Algarrobo, just passed it in the bus.

'I don't know. I never went. I don't go out with married men.'

Thwarted, they tried another tack.

'Where did you treat Gutierrez?'

'In a private house.' That at least was true.

'Who owned the house?'

'Miguel Rojas.'

'What does he do?'

'He's an architect.'

'Where does he live?'

'I don't know.' Again I knew their anger, and again, and again, as I tried desperately to think what to say.

'It was night. I didn't see the name of the street.'

'How did you get there?'

'I was taken by car.'

'What sort of a car?'

'A Peugeot.' (The convent car had been a Peugeot.)

'What colour?'

'White.'

'What colour was the upholstery?'

'Blue.'

I heard them repeat it: 'A white Peugeot. Blue upholstery.' Now they were getting somewhere. They began to look up Rojas in the telephone book and I heard them turn the pages in excitement.

'How did they contact you?' Dear God, was there no end to it?

'They phoned me.'

'Who phoned you?'

'The doctor phoned me.'

'What did he say?'

'He told me to wait at the garage on the corner of Vicuña Mackenna and Rancagua.' (Vicuña Mackenna is a main street near my house.)

'Who was in the car?'

'A man.'

'What did he look like?'

'He had a moustache.'

'What else?'

'I didn't notice.'

'What was his name?'

'I don't know. He didn't tell me.'

'Where did you go?'

'I don't know.' This wouldn't do and, the stepped-up current told me clearly that I must do better.

'Where did you go?'

'He told me not to look.'

'You must have looked. Women always look.' How right they were.

'I didn't. He told me not to. He said it wasn't in my interest to know where I was going.' This seemed plausible enough but they were determined.

'Which direction did the car take?' Quickly I thought

and chose the direction that led furthest away from Helen's house.

'Towards the Central Station.'

'And then?'

'Below the station.'

'And?'

There was no answer. This was an area that I didn't know at all, a big highway leading out to the airport. There were residential areas on either side. Or were there? Was it only waste land? I didn't know.

'Where did you turn off?'

So we must have turned off. But where.

'I don't know.'

This was the answer they didn't like and I knew it at once. I heard them looking at the map and they were obviously plotting my route. I heard the words '*Obispo Subercaseaux*' and latched on to them.

'Where did you turn?'

Mentally I tossed for it. 'Right.'

'What was the street called?'

'I don't know.'

'Of course you know.'

'*Obispo no sé cuánto.*' (Bishop something or other.)

'You said you couldn't see.' Dear God, was there no pleasing them?

'I think it was called Bishop something.'

'Bishop what?'

'I don't know.'

'You do know.'

'I don't.'

'You do.'

'I don't.' This was dicey. If I named the street they could prove me wrong and if I didn't it seemed they'd never stop. I stuck to my guns.

'*Obispo no sé cuánto.*'

They tried a different tack.

'What was the house like?'

'A big house.'

'What colour?'

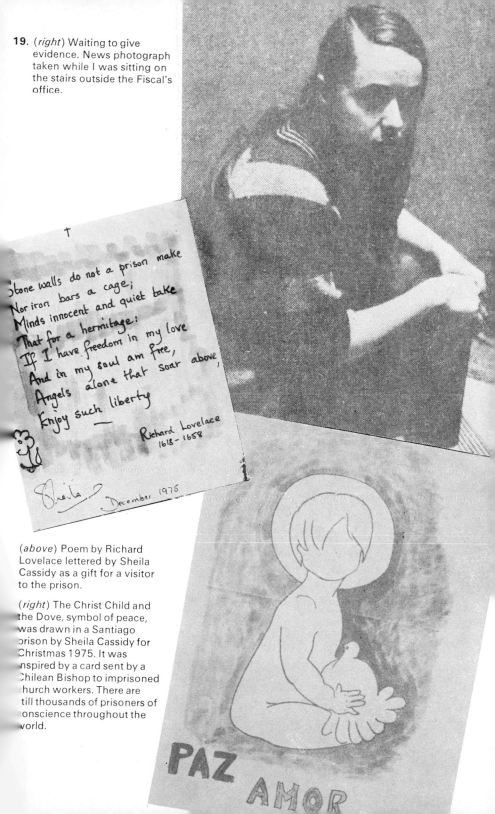

19. (*right*) Waiting to give evidence. News photograph taken while I was sitting on the stairs outside the Fiscal's office.

Stone walls do not a prison make
Nor iron bars a cage;
Minds innocent and quiet take
That for a hermitage;
If I have freedom in my love
And in my soul am free,
Angels alone that soar above,
Enjoy such liberty —

Richard Lovelace
1618-1658

Sheila December 1975

(*above*) Poem by Richard Lovelace lettered by Sheila Cassidy as a gift for a visitor to the prison.

(*right*) The Christ Child and the Dove, symbol of peace, was drawn in a Santiago prison by Sheila Cassidy for Christmas 1975. It was inspired by a card sent by a Chilean Bishop to imprisoned church workers. There are still thousands of prisoners of conscience throughout the world.

PAZ AMOR

Solución para el caso de la doctora Cassidy

Un vocero del Ministerio de Relaciones Exteriores dijo que "posiblemente entre hoy y mañana" quede resuelto el caso de la doctora británica Sheila Ann Cassidy, detenida por la Ley de Estado de Sitio desde el primero de noviembre.

El informante dijo que "debe haber una resolución (del fiscal militar o del Ministerio del Interior) en las próximas horas". Señaló, además, y reiterando lo manifestado por el propio Canciller, vicealmirante Patricio Carvajal, que en caso que se encuentre culpable a la médico británica de algún delito menor, podría serle conmutada la pena impuesta por la expulsión del país.

Por su parte, el Secretario de Prensa de la embajada británica, Patrick Langmead, dijo que se esperaba una solución para antes de Navidad.

LA DRA. británica Sheila Cassidy.

CURT
Noviembre de 1975

EN LA FISCALIA.— A...
doctora Sheila Cassidy y el sacerdote R...
orden del fiscal militar. Esta resolución e...
tarde de ayer, después que ambos de...
horas. Se les ve cuando dejan ...

ACTA DE LIBERTAD

EN SANTIAGO, a _once_ días del mes de _Noviembre_ de mil novecientos setenta y _cinco_, y visto los antecedentes que obran en poder de la D.I.N.A., se procede a dejar en libertad en las proximidades de su domicilio a _Dra. Sheila Anne Cassidy Drew_, por no haberse configurado cargos en su contra, que permitan someterlo a juicio por violar la Ley de Seguridad Interior del Estado.

En el momento de su libertad, se le devuelven sus especies particulares sin observaciones, ni reclamos que formular.

Además, tengo que declarar que _mientras estuve detenida en el campo de detenidos 4 álamos, no he sufrido torturas ni malos tratos. Además no he sabido personalmente que a otros detenidos se les haya torturado, flagelado o maltratado, y hago presente que me encuentro en perfectas condiciones física y mentalmente._

Leída que le fue y sin presión de ninguna especie, procede firmar la presente Acta.

7.4 76. 4.67 - Stgo.

22. (*above*) Newspaper report a few days prior to my release. The headline is 'A solution for the case of Dr. Cassidy.' The photograph was one taken for identification purposes while I was 'incommunicado'.

23. (*centre*) Press cutting from El Mercurio, Santiago's main newspaper showing Father Rafael Maroto and myself leaving the Military Court. The caption is 'Dr. Sheila Cassidy and the priest Rafael Maroto were sent to the Public Gaol yesterday at the order of the military prosecutor. They were transferred in the evening, yesterday, after both had given evidence for several hours. They are seen leaving the court.'

24. (*below*) Act of Liberty. This 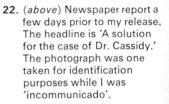 a photograph of a declaration that I was forced to sign by the D.I.N.A. when I was transferred to the Casa Correctional. It was published in a Santiago newspaper after I had left the country, as evidence that I had not been tortured. It is important to note that this is a cyclostyled form, indicating the number of prisoners similarly processed. It states that I was being set free, in the vicinity of my home whereas in fact, I was being transferred to another prison. The hand-written declaration that I had not been tortured was dictated to me by the chief the camp.

'White.'

'What style?'

'Colonial.'

'What colour were the gates?'

This was money for jam. 'Black.'

'Sheet metal or railings?'

'Sheet metal.'

'Who was in the house?'

'Rojas.'

'Who else?'

'His wife.'

'Who else?'

'The maid.' There would have to be a maid. There always was.

'Who else?'

'Nobody.'

'What's the name of the street?' Again it began.

'I don't know.'

They shoved the gag in my mouth. 'Raise your fingers when you remember.' Again it came, wave after wave, and I raised my fingers.

'Well?'

'I'll take you there. I'll show you.'

'What's the name of the street?'

'I don't know but I'll show you.'

I had no plan but anything must be better than this. There could be no future in going to look for a house which didn't exist, but by now I could see no future, only a haze of pain from which I must escape.

Suddenly it stopped. A voice said, 'Untie her', and I heard them move out.

I felt the bands on my wrists and ankles go slack and there was a new surge of pain as the circulation returned. I tried to sit up but couldn't lift my head. Gentle hands pulled me up and I sat blind and giddy on the edge of the bunk. They stood me up and caught me as I fell. I felt a chair pushed under me and then I heard a new voice.

This was a kind voice, educated and almost fatherly. 'Poor *gringa*,' it said. 'How do you feel?' For a moment I was overwhelmed with relief. This must be a senior officer who had come to take me away to the consul.

'How did you get mixed up in this, *gringa*?'

'I was asked to by a friend.'

'A fine friend to let you in for this!'

I was silent.

'You were very stupid to get involved.'

This was a friendly man who thought I was a stupid foreigner and I said pathetically, 'I was a fool.' He was pleased. 'Poor, stupid *gringa*. But now you are going to help us, eh?' So that was it. I was being softened up. Anger gave me courage.

'Oh yes, I'll do anything. Anything to stop this.'

'Good. Good *gringa*.'

Suddenly he stopped and I felt him touch my chest. 'What's that scar, *gringa*?' Of course! The scar. I'd forgotten. In Chile many young people have valve lesions following rheumatic fever and undergo operations to free valves that are stuck together or replace ones that are badly damaged. My scar was the legacy of an operation on my sternum but it could just as well have been the result of cardiac surgery. I said as convincingly as I could, 'They operated on my heart.'

'What was wrong with it?' He was obviously shaken. Here was my way out. If they thought I had a bad heart they wouldn't give me the shocks again. But quickly: what could I say it had been? What operation would leave me without a murmur? My mind went blank and I couldn't think of a heart lesion which would leave no signs. Lamely I said, 'I was very young. I don't know.'

'What could the electricity do to you?'

This was hopeful. 'It could give me ventricular fibrillation.'

'What?'

'It could make my heart go very fast.'

'And?'

'It could kill me.'

There was a pause while he thought. Then he said '*Gringa*, you're lying. Get dressed. You'd better help us or you'll be in trouble.'

He went and the men who had helped me off the bed now handed me my clothes and helped me as I fumbled with buttons and hooks and shoes that I could not see. They were gentle and patient with me and, helpless and unseeing, I felt the contrast so great that they seemed like friends.

(It was only after my return to England that I learned that the warmth of the friendly interrogator is part of a highly developed interrogation technique. After a session with aggressive interrogators, when the victim is shaken and demoralized, a new, apparently kindly 'father figure' is brought and the relaxation in defences so produced is often effective where the first method has failed.)

My captors led me out and I asked to go to the bathroom: they let me go but stood outside and when I went to drink from the tap shouted at me that I mustn't. (I learned later that drinking after the electrical 'treatment' can cause convulsions.)

We went outside and it was cold. They removed the bandage and taped my eyes shut with scotch tape, so that I could no longer see even the ground I walked on. I was led across the yard and pushed into a car. The gates opened and the car turned out and I felt the bump as we went over the bridge and drove down towards the town.

29

The False Trail

It is hard for those who live near a police station
To believe in the triumph of violence.
T. S. Eliot
Choruses from The Rock

I sat silent and unseeing in the front of the car, conscious of the gun on the lap of the man next to me and of a rising fear of what was to come. This had seemed such a good idea, but now I saw that there was no way out: no one could rescue me from this car speeding through the streets of Santiago and it would not be many minutes before they realized that I was lying. In perhaps ten minutes we were in the centre of the city and they pulled the tape from my eyes and said, 'Now, *gringa*, tell us where to turn off.'

We had just passed the Central Station and were driving down the wide road that led to the airport. I looked out of the car window and realized that there were very few turnings.

'How many blocks, *gringa*?'

'I don't know: maybe ten.'

We drove on and they got restless. 'Which way did you turn?' 'Right.' They were silent and as we drove I realized that there seemed to be no residential area to the right.

The driver turned to me and said roughly, 'We've gone twenty blocks, where do I turn?'

At a loss I said, 'We must have overshot it.'

He turned round and drove back, and as we reached the Central Station again he got angry. 'You're lying, *gringa*.'

'No. I just don't recognize the street. You'll have to go back again.'

He did another sharp U-turn and I realized that I couldn't stall any longer, so when we came to a big turn off to the left I said, 'Turn here.'

'You said right, *gringa*.'

'I made a mistake. This is it.'

They believed me and we drove on. Slowly we drove through streets while they asked again and again, 'Do you recognize it?' I looked out of the window and each time they asked me I shook my head and said 'No, not here.'

We spent nearly half an hour circling round the same area and they became obviously bored and angry; then one of them said in a matter of fact sort of voice, 'It really would be much easier if we killed you now.'

I said nothing, but I sat there and realized that perhaps I was going to die. It was a curious feeling and I thought, what then? Suddenly God and heaven seemed very unreal and very far away and I wondered seriously, almost for the first time in my life, if it was all a fairy story. It was as though I looked over the edge of a precipice and saw nothing and it seemed that there was nothing beyond. I can't remember what I thought over the next few minutes but I know that I came back quite calmly to the certainty that it was not all nonsense and that God did exist, but this was a cold-blooded intellectual decision and it brought me no warm Christian comfort.

As I faced the prospect of death I thought, 'What a very stupid way to die', but there seemed no alternative to what I was doing, so I sat there and somehow stretched out my hand to the God who seemed so far away.

The car had an intercom and after a while we stopped while the driver got out and went to speak to a man in another car behind us. They told me to get out and I stood with my captor in the shadow of a doorway, waiting for I knew not what. After a few minutes I heard voices and three young men passed, hurrying home before the curfew. They passed right in front of us and as they walked by I grabbed one of them by the jacket and said, 'Help me please, I'm a prisoner of the DINA.' A look of sheer terror crossed their faces and they moved on as quickly as they could; the jacket would have stayed in my hands had I not let it go. My captor struck me hard across the face and I knew that I had been very stupid. We went back to the car. In a little while we

were joined by the driver and another man who said '*Gringa,*
you're in luck; we've found the street.'

I felt sick with fear but pretended to be pleased. The
street of course was Obispo Subercaseaux, the one which I
had heard mentioned when I was being interrogated.' As
we drove along it the man who had joined us suddenly said,
'There it is, *gringa!*' And he was right: there on our left, in
a street of small dark houses, stood the house I had described. It was a large, white colonial house with massive
iron gates which were painted black.

It is hard to convey just how incredible was this coincidence. I had never been in this area and although white
colonial style houses are common in the wealthy suburbs of
Santiago they are not usually found in the poorer areas. So
the fact that we had found a house to fit my description in a
street called Bishop was indeed curious.

We stopped a little distance from the house and they
turned to me. 'Well, *gringa,* is this it?' I was now faced with
a difficult decision, for this was surely my last chance. They
would not go on searching and only God knew what they
would do when they found that I was lying. On the other
hand, how could I justify putting the people in this house at
risk? Fear led me to rationalize and I decided that the people who lived in such an elegant house must surely be very
rich and sure of themselves and they would quickly persuade
the DINA that they had nothing to do with the fugitive
Miristas. Hesitantly, trying to cover myself against all
eventualities, I said that I thought this was the house.

Their excitement was obvious. The driver spoke rapidly
into the intercom and let in the clutch. After a couple of
blocks we stopped and I was told to get out. We had stopped
alongside a Black Maria and they handcuffed me and told
me to get in. I sat in the back in the company of a couple of
drunks, and before long we arrived at what I presumed was
the police station. As I got out they pulled my sweater over
my head so that I could not see and led me into the building. I sat down where I was told on a bench. Through the
loose weave of my sweater I saw men running from one
office to another. An official came up to me and made to

slap my face; I flinched and he sensed that I could see and wrapped the thick curtain around my face. I could now neither see nor breathe properly and with my sweater around my head I was cold. I complained to the man who was guarding me and he loosened it a little.

The excitement and sense of urgency was palpable. Telephones rang, commands were shouted and men ran to and fro. I realized that they were mounting a big operation in expectation of finding Pascal and Gutierrez. I sat there fascinated, wondering when they would discover that I had deceived them.

After what must have been over half an hour we went out again and the driver parked the car in a side street so that we could see the house. We sat there and waited. It seemed quite unreal, like being in a film, waiting in a car without lights while a house was raided. After some time they came to fetch me and I was led to the house.

We entered the back of the house and I saw that, in contrast to its rich exterior, the house was very poorly furnished. Sitting pale and terrified on a bed was an elderly working class couple. It was obvious that the house was being remodelled and these people were living here as caretakers. I was appalled that my fabrication had put such defenceless people into this situation and said at once that this was not the house where I had treated Gutierrez. They did not believe me. I thought frantically for reasons and finally said firmly that the furniture in Miguel Rojas' house had been very elegant, whereas this furniture was cheap and of poor quality. Then came a moment so absurd that I could have laughed or cried in sheer desperation. One of the men called me over to where some of the furniture was covered by a dust sheet and said, 'What about this, *gringa*?'

There, under a sheet, were a group of the most elegant chairs I had ever seen! Fate, it seemed, was against me, but quickly I said, 'The furniture was modern.' It seemed logical that an architect would have modern furniture, but they were not to be so easily defeated. They said maybe the room that I had treated Nelson in was upstairs, and motioned me upstairs with the machine gun. Halfway up the stairs I became terrified and said firmly that the house had been of one floor only. Cursing me he turned back and said the words that were like doors closed against my path of escape. 'Back to the *parrilla, gringa.*' *Parrilla* means barbecue and I realized that I was in for another questioning session.

I don't remember what I thought as we drove back up the hill to the Casa Grimaldi. I was sick and afraid and was beginning to realize that many hours had passed since my arrest and that I was not going to be rescued.

30
The Epileptic Terror

If it comes to pass
that I get lost during the night
and don't find the road back home,
I want you to know the reasons for my absence.
I have learned and I have taught
that a person is free,
and now I awaken to the rattling of irons and bolts.
Because I loved culture
and humanity's inheritance
the flames have fed themselves with my books.
I did not stain my spirit with hatred,
but I have seen the anguish
and the epileptic terror
of naked men electrocuted.

Speaking with the Children
written in a Chilean concentration
camp, 1974

The journey back to the Casa Grimaldi was made at speed
through deserted streets. Now I know the terror of those
arrested during the hours of curfew. The familiar streets,
usually thronged with friendly people, were empty and the
citizens of Chile hidden away behind shutters and locked
doors. Like the three wise monkeys they saw and heard no
evil and they kept their thoughts to themselves. A light
sleeper, I had often risen from my bed to watch the cars or
trucks speeding purposefully through the empty streets and
wondered where they were going. The curfew provides a
clear four or five hours for the intelligence forces to impose
their will upon the city without fear of being observed. Now
it was my turn and I was as helpless in the centre of the city
as I was behind the locked gates of the Grimaldi. Even had I
been able to escape there would have been nowhere to turn,
for who would open their door in the night to an unknown
fugitive from the DINA?

In less than fifteen minutes we were back and I knew that they were furious with me. Not only had I deceived them and made fools of them but they had lost precious hours in the search for their quarry, hours that might be decisive, for the news of my arrest had surely spread rapidly among my friends scattered throughout Santiago.

I learned later that as they led me away the DINA agents had pulled the telephone from the wall in the house in the Larraín Gandarillas so that Father Halliden would be delayed in calling for aid. He informed the consul as soon as he was able to use a neighbour's telephone and by eight o'clock the following morning the ambassador was in full possession of the facts and representations had been made to the Chilean government. It was only ten hours, but for me it was an eternity.

They took me at once to the room with the bunk and again I was told to undress. The hands that secured me to the metal bed frame were rough and the ropes or straps tied so tightly that my circulation was severely impeded. I asked them to loosen the bonds but they made no response. During the first interrogation I never knew where the electrodes had been placed and the pain was generalized. Now they became more sophisticated for one electrode was placed inside my vagina and the other, a wandering pincer, was used to stimulate me wherever they chose.

From the first moment it was different. The pain was appalling and, determined not to be deceived again, they questioned me with a speed and ferocity that allowed no possibility of fabrication. I don't remember a moment in which I decided to talk but I know that after a while it seemed less likely that my friends would be killed and therefore less urgent to lie. Indeed, I found it quite impossible to lie for the shocks came with such frequency and intensity that I could no longer think. So, they broke me. Little by little I answered their questions. It was a slow and painful business for I told them as little as I could, always hoping that a minimum of people would be involved.

The irony of it all was that they found the truth more difficult to believe than the lies I had told them at first, and I received many gratuitous shocks because they could not believe the nuns and priests were involved. Their disbelief was very hard to bear for there seemed no escape from the white hot sea of pain in which I found myself. Terrifying, too, was the increased callousness of the interrogator. Each time they passed the current a gag was forced into my mouth and I was told, 'Raise your finger when you are ready to talk.' Unable to cry out and with my hands nearly paralysed I could call for relief only through the upward movement of my finger and this they ignored, filling me with a desperation the like of which I have never known.

How long it went on I don't know: perhaps an hour, perhaps longer. I told them that I had treated Nelson Gutierrez in the house of some American nuns but I did not know the address, for although I knew the street name I had no idea of the number. Still furious they realized that in truth I could not tell them where to go and once more they untied me and lifted me off the *parrilla*.

This time I was much weaker and needed their help to dress myself. Again there was the contrast of their gentleness with the brutality of the interrogators. I see this as a genuine compassion rather than a psychological trick, and think that there must be many men caught up in the nightmare of the torture machine who are distressed by the deliberate infliction of pain. I have been told that it is virtually impossible to withdraw from the service of the DINA and it is not difficult to imagine that resignation from a torture squad might be viewed with suspicion and disapproval. The damage wrought upon the personality of the torturer must be far greater than that caused to the person tortured for it must be hard indeed to blot out the sight and sound of tortured men and women from an overactive memory on a sleepless night.

Again they sealed my eyes with scotch tape and we went out in search of Helen's house. This time I sat in the back and as we drove to find the house I felt sick with humiliation at my betrayal. I said to the man who sat beside me, 'Does everyone talk, or am I weak?' and he replied. 'Everyone has their breaking point.'

This is something that I often think about, now that it is all over, but I feel no shame or guilt that I told what I did for I know that I could take no more. How much longer I would have been able to hang on if I had known that my talking would lead to the death of someone I love I do not know. Perhaps I would have had the courage to die: perhaps not. I learned later that I had been stronger than some, weaker than others and that there were many men and women who pay the ultimate price for what they believe to be right. In the midst of sadness that men can treat their fellows in this way there burns the flame and inspiration of their example.

They have not died! They stand in the midst of the gunpowder like burning fuses.

Pablo Neruda

There was an unpleasant moment when the driver mistook the street and I could not point out Helen's house. They thought I was lying again and became very unpleasant until they found the right street and I was able to show them the house. I knew that neither Helen nor her friend were at home for there was a meeting of one group of nuns out of Santiago that weekend and Helen was in someone else's house to keep a friend company for the night. I had gleaned this information by accident earlier in the day when I had met a friend who had come to visit Susie. This particular girl (let's call her Margaret) worked in the provinces and was in Santiago quite by chance at the time of Nelson's 'visit'. She had been staying with Helen and had therefore helped in the hiding of the fugitives and as she had some nursing experience had helped to dress his wound. Thus when I met her outside the house in Larraín Gandarillas I asked her if she had any news of Nelson and she told me that there was no news but that the priests who had driven Nelson and Mariella to safety had been trying to get Andres Pascal and Mary Ann into an embassy. An attempt made the previous night had failed and a further attempt was to be made this night or on Sunday. This information, so casually gleaned, perhaps saved my life but was nearly responsible for another's death for it led to the arrest of an American priest and of Martin Hernández, another member of the MIR who was being sheltered by him, and of whose presence there I had no knowledge.

When we returned to the Casa Grimaldi I was led to an office where I was interrogated by men who judging by their manner of speaking I took to be senior officials. The fact of my earlier lies had obviously stung them for from now on they repeatedly called me '*La gringa mentirosa*' – 'the lying gringa'. I was made to tell again in detail the story of how I had been asked to treat Gutierrez and where I had attended him. They had obviously expected to find Nelson in the house where I had treated him but when I told them that he had been given asylum in the Nunciatura they were enraged. I heard one of them suggest that the Nuncio's house be raided but the other told him that there were orders from above to the contrary.

They were anxious to know the whereabouts of the baby but mercifully believed me when I said I didn't know. While I was there they spoke on the telephone to Helen's house and I was momentarily filled with terror when he said to me, 'the nuns don't know anything about Gutierrez.' Desperately I said, 'They are lying', but he said simply, 'But a nun would not lie, *doctora*.'

In retrospect it is almost funny because so many people had become involved that it was impossible for the DINA to decide whom to arrest. The North American missionary nuns in Santiago must number over forty and though they belong to different congregations they are all friends and often visit each other's houses and, because of the difficulty of transport, spend the night there. They are nearly all in their early or middle thirties and many have short fair hair, wear jeans and anoraks and have names like Jean or Joan or Jane or Janet or Jo. Even had they all spoken the truth it would have been difficult to unravel the tale and explain why one nun who was a Holy Child nun had been spending a week with some friends of the Notre Dame community but was no longer in the same house because she had gone to spend the night with a friend who was a Sister of Mercy in the house

of a Mary Knoll sister because the Mary Knollers were out
of Santiago for the weekend at a conference being held in a
retreat house run by the Society of the Sacred Heart! It is
small wonder that one officer cried out in disgust, 'Nuns,
priests, bishops, it's all too much!'

When my interrogators discovered that Gutierrez and
his lady had eluded them they turned their attention to
Andres Pascal Allende and Mary Ann. They could not
believe that I did not know where they were for they had
convinced themselves that I was working with the MIR. I
told them repeatedly that I had treated Nelson Gutierrez
because he was badly injured and that it was not within my
code of ethics to refuse to treat someone for ideological
reasons. They were floored. They sat one side of a table and
I stood blindfolded before them while they shouted at me
that I worked with the MIR and I repeated again and again
that Nelson was my patient, neither more nor less. Eventually, finding that the trail which had at first seemed so
promising was now cold, they returned me to the torture
squad.

For the third time I was stripped and bound to the bed. I
was completely desperate. They were convinced that I knew
the whereabouts of the MIR leader and I had no idea. I
don't know if they increased the strength of the current or if
the hours of torture had lowered my resistence, but the pain
seemed each time more terrible. My interrogators, too, were
sexually excited and the fear of being raped was ever
present for I knew that this was quite common. As it happened, I was lucky, because although a Chilean church
worker (an ex-nun) was raped in this same place just a week
later, I escaped.

Determined to break what they thought was my lying,
they interrogated me about the events of that day. Each
event was explored and I was questioned about all the people
I had mentioned. Eventually they came to the encounter
with Margaret and when I hesitated as to the subject matter
of our conversation they realized that I had something to hide.
Now there was no stopping them and piece by piece they
dragged out of me the last information that I had: that a

certain priest had been going to attempt to get Andres Pascal and Mary Ann into asylum the previous night.

When they found that this involved yet another church group in a completely different area of Santiago their exasperation and disbelief reached new heights but at seven or eight o'clock in the morning they went off to look for the priest as he celebrated his first mass of the Sunday.

While one group went off to search I was again taken before the senior officers. They shouted and reasoned with me alternately. They offered to take me to the British embassy if only I would co-operate. They showed me photographs taken at church functions to see if I could point out the priests I knew. They made me listen to a recording of a telephone conversation in English to see if I could identify the voice. Perhaps the most unnerving was the man who spoke kindly and with an educated voice and said, 'Doctor, you are a sensible woman. You have seen what three sessions on the *parrilla* are like. If you do not tell us what we want we will go on, and on, ten, twelve, thirteen times, and you must see that you will get weaker and weaker and that you will tell us in the end.'

Again and again they returned to the question, 'Why did you treat Gutierrez?' and again I repeated, 'He was sick. I am a doctor.' Exasperated, one of them said, 'But if I had a wounded leg you wouldn't treat me,' to which I replied, 'Of course I would.' There was a long silence and then he said slowly, 'I do believe you would.'

I don't know how long I spent being questioned by these men; not more than half an hour, I think, because after a while one of them insisted that I be returned to the *parrilla*. Twice more during the next couple of hours I was stripped and tied to the bed but it must have been at the time they were looking for the priest because though I spent what seemed like hours cold and afraid on the bunk they did not give me any more shocks.

I think it was during this time of waiting that I was conscious of praying. I remember little except that I prayed for strength to withstand the pain and for courage to die with dignity if that was to be my fate. Most of all I remember a curious feeling of sharing in Christ's passion. Sick and numb with pain and fear, and spread-eagled so vulnerably on the bunk, it came to me that this was perhaps a little how it had been for him one Friday so many years before.

When it was quite light they untied me once again and I was led stumbling across the courtyard. As we left they joked that their friend was going to sleep with me and, bruised and bleeding, it seemed too much to bear. I heard a door being unlocked and he pushed me gently on to a bed and covered me with a blanket. It was only then that I realized that they had been joking and that we were not alone, for he said, 'Look after her, girls, she's had a hell of a time.' The door closed and a key turned in the lock and for the first time in twelve hours I found myself among friends.

31

The Gates of Sheol

I said: In the noontide of my days I must depart;
I am consigned to the gates of Sheol for the rest of my
    years.
I said: I shall not see the Lord in the land of the living;
I shall look upon man no more among the inhabitants of
    the world.
My dwelling is plucked up and removed from me like a
    shepherd's tent;
like a weaver I have rolled up my life;
he cuts me off from the loom;
from day to night thou dost bring me to an end;
I cry for help until morning;
like a lion he breaks all my bones;
from day to night
thou dost bring me to an end.

The Canticle of Hezekiah
Isaiah 38.9–19

I lay on the bed without moving, still blindfolded and terribly afraid. For a while there was no sound and then I felt a gentle hand on my shoulder and a voice whispered in Spanish, 'How are you?'

My fears found speech. 'Are they going to kill me?'

How could she know? Indeed, who was she, this voice in the darkness? Incredibly, she knew about me and she said at once, 'No, it is all over. But you must work to keep well mentally.'

This was Francisca, and in that incredible meeting as I lay there in pain and fear she took me to her heart. She was just nineteen, a young socialist who had been arrested and tortured a few days earlier. Her adolescence cut short by war, she had a maturity far beyond her years. That Sunday morning we forged a bond of friendship that can never be broken.

For the next twenty-four hours Francisca nursed me as if I had been a sick child. She moistened my lips with cotton wool, for they were dry and had a split from the blows to the face. She replaced the thick cord which was tied tightly around my eyes with a strip of white cloth so that my eyes no longer hurt and I could see the ground under my feet when I walked.

Perhaps half an hour after I had been shut in they came for me again. 'Quickly, *gringa*,' they said, and hustled me to the door, for I could not walk unaided. I was led across the courtyard to the office and once more interrogated by senior officials. This was the first of many interrogations that I was subjected to that Sunday. I am confused as to the number and the sequence but I remember clearly the fear that welled up inside me each time I heard the key turn in the lock of our cell. I remember, too, the anguish that possessed me until I knew where we were going, for after the first few yards we either turned left to the room where I had been tortured or continued straight across the courtyard and through the steel gates to the main office.

The fear of being returned to the *parrilla* possessed me like some demon and made me feel sick and ill. They never told me where they were taking me and always there was great urgency so that I was made to hurry. I learned the meaning of 'to be led like a sheep to the slaughter', for each time I was taken unseeing to what could have been my release or my death. There was no need for sophisticated psychological torture, for to live in constant fear and uncertainty, to be constantly hurried and harrassed, to be denied access to the bathroom, quickly induces a condition of profound mental anguish.

On my visits to the officers I was questioned about many things. They gave me photographs to identify and asked endlessly for descriptions of all the people I had named, and if I did not appear to be co-operating I was struck across the face and threatened with another session on the *parrilla*. Once they asked me if I spoke Russian and I found the idea that anyone should think me capable of learning Russian so funny that I laughed, which made them very cross. Beneath my bandage I saw that they had a cardboard box full of the contents of my desk but, as I had no incriminating documents, this was only a minor irritation.

After what must have been half a dozen or more interrogation sessions I was led to the little room where I had
been tortured, but this time they sat me at a table and giving
me paper and pen said, 'You are going to make a statement. This is what you are going to say.'

So, for nearly two hours, I wrote out the statement that
they dictated to me. It ran into eight or nine pages and
began something like this: 'I, Sheila Cassidy, an Apostolic
Roman Catholic, swear that this statement is made without
any form of duress . . .' On and on it went, telling the story
of how I had been asked to treat Gutierrez, and all the
people involved. I had difficulty in writing but they hit my
hands to make me write with greater care. When it was
finished I signed it and they carried it off in triumph.

It could be argued that I had signed a false statement,
for this was certainly made under duress, but the account of
my treatment of Gutierrez and of the other people involved
was quite true, so I had no qualms about signing it. To
refuse to sign a statement written at gun point after one has
been tortured would be an act of great heroism. Frankly, it
did not cross my mind to refuse. In the weeks that followed
I signed six other statements: one was a typed version of the
hand-written one and the others, made in different prisons,
were duplicated declarations which stated that the person
signing had not been tortured nor had they seen anyone else
being tortured. These statements were published in the
Chilean newspapers as evidence that I had not been
tortured! In actual fact, as I was not tortured again after
leaving the Casa Grimaldi, the statements were true, but the
very fact that duplicated forms of this type are used must be
seen as evidence against the DINA.

Some time during the course of the Sunday – I couldn't
say at what hour – we heard a man being tortured. The little
room with the bunk was directly behind the women's
dormitory and we could hear the raised voices of the
interrogators and the muffled screams of the subject through
the sealed-off door which had once connected the two rooms.
It was in this way that Francisca and the two other girls in
the dormitory had heard my interrogation, so that when I

was brought to join them they already knew the whole story.

The man was almost certainly Martin Hernández, a senior member of the MIR, who had been arrested when the DINA went to look for the priest who I had been told was helping Andres Pascal. On one of the many visits which I made to the office I saw him being half dragged, half carried, across the courtyard. He was wearing only his shirt and he seemed to be unconscious. I learned much later that he had been severely tortured and was very ill for a long time with a kidney infection which was a direct result of the torture. He is still in prison as I write (November 1976).

My memories of that day are hazy, a series of islands in a sea of pain and fear. I remember most the terror with which I was filled each time the door was unlocked, and the harsh voices saying, '*Gringa*. Hurry up, you're wanted.' Paradoxically I only felt safe when I was locked in my cell: a feeling that was to persist until I was released two months later. In between questioning sessions I lay huddled on the bed under the blanket, numb and unseeing. It was as though I was suspended over a pit: the past had no relevance and I could see no future. I lived only for the minute that was and in the fear of further pain.

Darkness fell and the girls went to bed, sleeping under spare mattresses as they had given me the blankets. Still I lay there and listened to the shouts of the men and the continual comings and goings outside the room where we were locked. I must have dozed for I woke suddenly with the feeling of terror that they had come for me once more. But this time the door was locked again without anyone's name being called. I heard someone moving about and then settling down for the night: it was the wardress who had come to bed. Suddenly I felt different and hope gently seeped back into my heart; at first I could not understand why I was no longer so afraid and then I realized that for the first time in over twenty-four hours the shouting and movement outside had stopped.

The urgency of the chase had abated and for a few hours peace fell on the Casa Grimaldi.

32

The Will Which Says 'Hold On!'

If you can force your heart and nerve and sinew
To serve your turn long after they are gone,
And so hold on when there is nothing in you
Except the Will which says to them, 'Hold on!' . . .
Rudyard Kipling
If

The next morning I awoke stiff and sore but very much
alive. There was a loud knock on the door and, cursing the
shortness of the night, the wardress got up. I looked at her
from under my blindfold: a girl of less than thirty with long
hair and dressed in jeans and a sweater. She had slept in her
clothes and now rose to do her hair and put on her shoes.
When she was ready she knocked on the door and the man
let her out. After a little while the door was unlocked again
and a voice said, 'Time to go to the bathroom, girls.' We
filed out, Francisca helping me as I had difficulty in walking. There was a small bathroom where one by one we
washed ourselves as best we could in the icy water and dried
ourselves on a rag which served as towel for the four of us.
I felt very sticky and dirty for I had bled a good deal on the
parrilla, but I had only the strength to wash my face and
return to the dormitory.

Francisca and the other two girls busied themselves
sweeping the dormitory and then the broom was taken
away and the door closed again. Perhaps half an hour passed
before there was a clatter outside and Francisca said, 'It's
breakfast!'

The door opened and the girls went forward to receive a
tin mug and a piece of bread. I had drunk nothing since tea
time on Saturday because of the danger after the electricity.
(I still don't understand clearly what happens, but neither my
gaolers nor my fellow prisoners would let me drink anything

during the Sunday.) Now on Monday morning I was allowed my first drink and never had a cup of coffee tasted so good. It was hot and syrupy with sugar, and had a curious flavour which bore a faint resemblance to coffee. The bread was dry and pretty nasty but by breaking it into small pieces and dunking it in the coffee I managed to eat a small quantity.

Breakfast over, I lay down again, and the girls sat around my bed to talk. It seemed that they were friends and that they had been arrested on the same day. They told me nothing of their political activity except that they were socialists and that they worked at the university. Francisca was still a student, as was Magdalena, and Esther was a teacher of English. They told me that they had listened at the door throughout my interrogation and they were delighted at the wild goose chase which had occupied so many of the members of the DINA during the night. Little by little I realized that they were surprised and fascinated that someone who was not a committed revolutionary should have resisted torture as I did. It is important to say very clearly that I behaved neither more nor less bravely than the majority of the girls whom I was to meet during my time in prison, but the very fact that I had suffered to try to protect my friends was an act of witness which made them look enquiringly at an ideology which they had long since discarded: the Christian belief. My baptism by fire had given me an entry into their society which I could have achieved in no other way. If the fact of my being British and a future nun had protected me from the torture I would have been set apart from them and though we would surely have become friends we would never have been equals.

Francisca, though she was the youngest, assumed the leadership of our little group. She told me that it was very important that we discipline ourselves so as to be as fit as possible mentally and physically to withstand whatever might happen to us. Sleep, she insisted, was of prime importance. We must not allow ourselves to sleep during the day because this would make it difficult to sleep at night, and anyone lying awake in the dark would be likely to give in to depression and fear. We were to occupy ourselves during the day and each person must make her contribution to the entertainment of the group. We were to think of films that we had seen or books that we had read and tell the others about them.

I had not been to the pictures for many months and could think of nothing to relate, but asked if they liked poetry. They were delighted and I searched my addled memory for some poem that would please them. I have a large store of snippets of poetry that stay in my mind because they please me but there are few poems that I know in their entirety. Curiously, Burns' 'My luve is like a red, red rose' sprang to the fore and I recited as movingly as I could from the horizontal position on my bunk:

> O my Luve's like a red, red rose
> That's newly sprung in June.
> O my Luve's like the melodie
> That's sweetly played in tune.
>
> As fair art thou, my bonie lass,
> So deep in luve am I;
> And I will luve thee still, my dear,
> Till a' the seas gang dry.
>
> Till a' the seas gang dry, my dear,
> And the rocks melt with the sun;
> And I will luve thee still, my dear,
> While the sands o' life shall run.

They were pleased with the musical sound of it and made me translate it and then recite it again. I learned then that the English poem most dear to the revolutionary's heart is 'If', and they were sad that I could only remember a few lines. It is only a few days ago that I read how Che Guevara shared his love of it with his first wife, Hilda, who was a Peruvian revolutionary. It is curious to think of Kipling, who seems almost scorned in England, being read and loved by fiery young Latin Americans so many years after his death and so far away from England. It is not, however, difficult to see the appeal:

If you can dream – and not make dreams your master,
If you can think – and not make thoughts your aim,
If you can meet with Triumph and Disaster
And treat those two impostors just the same;
If you can bear to hear the truth you've spoken
Twisted by knaves to make a trap for fools;
Or watch the things you gave your life to, broken,
And stoop and build 'em up with worn out tools.

Perhaps it was the time on the *parrilla* which made them
claim for their own:

If you can force your heart and nerve and sinew
To serve your turn long after they are gone,
And so hold on when there is nothing in you
Except the Will which says to them, Hold on!

After a while we fell silent. Francisca, determined to
occupy herself, took a scrap of cloth from a box of rags and
clothes in the corner of the room and began to pull out the
threads. Then, with a collection of threads, she proceeded to
'draw' on her bed and every so often we were invited to
inspect her work. She drew flowers and birds and people
and soon the others joined her in seeing what they could
produce. I gained much kudos by inventing a title for this
new form of prison art – 'pelusagraphia'; a *pelusa* being a
scrap of fluff or thread.

In the afternoon the guards came for me again and the
courage which our morning together had given me ebbed
away. I was taken to the little office with the bunk and told
to sit down because I was to make another statement. Once
more I went through the story, dictating while the man
typed. It took a long time and we became almost friends
after a while. My bandage was loose and by tilting my head
I could see him quite clearly. After a while he said, 'You
know, doctor, you are far too fond of looking. It is not in our
interest nor in yours that you should recognize us.' The cold
logic of what he said hit me and from then on I made no
effort to look at my captors.

In the middle of my interrogation they came to tell me

that the doctor had arrived and that if I wished I might see him. Although I had a lot of muscle pain I had no real need of a doctor, but I was fascinated to see if it was anyone I knew so I accepted their offer.

They tightened my bandage so that I could see only the ground and led me into an adjoining room. I saw a pair of suede shoes and the bottom of a white coat over his trousers, and though I did not recognize the voice I was appalled at the aggression and coldness of his manner. I told him that I had a lot of pain from the 'electrical treatment' and I asked him if he could give me some cotton wool as I was still bleeding and had no means of protecting my already filthy clothes. His answer, surely intended to humiliate me, is difficult to believe when one thinks that this was a man to woman, doctor to patient and doctor to doctor conversation: 'Menstruation, *doctora*, is normal in women.' I don't know what I had expected but certainly not this gratuitous incivility. He gave me some suppositories for the pain and I left with my escort.

The involvement of doctors in torture is a subject which causes much concern in the profession. From the evidence available (collected by the Church, the United Nations and other humanitarian organizations) there seems little doubt that in some cases doctors are present while prisoners are being tortured and tell the torturers how far they may go without killing them. It is known that in Santiago there is a clinic where detainees who have become severely ill under torture are taken to be resuscitated. It is in the centre of the city, next door to the offices of the British Council, opposite a small hill called the Santa Lucía. I used to pass it on my way home from work at the Posta and I remember well that I could see a man stationed at each window on the four floors and outside there was always parked a National Health Service ambulance from the Posta. This may not sound curious but in Santiago patients in private clinics are transported by private ambulances and an NHS ambulance has no cause to be parked consistently outside a private clinic.

When the statement was finished I was returned to the

dormitory. After supper we lay on our beds and waited for the men to be taken to the bathroom. Three times a day the male prisoners passed by our window on their way to the bathroom. There must have been twenty or more of them and they walked slowly past in single file, blindfolded and with one arm on the shoulder of the man in front. They passed so close that we could have touched them through the window and it would certainly be possible to identify with certainty anyone whom one knew. The fact that this is so has great importance, for there are many prisoners who have been detained and later seen in the Casa Grimaldi or other interrogation centres and who are never seen again. It seems that some people die under torture and it is presumed that others are executed, for of a group which spends

*View from the window of the women's room
in the Casa Grimaldi*

days or weeks together some are taken away and nothing further is heard. One of the girls in my room at Tres Alamos (my final place of detention) had been in the Casa Grimaldi with people who had just never re-appeared. Two of the six girls had been detained with their brothers who were still missing and one girl had spent over a week with an elderly woman, the mother of another prisoner who also disappeared.

One of the most blatant mass executions took place not long after my arrest although I was by this time in another prison and only heard about it afterwards. Piecing the details together from the various reports it seems that 27-year-old Roberto Gallado disappeared on the night of Monday, 17 November. The following night, Tuesday the 18th, his wife, Mónica, and his two sisters Isabel and Catalina, were arrested. On arrival at the police station Isabel saw her father, Alberto, her mother, Ofelia, her brother, Guillermo, and her nine-year-old niece, Viviana. The following morning Isabel, Guillermo, their mother and the child were released; they were informed that Roberto had died in a street fight on the 17th and that Alberto, Catalina and Roberto's wife Mónica, were in the custody of the DINA. That same day it was announced on the radio that Alberto, Catalina and Mónica had died in an armed confrontation with forces of the DINA on the outskirts of Santiago. The bodies were later identified in the city morgue by members of the family and showed clear evidence of torture.

Also named as having been killed in the same encounter was Luis Ganga. His mother and three other members of the family were arrested and taken to the Grimaldi on Wednesday 19 November where the mother heard her children screaming. She was made to take members of the DINA to the house where her son Luis was hiding and he was arrested and later that same day his death in the fight was announced.

The events described above are not easy to follow but they show the terrifying disregard for law and human life by the DINA. Javiera, an eighteen-year-old girl with whom I later shared a cell, was in the Grimaldi with the Ganga family and heard the report of their death on the radio which the guards had on loudly outside the dormitory.

The night of Monday 3 November was quiet and once again the girls gave me the only blanket. It was very cold and I slept with a mattress on top of me as well. The next day I felt a good deal better. I had a lot of severe muscle pain in all parts of my body: even my jaw was very stiff indeed. I had bruises on both my arms where I had been secured to the bed and minute haemorrhages on my abdomen and legs where they had touched me with the pincer of the *picana*, the wandering electrode.

While we were waiting outside to use the bathroom I was suddenly approached by a young girl who gripped me quickly by the arm and whispered, 'Keep up your spirits, *Compañera*! The Resistance will triumph!' (The word *compañera* means friend, ally, workmate, rather than the politically loaded 'comrade', and was used much during Allende's time.) She vanished as mysteriously as she had appeared but later in the morning was brought to join us in the locked dormitory.

This was Javiera who was just eighteen and a member of the MIR. She had been arrested some two weeks earlier and after spending a week in the Grimaldi had been transferred to Cuatro Alamos, the incommunicado part of Tres Alamos, the big detention camp in Santiago. Now she had been brought back and was to be taken out to try and trap a man with whom she had a meeting arranged for this day. This was a favourite technique of the DINA: when they picked someone up they tortured them until they told the name of their 'contact' in the MIR and the date and site for their next meeting. These meetings were sometimes in the street and sometimes in cafés and the prisoner would be taken to the site of the meeting and left sitting at a table apparently alone but in fact completely covered by armed men. He was forced to sit there until the contact arrived and walked straight into the trap. It was a very bitter event, for if the prisoner made any false move he or she would very likely be shot, so that they were faced, in effect, with betraying a friend or committing suicide.

After lunch they came for Javiera. She went off apparently cheerfully and we kept watch for her wondering if
she would return. About two hours later she was back and
when the door closed behind her she told us jubilantly that
the contact had not turned up. She was exuberant and
thankful that she had not been forced into the position of
choosing between death and betrayal, but we knew that
this might well mean a further session of interrogation.

Sure enough they came for her again and an hour passed
while we waited for the now familiar sound of the squad
with the *parrilla*. There was no evidence of its use, however,
and after about an hour Javiera returned. They pushed her
inside the door and slammed it shut and though she said
nothing we knew by the way she walked and the look on her
face that they had hurt her. As she neared the bed she almost
fell and Francisca and Esther caught her and laid her down.
Now it was my turn to relinquish the pillow and blanket
and when she had been made comfortable she told us that
they had given her the 'telephones'.

This is a very hard and sudden blow to both ears applied
simultaneously with the flat of the hand. The subject being
blindfolded it catches him by surprise and damages not only
the hearing but also the balance mechanism of the inner ear,
producing deafness and vertigo. Javiera could no longer
hear normally and was subject to sudden violent attacks of
giddiness which caused her to fall. She told me that she had
a loud noise in her ear and when I listened I too heard a
curious noise which accompanied her pulse beat.

Down but by no means out, Javiera lay on her bunk as
we sat beside her and talked. She told us that she and her
husband Andres had been arrested at her parents' home two
weeks before and that she believed that Andres was still here
in the Grimaldi for there had been no news of him at
Cuatro Alamos. She explained to us that although inmates
of the different cells at Cuatro Alamos were never allowed
out simultaneously, so that there was no possibility of their
seeing each other, they managed to scratch messages on the
walls of the bathroom in the brief time that they were
allowed out and in that way they could know of the arrival

of a friend or loved one. Now that she was back at the Grimaldi she was waiting with mixed hope and fear for the evening passage of the men past the window for then she would know at least that Andres was still alive.

After supper we heard them approaching and, made bold by Javiera, who seemed to have no fear, stood near to the window and peered through the half-closed shutters. Slowly they passed, nearly all young men, with the uncertain shuffling gait of the unseeing. Suddenly Javiera hissed 'Andres!' and we saw a dark head turn and a thin face illuminated with joy before it passed out of sight.

33

Barbed Wire Besets Me

Lord O Lord my God
why have you left me?
I am a caricature of a man
People think I am dirt
   they mock me in all the papers

I am encircled
   there are tanks all round me
Machine-gunners have me in their sights
   there is barbed wire about me
   electrified wire
I am on a list
I am called all day
They have tattooed me
   and marked me with a number
They have photographed me behind the barbed wire
All my bones can be counted
   as on an X-ray film
They have stripped me of my identity
They have led me naked to the gas-chamber
They have shared out my clothes and my shoes.

Ernesto Cardenal
Why Have You Left Me?

Wednesday morning dawned crisp and cold and we busied ourselves tidying the dormitory. Incredibly, we had flowers, for one of our gaolers had given us some discarded roses and they sat, blown but still lovely, in a Nescafé tin on the window sill. After breakfast a man came to the window and called Javiera: he had brought Andres and she leaped on to the broad window sill and was able to kiss him through the bars before he was called away. A few minutes later the door opened and one of the gaolers said, 'I need someone to help with the washing up.' Before we could answer Javiera was at the door and we realized that she was being given an opportunity to speak to her husband.

She was radiant when she returned and said that Andres was well, though he was very thin, and that the other men sent their love to us all.

We spent the rest of the morning alone, being disturbed only to receive our 'numbers' which were written on pieces of cardboard and hung round our necks. There was one other interruption when a request was made for someone to wash a shirt. Esther went and returned a quarter of an hour later and told us quietly that it had been soaked in fresh blood.

I lay on my bunk and looked at the metal bands of the mesh which supported the mattress of the upper tier. I had long ago learned to look for the sign of the cross in doors and windows and all things square, for it reminded me of Christ and helped me to focus my attention on him and pray in unlikely places such as the bus or the hospital. At the Posta there had been a long corridor with a door at the end and I used to walk slowly down the passage with its yellowed tiles and look up towards the 'cross' as if I were walking down the aisle of a church. This walking 'towards the cross' was a regular pilgrimage on my nights or long Sundays at the Posta and in some unspoken way I was presenting the blank cheque which had now begun to be cashed. As I lay now and looked at the cross above my head I longed to leave some Christian sign upon this terrible place and wondered how I could mark for others the cross that I could see so clearly in the metal above me.

Francisca was working quietly at her pelusographia and I went to the box to see if I could find some suitable 'drawing materials'. I found a strip of black woollen cloth that had once been a blindfold and returning to my bunk I began to pull out the threads. Then, working slowly and painstakingly, I began to wind them round the central band to make the upright of my cross. The girls asked what I was doing but I didn't have the courage to explain and said that I was just playing. Much later, when we were all together again, I was forced to speak openly about my belief in God and my vocation to be a nun and it came as a surprise to find that these girls, although they no longer believed in God, understood the concept of commitment and total giving far better than the average Christian, for they, too, had made the decision to give themselves without reserve.

25. (*above*) Saying goodbye to friends on the airport balcony. The blouse was embroidered in prison by my fellow prisoners and the white cross is the bone one which I carved.

26. (*left*) A last farewell from the bus.

27. At home in Devon. December 30th, 1975.
Photograph : courtesy of The Kingsbridge Gazette

Late in the morning we were quietly lying on our bunks talking and working when the door opened and Francisca, Magdalena and Esther were called and told to bring their things with them. I couldn't believe that it was them rather than me, but there was no mistake. We hugged each other goodbye and they were gone. We had all been so sure that I would be released, for now the men were starting to treat me with deference and I was called *doctora* more often than *gringa*. I had learned the telephone numbers of the four girls so that I could notify their families as to their whereabouts but now I was left behind with Javiera.

I was very unnerved to be separated from the others, for there had been a sense of security in numbers although we were only five. Javiera seemed very much more at risk than the other three, and although she was good company I did not feel protected by her as I had by Francisca. We sat closely together and talked as we ate our lunch and she told me about herself. She had gone to one of the best schools in Santiago and had been very active in politics when she was only sixteen. Immediately after the coup she was arrested and held for nearly a week in the Estadio de Chile. She told me how they had all lain on the ground while the soldiers fired over their heads, and of the Russian roulette in which groups of students were fired upon by soldiers using revolvers in which only some of the chambers were loaded. At sixteen she had seen women violated and tortured with animals and had seen men die. It took many months for her to emerge from the state of shock produced, but she had done so with a conviction in the revolutionary cause that could not be broken. Andres, like Javiera, was a member of the MIR. They were arrested on the same day and were tortured, each in front of the other, and it seems that Javiera had been on the *parrilla* many times. I marvelled at her cheerfulness and bravery and when the men came past the window after lunch we sat together and sang to them the 'Hymn of Joy', the song which gained enormous significance and popularity after the coup. It is sung to the music of Beethoven's Choral Symphony and speaks of joy and of the day when all men shall again be brothers:

Listen my brothers,
to the Song of Joy,
to the glad song
of those who await a new day.
Come! Sing! Dream Singing!
Live dreaming of the new sun
of the day when all men shall be brothers.

This song was to become our theme song and was sung
night after night in Cuatro Alamos. It is a measure of just
how indomitable is the human spirit that within days of
being tortured, and uncertain of the future, we were able to
sing to raise the morale of our fellow prisoners.

In the middle of the afternoon they came for me again
but this time I was told to bring my things. Not knowing
what to think, but with a rising certainty that I was to be
released, I bade farewell to Javiera and followed them. At
first we went into the small office next door to the dormitory
and I was given back my belt, my watch, and the silver
cross which always hung around my neck. Then I was taken
into the yard where they sat me down on a low wall. After
removing the blindfold they closed my eyes with tape and
then, having taken a photograph, led me through the iron
gates into the courtyard.

It is hard to convey the horror of being totally blindfolded. The cloth around the eyes permits one to see the
ground so that walking is comparatively easy and one re-
tains to a certain extent one's orientation in time and space,
for it is possible to distinguish night from day and indoors
from outdoors and so on. With the scotch tape, however, I
was totally blind. I walked slowly and fearfully, stumbling
as they forced me to walk faster than I wished. I heard
much later of prisoners from the provinces who remained
for over a week with their eyes closed with adhesive plaster
and their accounts of how they lost all sense of night and day
and became extremely distressed were not difficult to believe.

After we had walked some distance from the gates which
separated the front courtyard of the Grimaldi from the rear
portion where the prisoners were kept, I was told to stand

still and the man who had been leading me let go of my arm. I stood transfixed, unable to see and afraid to move. Then suddenly I heard an engine revving up and was filled with terror as I heard them drive towards me. In that instant I remembered the stories of prisoners who had had their legs run over and I wondered if they were going to kill me in this way and pretend that I had died in an accident. My fear, though acute, was mercifully short-lived, for the car stopped by my side and I was told to get in. It was a small incident, but I can remember the nightmare of terror as if it had just happened.

Once in the vehicle (it was a Chevrolet pick-up which I was to get to know well) I was sandwiched in between the driver and a man with a gun and they put a pair of sunglasses on my face and set off. As we drove out of the villa the driver asked me casually, 'How was Andres when you last saw him?' He must have thought to trap me into an admission of my complicity with the MIR and seemed cheated when I told him that Andres Pascal and I had never met.

As we drove along I knew that they must be taking me to the British embassy and I rejoiced in the certainty that I would soon be amongst friends. I thought it must be so for nearly five days had passed since my arrest and they could not keep me a prisoner for ever. I had never been to the embassy but knew that it was somewhere in Providencia and not far from the Grimaldi. As the minutes passed my certainty diminished and when we suddenly started to go much faster I realized that we could no longer be in the residential area. Again I was filled with fear and uncertainty, but consoled myself that they must be taking me to some spot where I could be handed over to the consul without causing any comment or publicity. After nearly half an hour's driving we slowed down and once more I heard the unbolting of heavy iron gates. Still I did not give up hope, for embassies in Chile have enormous gates and long drives; perhaps we had come a roundabout way for some reason. They told me to get out and then my glasses were removed and the tape ripped unceremoniously from my eyelids, so that I opened my eyes to see, not the well kept green lawns of an ambassadorial residence, but long grey barracks and armed soldiers.

This was Tres Alamos, the detention camp on the outskirts of Santiago, where over six hundred political prisoners were held without charge in accordance with the law of the State of Siege. Speechless, I took in the bleak buildings, the high wall with its barbed wire and the sentries in high boxes at each of the four corners of the enormous enclosure.

My captor called to me to come with him, and with my heart in my boots I walked down a concrete path into my new prison.

34

The Breaking of the Shell

Your pain is the breaking of the shell that encloses your
    understanding.
Even as the stone of the fruit must break, that its heart
    may stand in the sun,
So you must know pain.
And could you keep your heart in wonder at the daily
    miracles
of your life, your pain would not seem less wondrous
    than your joy;
And you would accept the seasons of your heart, even as
    you always accepted the seasons that pass over
    your fields.
And you would watch with serenity through the
    winters of your grief.

Kahlil Gibran
The Prophet

We entered a small office and they motioned me to sit down.
I felt neither relief at being out of the Grimaldi nor fear at
my new surroundings, just a numbness born of weariness
and shattered hopes. My name was entered in a ledger and
my watch and cross once more taken from me and put into
an envelope which bore my name. At least it seemed that I
existed as a person, and, for the first time, I could look at the
faces of my captors.

Cuatro Alamos, which stands within the grounds of Tres
Alamos, is a 'half-way house' for political detainees. Until
recently its existence was not publicly acknowledged for it is
run by the DINA and they do not like to admit to having
someone in custody until they have completed their investigations. Thus prisoners who have apparently given all
the information in their possession are held 'incommunicado'
while this information is processed and acted upon. If it
emerges (by interrogation of a new prisoner) that a given

detainee has further information of importance he is returned to the Grimaldi, as happened with Javiera.

The actual building is a former noviciate and the 'cells' were presumably the rooms of the novices. There are about fifteen rooms in a row off a long corridor with a bathroom in the middle of the block. Prisoners are held either alone or in groups. They are locked in their cells for the twenty-four hours of the day except for three visits to the bathroom. There are three armed guards on duty both day and night, and no one group of prisoners is ever allowed out at the same time as another. Food is brought to the door of the cell and passed to the prisoner who eats it in his cell. There is no exercise period and the prisoners do not go out unless they are being taken for some specific reason.

I was put into Room No. 4 and I was alone. The room held two metal bunks and a chair, and the beds had

Solitary Confinement in Cuatro Alamos

mattresses and pillows and grey army blankets. The window was quite large but was barred and looked out on to a small grassed yard and a high concrete wall surrounded by barbed wire.

I took stock of my surroundings and tried to regain my spirits. This was surely an improvement and a step towards liberty. Perhaps I would be released in a few days, for there could be no possible reason to detain me further now that they had the information they wanted. I wondered if Francisca and the others were here. As I sat on the bunk I heard a knock on the wall. I knocked back, the three short beats and a long one of the famous passage from Beethoven's Fifth Symphony. This was to be my signature tune and I communicated in this way with greater confidence as the days turned into weeks.

That night, however, I was new and fearful of the unknown. It was not long before I received a visit from the 'doctor'. Javiera had told us that there was a man who said he was a doctor and who tried to hypnotize all the prisoners. So when he told me he was going to help me to relax I realized that he was going to attempt it with me. At first I resisted and told him that I was quite relaxed but he persisted and making me lie down, loosened my clothes and covered me with a blanket. He talked gently and told me to breathe deeply and when he thought that I was settling slipped quietly away. I lay there wondering what would happen next until I heard someone at the window. So I looked around. He had obviously sent someone to see if I was asleep, for he came back and said that he would try again after supper.

Javiera had told us also that the food was not up to the standard of the Grimaldi (where we had been fed from the soldiers' kitchen), and I soon learned how right she was. Supper consisted of soup and bread and a cup of tea. The soup was thin and greasy and tasted of nothing in particular. At least it was hot and the bread was fresh, so that my hunger was satisfied, but I was soon to learn that this was the standard meal. For breakfast we had tea and bread, and for lunch and supper we had soup and bread, and that was that. There was no fruit and no vegetables and the soup contained for practical purposes no meat or fish. (I soon learned that the stew bones which looked so meaty were a snare and a delusion for they displaced the soup and what looked like meat was inedible gristle.) Once a week we had a plate of beans and once a week some spaghetti. This was a diet which was enough to maintain life but anyone living on it for any length of time would become rapidly depleted of protein and vitamins.

I later discovered that this was the staple diet for the whole camp and was the only food supplied to the long-term prisoners, some of whom had been detained for over two years. This criminally inadequate diet placed an enormous burden on the families of the prisoners who, already deprived of a breadwinner, had to bring fresh fruit and vegetables and tinned fish to stop their loved ones from becoming ill with protein malnutrition and scurvy.

After supper the doctor returned, this time in his white coat, and led me down to his office. Having been conditioned to expect the worst I was very frightened and thought he was going to give me drugs. I had heard tales of people who were given intravenous Pentothal very slowly so that they were no longer able to guard what they said and thus betrayed their friends. Trying desperately to stall I sat bolt upright on the bed and talked to him, but after a while he told me that I must lie down. He softened the lights and told me to breathe slowly and deeply. As soon as I realized that he was not going to use drugs on me I was not really afraid because I know quite well that it is impossible to hypnotize anyone against their will. I lay there and tried to give all the appearances of co-operating whilst keeping my mind active and alert. It was surprisingly difficult for he made me breathe slowly and deeply so that I relaxed whether I wanted to or not. All the time he talked, rambling on and on, and I think he realized that he was not going to achieve his end for he changed to a different tack. At first I was angered by what he said and then I realized that perhaps he was trying to get me to understand something very important, for he told me to forget what had happened to me. 'You are going to be a nun,' he said. 'It would not be good for you to talk of such unpleasant things, it would not sound well. Nuns do not talk of these things.' He continued for some time and then repeated again and again, as if it were some kind of spell, 'They were so kind to you. They treated you so well.' My eyes shut and my voice hazy, I repeated to him that they had treated me very well, and after a while he took me back to my room. Slowly it dawned on me that they were trying to make me forget the torture and that I would have a much greater chance of getting out if they thought that they had succeeded.

Soon it was time to go to bed. I was escorted to the washroom by one of the guards, who sat with his pistol in his hand outside the open door while I washed my face in the cold water and swilled out my mouth. I had no tooth-brush and nothing to do my hair with, and I had now worn the same heavily blood-stained clothes day and night for five days. We had had one tooth-brush between us at the Grimaldi and it had been a great luxury. Never a particularly obsessive tooth brusher I found that I missed this most of all the simple things that one takes for granted.

When I was back in my room the doctor brought me a present: a battered part of the Bible and two old *Reader's Digests*. This was riches indeed, for they were to be my only company for many days.

One of the things for which I am most grateful is the fact that I was able to sleep so well in prison. It is a curious thing, for I do not always sleep well and am easily upset by strange surroundings or by having to share my room with another, but by some gift of God or subconscious defence mechanism (however one chooses to see these things), although living in a state of constant fear I slept much better than I did in my own home.

The next morning I woke early to the sound of the men being let out to the bathroom. The guards were aggressive with them and made them run down the corridor so there was no sleeping once they began. It is to some extent understandable, for even by making everyone hurry it took over an hour to let us all out. I think there were over fifty prisoners in Cuatro Alamos, for the cauldron of tea and the basket of bread were very large indeed. While I waited to be let out I sat on my bunk and looked out at the mountains. It was just possible to see the peaks of the Andes over the wall, and I found that if I stood on my chair I could see the sunrise. The sight of the sun on the snow-capped mountains became the most important moment of my day and despite my dreary surroundings and uncertain future my heart rose within me to greet the Light Invisible.

> O Light Invisible, we praise Thee!
> Too bright for mortal vision.
> O Greater Light, we praise thee for the less;
> The eastern light our spires touch at morning,
> The light that slants upon our western doors at evening,
> The twilight over stagnant pools at batflight,
> Moonlight and starlight, owl and moth light,
> Glow-worm glowlight on a grass blade,
> O Light Invisible, we worship Thee!

> T. S. Eliot
> *Choruses from The Rock*

They brought us breakfast: a cup of tea and a piece of dry bread, and I sat on my bunk and I tried to eat it. I ate it slowly and dipped it in the tea, but after I had eaten only a quarter of the bread I knew that if I ate any more I'd be sick. This became a familiar pattern and I learned to save half my tea and drink it cold in the middle of the morning, for by that time hunger had overcome the nausea.

After breakfast I sat on my bunk and gave myself seriously to thinking. God was very real to me, and I asked myself and Him just what it was He had in mind. There was no blinding light or voice from behind the mountains (in my experience there never is!) but it seemed to me that if I was going to spend all day alone I must spend a great deal of it in prayer. There was absolutely nothing else that I could do to be of any use to anybody, so apart from doing everything within my power to maintain my health and sanity I must pray.

I was not unused to spending several hours in prayer, for

I had often spent four or five hours sitting on my mountain top, leaning against the wall of the Benedictine monastery and giving myself to the love and praise of God. It was not easy, however, in a prison cell, and I soon realized that this was going to be very hard work for it was much easier to read the *Reader's Digest* or lie on my back on the bunk and think. Not by nature an orderly person, I knew by some instinct that if I was to survive being alone twenty-four hours a day I must keep myself busy. I therefore mentally divided the day up and made myself a sort of timetable so that I had periods of prayer, of reading, of exercise and of rest. I rationed the *Reader's Digest*s very strictly to two or three articles a day, for they were my only escape from the grim reality of the cell.

When I tried to pray I found that it was very difficult to be quiet before God, for I was filled with fear and anxiety for the future. Unable to be at peace, I presented Him with my anguish and with that of all the other prisoners, with whom I felt an enormous bond. Although I was so alone and so far from my friends and family, I felt curiously united with many people.

I thought of my friends the Benedictines. I could see them gathered in choir praying, and I added my voice to theirs and found that we were joined by all the other monks and nuns all round the world in a great river of prayer. It is difficult to explain just how this was: it wasn't an emotionally comforting experience and I didn't 'feel' (as it seems other people have felt in similar circumstances) the prayers of others for me, but I knew that I was not alone in my worship, that I was part of the Body of Christ.

> When you pray you rise to meet in the air those who are praying at that very hour, and whom, save in prayer, you may not meet.
>
> Kahlil Gibran
> *The Prophet*

I examined the Bible the doctor had brought me. It was half of a New Testament in a popular paperback edition, and contained St John's Gospel, the Acts of the Apostles, and the letters of St Paul. It was illustrated with charming line drawings and, leafing idly through it to look at the pictures, I came across a drawing to illustrate the famous passage in St Paul's letter to the Romans:

> Who, then, can separate us from the love of Christ? Can trouble do it, or hardship, or persecution, or hunger, or poverty, or danger, or death? As the scripture says,
>> 'For your sake we are in danger of death the whole day long,
>> We are treated like sheep that are going to be slaughtered.'
>
> No, in all these things we have complete victory through him who loved us! For I am certain that nothing can separate us from his love: neither death nor life; neither angels nor other heavenly rulers or powers; neither the present nor the future; neither the world above nor the world below – there is nothing in all creation that will ever be able to separate us from the love of God which is ours through Christ Jesus our Lord.
>
> *Romans 8: 35–39*

When I looked at the drawing I knew what he meant, for there was a man, naked and on his knees, buffeted by wind, shielding his head from hurled stones and flying arrows. Shooting across the page were the jagged lines which are often used to represent lightning, but for me they were the electricity and there, stretched down to him, was the hand of God.

> . . . and yet
> He was there.
> I could only
> close my eyes
> and hold his hand
> and grit my teeth
> and know
> with that cold, dark naked knowing
> that He was there.

Incredibly, in the midst of fear and loneliness I was filled with joy, for I knew without any vestige of doubt that God was with me, and that nothing that they could do to me could change that. I knew, too, that in some strange way the pain which I had suffered was his gift, and that far from being a sign of his lack of care or wrath, it was an unmistakeable sign of his love. In some mysterious way I had been permitted to share in the mystery of life and death, of the Incarnation and the Cross.

> When you carry the Cross
> of Christ
> willingly
> He loves you.
> You have in your hands
> His gift.
> You have the cup
> Which you may drink
> or not
> for the Salvation of the world.

On Friday evening the consul came. I was told simply that I had a visitor and they sent me to do my hair and then led me into the office. When I saw Derek Fernyhough standing there looking so incredibly British, all the bottled-up anguish of the past week overflowed, and I burst into tears on his shoulder. The prison commander was not pleased, and said sharply that he didn't know what I was crying about. He said immediately that the interview was to be conducted in Spanish, and I knew from the tenseness of his attitude that he was waiting to see what I would say.

In that small office with the colonel and the doctor looking at us and the men with machine guns just outside the door, I knew that Derek was just as helpless as I was. On that first night I had imagined him sweeping up in the ambassadorial car like a knight on his charger and carrying me off. The reality was very different and I realized from his manner that he was completely powerless to rescue me by force and that we must both resort to the famous diplomacy of the British.

I choked back my tears and asked him if he had a handkerchief, and when he handed me the traditional clean
white handkerchief that all well bred English gentlemen
carry for maidens in distress I didn't know whether to laugh
or to cry all the more. For the rest of my time in prison that
hanky with its Cash's name tab was to me like a child's piece
of blanket, a link with the British way of life and a country
where policemen were one's friends.

When the initial tide of emotion had ebbed, Derek asked
me how I'd been treated. Acutely conscious of the two
Chileans watching me, I replied that I had been treated
very well. Their sigh of relief was audible, and the colonel
smiled and agreed in a jovial voice that I was being very
well cared for. For nearly an hour we talked, and slowly the
outside world took shape. There was much press interest in
England, there were cables from many different countries
and there were messages of love from my family. He read me
a list of the names of people who had cabled and I was
moved again to tears to hear the names of the professors who
had taught me at Oxford and of old friends, now themselves professors, who had sent messages of support and encouragement from different parts of the globe.

Just how many people worked for my release and prayed
for my safety I think I shall never know. Wherever I have
gone in this past year I have met people who wrote letters to
their Members of Parliament or to the Chilean Embassy or
who prayed that I might be released. Never will I forget
going to meet a group of university students in Oslo and
being told by the Norwegian Dominican priest and Lutheran
pastor that they had all prayed for me. It has given me a
sense of having been ransomed that I think I shall never
lose.

Suddenly the telephone rang. The line to the chief's
office at Cuatro Alamos was a bad one and he always had to
shout; and now as he struggled to get whatever he had to
say across, I leaned forward until my face was very close to
Derek's and said 'Mains, Derek; mains', three times.

It was all I dared, for the words 'electricity' or 'torture'
in Spanish are practically the same, and the doctor would

have caught what I said. I learned later that Derek, although he knew that I was telling him something, didn't realize what I meant, but he relayed my message to the Foreign Office in London, where they understood at once that I had been subjected to electrical shock. Thus it was known in England from the very first interview that I had been tortured but it was decided that it was more likely that I would be released quickly if appearances were maintained.

When Derek had gone they took me back to my room where I clasped his gifts of cologne and soap and cigarettes as proof that his visit had not been a dream. They had said that he might come again on Monday: there was light at the end of the tunnel.

35

The Visit to the Fiscal

When love beckons to you, follow him,
Though his ways are hard and steep.
And when his wings enfold you, yield to him,
Though the sword hidden among his pinions may
   wound you.
And when he speaks to you, believe him,
Though his voice may shatter your dreams as the north
   wind lays waste the garden.

Kahlil Gibran
The Prophet

On Monday, 10 November, nine days after I had been arrested, I was taken before the Military Prosecutor, the Fiscal. It was about six o'clock in the evening when I was suddenly told that I was going out. I sat in the big Chevrolet pick-up between the colonel and one of the guards and we drove off to Santiago. Terrified that they were taking me back to the Grimaldi, but gaining courage from the fact that they did not blindfold me, I asked them repeatedly where we were going. After a while the colonel became irritated by my questions and said, 'We are taking you before the Fiscal.'

This was progress indeed. If I was to appear before a court, then surely it could only be a matter of days before I was on a plane for England. My spirits rose and I began to enjoy the drive.

Tres Alamos is in the suburb called Departamental on the outskirts of Santiago. As we sped along the highway the city was stretched out before me and I looked for familiar landmarks. Suddenly my heart leaped as I recognized the twin towers of the Church of San Ignacio. Once again the fact of my being a prisoner took on the dream-world quality of a film and I had fantasies of being rescued or escaping.

As we drove into town the colonel told his men that there

would be photographers and that although it didn't matter if I was photographed, the pictures were on no account to appear in the papers. When we alighted from the vehicle they made me walk separately and when one man took a photograph of the colonel, he quickly ordered it to be confiscated, and we waited at the foot of the stairs while the film was destroyed.

The military court was a small and shabby department in a large building in the very centre of town. I was taken by the colonel and left in the office of the military prosecutor. For a little while I was alone and then he hurried in, a tall army lawyer in civilian dress, and, sitting at his desk, he began to interrogate me. His first question was about how I had been treated, and, trusting no one, I said that I had been well treated. If he was surprised he didn't show it. After a few questions establishing that I had treated Gutierrez, he began to question me about the incident at the house in Larraín Gandarillas.

At first I was quite at ease and told him how I had been sitting with Susie when I heard the maid scream and how I had rushed down to find her lying in a pool of blood. He asked me who had been in the house with me and I told him that there had only been the four of us, Susie, Father Hallidan, the maid and myself. To my surprise he pressed the matter and repeatedly asked whether or not there could have been someone hiding in the house, and whether or not I had had a gun. I was at a loss, for it seemed absurd that he was asking questions to which he must surely know the answer, for had not the DINA searched the house and found no one?

On and on he went, and it gradually became apparent that he did not wholly believe what I said. Then the purpose of his questions became abundantly and frighteningly clear, for he told me that one of the members of the DINA had been shot in the arm and if it wasn't I who had shot him, who had?

As I sat there before this apparently just and reasonable man I realized that he had been told that I had been captured in a gun battle in which a policeman had been shot and that either I had had an accomplice or I fired myself. The most terrifying thing of all was that the capture of an armed revolutionary was much easier to believe than what had actually happened: the unprovoked attack on a religious house in the centre of Santiago.

The nightmare quality of the events following my arrest had made me forget the totally unjustifiable behaviour of the security forces at the house in Larraín Gandarillas. They had shot and killed a defenceless maid and had fired without ceasing for nearly fifteen minutes on a house from which not one shot had been fired in response. Now they had been called upon to account for the episode and were seeking to justify their actions. Their behaviour could only be justified if someone inside the house had fired the first shot and they were anxious to prove that this was me.

Still unbelieving, I protested that I had no weapons and I told him that someone must have made a mistake and fired on Enriquetta when she opened the door. He looked at me unbelievingly and told me that was all for now, and that he would continue to question me the next day.

As I rose to leave I said to him, 'I'll be deported, of course, won't I?'

His reply, as he looked up from his papers, brought a new dimension of horror to this still incredible drama, for he said, 'I haven't heard anything to that effect, doctor. You will be tried and sentenced according to Chilean law.'

36

Now Done Darkness

> ... That night, that year
> of now done darkness I wretch lay wrestling with (my
> God!) my God.
>
> Gerard Manley Hopkins
> *Carrion Comfort*

I lay in the dark long after the transistor radio had been switched off and the muffled conversation of the guards in the next room to me had ceased. 'Tried according to the Chilean law.' What did that mean? How great was my crime in their eyes? It had never occurred to me that I was guilty of a crime, but I had treated one of the most wanted men in Chile and had deliberately refrained from notifying the police as to his whereabouts. I had seen this as a breach of the regulations which would result in my being expelled from the country, but now I was to be tried as a criminal.

Alone and sleepless in the dark cell my imagination ran riot. They would certainly find me guilty, for I had never denied treating Gutierrez. What would be the penalty? Presumably it would be prison. At the back of my mind I recalled reading about an English schoolteacher in East Berlin who had been sentenced to prison for helping people to escape. Could it really be that I was going to spend the next five or ten years of my life in a Chilean gaol?

Suddenly, like a cold wind, a new thought came to me: perhaps they would sentence me to death. Perhaps the helping of terrorists carried the death penalty, or perhaps they would find me guilty of Enriquetta's death. It seemed absurd and incredible: but was not the whole situation beyond reason and belief? If they could arrest me at gun point in the presence of Father Halliden, carry me off blindfolded to a secret place and torture me for twelve hours, could they not just as baldly fabricate a case against me so that I was found guilty by a court of law?

Bewildered and afraid, I faced God. I had been so sure of his plans for me: I was to return to England and become a nun, to dedicate my life totally to his service. Had he changed his mind? Or perhaps I had read the signs wrong. That my life was to be one of service to him I knew beyond any doubt, but it had never occurred to me that that service might be undertaken somewhere very different from where I had chosen.

I lay there and struggled with the idea. I had written my blank cheque and invited him to do what he willed with me, yet now that the crunch had come I was afraid. All night I lay there and argued with myself.

You offered yourself freely. No one forced you.

Of course.

Well, then? Now your offer's been accepted.

But I didn't think it would mean this.

What did you think, then?

I don't know. I thought it meant being a nun.

Perhaps he doesn't want you to be a nun. Not yet, anyway. Perhaps he wants you here in Chile.

But why?

Who knows? Perhaps he wants you just to be here amongst the prisoners. A Christian presence.

I hadn't thought of that.

I know you hadn't, but it's not so impossible, is it?

I suppose not. But five years!

So what. You offered yourself. Was it only a short term offer?

No, no! It was for always, for anywhere.

Well, what are you worried about, then?

Nothing, I suppose.

Relax, then.

For a while I was quiet, then it began again.

What if they execute me?

Well, what if they do?

What do you mean?

Well, you believe in God, don't you? Does it matter if you die now?

I suppose not. But I'm afraid.
What are you afraid of?
I'm afraid of dying.
Why?
I don't know.
What is there to be afraid of?
If you put it like that, nothing, I suppose.
Well, then.
Could it really be that this is going to be the end of my life?
Of course it could.
But I thought I'd only just begun it. I've got so much to do.
Who says? I thought you had handed the reins over.
I have. But I thought . . .
You thought! It's what he thinks, isn't it?
I suppose so.
Well then! Stop struggling, let go.

> Go down
> into the plans of God.
> Go down
> deep as you may.
> Fear not
> for your fragility
> under that weight of water.
> Fear not
> for life or limb.
> Sharks attack savagely.
> Fear not the power
> of treacherous currents under the sea.
> Simply do not be afraid
> let go. You will be led
> like a child whose mother
> holds him to her bosom
> and against all comers is his shelter.
>   Helder Camara
>   *The Desert is Fertile*

I tried to pray.

'Dear God! Help! Please get me out of here!'

No, this wouldn't do. This wasn't joyful acceptance of whatever he had in mind. I tried again.

'Please, God. Help me to be brave. I'm very frightened. Please help.'

That was better.

'Lord, I don't know what you have in mind. I'm afraid. I don't want to die. Help me to accept whatever you send.'

Never had a night seemed so long. Wearily I fought the urge to cry out to God to be freed. At some very deep level I knew that this was a time of testing and that I was at liberty to accept what he sent or to ask to be spared, and I knew that if my offering of self had any meaning at all it must be unconditional and I must leave him free to use me as he wished. The moment had come when I was invited to walk upon the waters, to show that I had the faith to trust him utterly, to abandon myself to him.

> Abandonment is managing nothing,
> blocking or blotting out nothing,
> expecting nothing.
> Abandonment is receiving all things the way
> one receives
> a gift
> with opened hands.
> and opened heart.
> Abandonment to God
> is the climactic point in any man's life.
>
> Anonymous
> from *Disciples and Other
> Strangers* by E. J. Farrell

When the light came I was sick and spent. Numbly I washed and drank my tea, and waited for the sound of the bolts on my door which would herald the arrival of my escort. I didn't have long to wait, and feeling as though I had already been condemned I followed the colonel out to the car.

37
Trial

If you try me
send me out
into the foggy night,
so that I cannot see
my way.

Even if I stumble,
this I beg, that I
may look and smile
serenely,
bearing witness
that you are with me
and I walk in peace.
Helder Càmara
The Desert is Fertile

When I was led out to the pick-up I was surprised to find
that there was another prisoner, a man of well over sixty
years. He was terribly thin and looked ill and miserable,
trying to hold up beltless trousers that were too large for him
and stumbling in shoes from which the laces had been removed. We sat packed tightly together in the cabin of the
vehicle, sandwiched in between the colonel, who always
drove, and a guard with a machine gun. We drove in
silence while I wondered numbly what the day would bring.
As we passed through the crowded shopping centre I looked
at the people hurrying by. There was a street vendor with
his barrow laden with fruit; it was impossible to believe that
less than two weeks before I had bought strawberries from
this same man.

The photographers were present in full force as we entered the back door of the building which housed the court,
pursued by flashing lights. Once inside the building we were
hurried down to the basement where the Second Military
Court had its offices, and told to wait. My turn came first. I

was shown into a large office where two young men were seated at desks. One of them explained to me that he was the Fiscal's assistant and that he had been instructed to take my statement. His companion, it emerged, was to type what I said, so after I had sworn that what I was about to declare was the truth, we began.

It was a slow business, as each question and answer had to be typed out as we spoke it. After a couple of hours the Fiscal came in. He greeted me politely and turning to his assistant said, 'Have you offered the doctor a cup of coffee?' So accustomed had I become to the treatment of the last week that I had forgotten how normal civilized people behave. My heart warmed to this man who showed me such consideration and I began to feel some sense of my identity once more. The thought of the coffee made me realize that I was hungry and I summoned the courage to ask, 'Please do you think I might have a piece of bread?' The Fiscal was angered and embarrassed and exclaimed, 'Good God, *doctora*! Have they not fed you?' I explained that the prison breakfast made me feel sick and, pulling a banknote from his pocket, he sent one of the office workers out to buy me a sandwich.

We continued with the statement for the rest of the morning. I sat crouched over the hot coffee trying not to spill it over the kindly Fiscal's desk, for my hands shook so much that I had to take it in both of them.

At six o'clock in the evening we were still there. My statement had been taken until mid-afternoon and now they were questioning my companion. As we sat there after lunch I had whispered to him, 'What are you here for?' to which he replied, 'Same as you', and I realized that he must have been involved in the hiding of Andres and Mary Ann. It wasn't, however, until the Fiscal came out of his office and addressed him as 'Padre Carlos' that I realized that my fellow prisoner was a priest. Much later, when I was in Tres Alamos, they told me that this man who was so thin and poorly dressed had once been one of the most important of the Cardinal's assistants, but some ten years before he had left his post to become a worker priest. He had worked for

several years in the copper mines and now was a labourer
in one of the poorest shanty towns of Santiago. It was small
wonder that a man who felt so called to carry the cross of the
people he served should one day find himself stretched upon
it. Carlos, of course, is not his name, and he has returned to
his life of obscurity, a gentle Nazareth presence among the
people he loves.

As I sat there, between two men with pistols, a young
reporter walked down the stairs into the hall outside the
court, and engaged my guards in conversation. He and the
other reporters had been waiting outside the court all day
for news of the Fiscal's verdict, and he had managed to slip
past the guards at the entrance and had found his way inside.
After talking for a while to the men beside me he said that he
was going off to get a sandwich. Something about the look
of longing on my face must have touched him for he asked,
'Would you like one?' It wasn't only that I was hungry
again but this was a link with the outside world and normal
existence. So I said 'I'd like a hot dog with mayonnaise and
mustard, please.' It is not possible to put into words the
experience of actually choosing what sort of sandwich I
wanted, not to mention being able to request an embellish-
ment such as mustard! The ordering and the eating of that
sandwich was one of the most memorable events of my two
months as a prisoner! After I had carefully wiped the last
of the mayonnaise off my face and fingers with the by now
rather grubby consular handkerchief, I posed for photographs, and his generosity was rewarded by getting an
exclusive for his newspaper, a small weekly in the south of
Chile.

At last they finished interrogating Father Carlos and I
was called into the office once more. The Fiscal told me that
I was now under the jurisdiction of the military court and
that until my case was decided I was to be moved to the
Casa Correccional, the House of Correction which was the
women's common gaol in Santiago. In other words, I was
no longer under the jurisdiction of the DINA. I could have
kissed them all but I restrained myself and asked if I might
be taken to the new prison immediately as I did not wish to

spend another night at Cuatro Alamos. They told me that
this had already been arranged but that I must return
briefly so that the necessary papers could be completed and
my personal belongings returned to me.

It was well after eight when we arrived back at the
prison but nothing was said about the transfer. Shut in my
room once more I wondered if they were discussing how
they could keep me, and the fear that was never very far
below the surface took hold of me once more.

They kept me waiting in suspense for two hours, but
around ten o'clock I was told to come and bring my things.
My only possessions were the clothes I stood up in and the
precious cologne, and clasping it firmly in my hand I
followed the guard into the office. The colonel told me that
there was a paper to sign and placing a cyclostyled form in
front of me told me to sign it. I read it through slowly while
he waited with ill concealed impatience. The form was that
of an Act of Liberty, presumably used for all prisoners
detained by the DINA, and it stated that I was being freed
in the vicinity of my home as charges of violation of the law
of security of the state were unproven. The first part of the
form was printed but the second part was blank and the
colonel dictated to me, 'Furthermore I declare that while I
was detained in Cuatro Alamos I have not suffered either
torture or maltreatment.' I paused here and looked up at
him, whereupon he smiled and said, 'This only refers to
here.' He continued to dictate, 'Furthermore I have not
known personally that other detainees have been tortured or
maltreated and I declare that I am in perfect physical and
mental health.'

At the bottom of the page was printed, 'Having read the
above I declare that I sign it without pressure of any kind.'

This document, in company with others that I signed on
leaving other prisons, was used as evidence that I had lied.
(It is because a facsimile of this form bearing my signature
was published in a Santiago newspaper that I am able to
reproduce accurately the contents of the form.)

Father Carlos was also to be transferred to another
prison and the two of us once more climbed into the DINA

pickup. The colonel was in jovial mood and talked to us as we drove along. (I have forgotten the conversation, but recall that he engaged in some kind of religious dispute with Father Carlos.) The Casa Correccional is very close to the Tres Alamos and it did not take many minutes to get there. I was taken into the office and handed over to the grey-uniformed prison officials by one of the guards and, bidding me farewell, they drove off.

After they had entered my name in the register the man at the desk telephoned for someone to come and collect me. The woman who came was between thirty and forty and wore the pale green uniform of the prison service. She complained to the warder that they were working her too hard and, bidding me to follow her, unlocked the door that led into the prison.

I think I was expecting something like my idea of Holloway with floors of barred cells and metal staircases, but I found that we were once more in a garden. As I followed the wardress down the path, five white-robed figures materialized out of the gloom and I wondered if I had died without realizing it and was in heaven, for I suddenly found myself being hugged and kissed by a group of nuns!

38

The House of Correction

Teach your child from infancy
To love open spaces,
widen his mind.
He will be glad of this,
especially if later
he must endure
a life confined
by a slit window's littleness
to one small patch of sky.

Helder Càmara
The Desert is Fertile

One by one they hugged me, and motioning the wardress to go, led me down the path. Nor did the dream-like quality of what was happening pass when they spoke, for they said, 'We've been waiting for you so long.' Perhaps if I hadn't eaten that hot dog and so, for a brief moment, proved to myself that I was still in Chile in 1975, I might truly have wondered if I had passed without knowing it into another life, for never have women seemed so much like angels. Completely dazed, I allowed myself to be borne along and led into a large building which seemed more like a school than a gaol. As we walked along a tiled corridor I found that only one of my angels remained, and she led me into a small room and closed the door.

As if it wasn't sufficient to be met by nuns when expecting men with guns, I now blinked in total disbelief for there on the floor was a large cardboard box full of baby ducks! It was too much. I sank down on a chair and all the unshed tears of the past week poured down my cheeks and on to the floor as I fumbled for Derek's handkerchief.

After a while I discovered that I was weeping on to a red jersey and that the wearer, a slim, dark-haired girl in her twenties, was gently stroking my hair. I pulled myself together and after stealing another look at the ducks to make sure that they were real, looked up at the inhabitants of this strange outpost of heaven. Delighted to see these signs of returning life they greeted me anew and I was introduced to Antonia, Maria and Sister Augusta. They repeated that they had been waiting for me for days, and when I said that I did not understand, they showed me a pile of newspapers, and there in that evening's paper was a large photograph of my bedraggled figure entering the court. As they showed me the newspapers of the past week, I realized for the first time that my arrest had been headline news for days, and that the whole of Santiago was in an uproar over the involvement of so many priests and nuns in the hiding of the revolutionaries. It was not, however, until much later that I learned just how great were the repercussions of our actions.

As I scanned the newspapers, completely fascinated by the mixture of truth and lies which had been published, I heard a magic word: 'shower'. I looked up and found that they were handing me soap, towel, shampoo, tooth-brush, clean clothes and telling me that I was to have a hot shower. Still not quite able to believe that it was all true, I followed Sister Augusta down the corridor and listened to her instructions about the way the taps worked.

It was eleven days since I had been arrested and I had lived and slept in the same shirt, sweater and jeans which had been soaked in Enriquetta's blood, as it had ebbed away from her while she lay on Father Halliden's floor. Thankfully I peeled them off and revelled in the luxury of the warm water and the smell of soap.

When I returned to the little room my dirty clothes were whisked away, and while Antonia dried my hair and Maria boiled eggs on an electric ring, we talked. They explained to me that all prisoners whose case was being processed or who had been sentenced were held in this prison, and that those who were detained without charges under the laws of the state of siege were held in the detention camp at Tres Alamos. Antonia had been in prison since the time of Allende, for she had been a member of a small far left revolutionary party that had 'disturbed the peace'. After

three years her case was still unresolved and there seemed
little hope of it being settled in the near future as the
numbers of prisoners awaiting trial was increasing every
day, and the legal departments worked very slowly. Her
husband was also in prison in the penitentiary and their
families had long since run out of money to pay lawyers'
fees. Maria was a long-stay prisoner and did not tell me why
she was there, but she appeared to be in a position of special
trust.

The nuns were members of the Good Shepherd congregation whose apostolate was with delinquent girls, and they
lived and worked within the state prison, trying to re-
educate the women and rehabilitate them. Sister Augusta
was an especially kind woman and did her best to make life
tolerable for people like Antonia.

The room we were in seemed to be an all-purpose room
for sewing and ironing and drinking coffee and was marvel-
lously cluttered with all manner of clothes and materials for
projects, not to mention, of course, the ducks. The poultry,
for there were also a few chickens, were Antonia's special
charge, and she had a small piece of garden in a neglected
corner of the prison grounds where she tended her flock during the day and brought them in for safety and warmth at
night.

After I had finished my supper and my hair was dry and
shining from Antonia's attentions I was told it was time for
bed. They explained apologetically that I would have to be
locked up again. This was indeed a prison and these two
hours had been stolen time, for I was still under order of the
court to be held incommunicado. They promised that they
would bring me my food the next day and hugged me goodnight as the wardress, who had mysteriously reappeared,
waited impatiently at the door.

I followed her down a dark staircase and through a basement room full of sleeping women and waited while she unlocked my cell. Appalled, I looked at her and then went in.
It was like a cupboard, just big enough for the bed and a
locker and nothing else, perhaps eight feet by five, and worst
of all there was no window save a small wired hole in the

door. I climbed slowly on to the bed and she locked the door and went away. Finding it difficult not to burst once more into tears, I told myself that at least I was safe in this place, and for the first time since I had been arrested was no longer in the power of the DINA.

They had done their best to make me happy, for the bed had sheets and so many blankets that I could hardly move. I lay down, and exhausted by the previous sleepless night and the hours of fear and conflict, fell asleep.

The next morning the wardress unlocked my cell and led me upstairs to the bathroom. I found that my brief period of privilege had ended and I joined about ten other women crowded into a small washroom. My idea of prison life, gleaned from films, had not been so wildly wrong, for here was a group of women herded unwillingly together, and submitted to the indignity of carrying their night receptacles to be emptied and washed. Their language was coarse and some of them were obviously mentally defective or un-balanced. I learned later that they were mainly prostitutes and thieves though a few of them were guilty of acts of violence including murder.

After I had washed I was returned to my room and got back into bed for I had no clothes and there was nowhere else to sit. I passed the whole day in bed except for visits to the bathroom and from time to time I had a visitor. One of the nuns brought me a Bible but there was so little light that I could only read by standing on the end of my bed and holding the book up to the small window set in the door. I quickly became tired and tried to resign myself to lying quietly in the semi-darkness.

When lunch time came my door was unlocked and Antonia and Maria came in with a plate of stew that they had prepared especially for me. It was the first meat (apart from my hot dog) that I had eaten for ten days, and I was very grateful. They were only able to stay a few moments but their visit raised my spirits, and I composed myself to be calm and patient. In the late afternoon my clothes were returned to me, meticulously washed and ironed by one of the prisoners. I dressed and, feeling more like a proper person, stood on my bed and peered out of the little window. The tiny cell was one of a block in a basement dormitory, and through the wire grille I could see the barred window and the passing feet of the prison officer who patrolled in the garden.

When the guard changed, a new and more friendly wardress came and told me that I could sit out of the cell for half an hour. As I sat on the window ledge looking at the wall outside and the grass which grew in the garden above it I realized that I was not alone. Softly a voice called from one of the other cells and then a pale-faced girl with red hair appeared at the window.

This was Lucia and we conversed in undertones, listening for the sound of the guard's footsteps on the gravel and the rattle of the key in the lock which would herald the return of the wardress. How different was Lucia from my cell mates at the Casa Grimaldi! She was a worker in a government office and had been a passing accomplice of a girl who had perfected a system of fraud. I don't recall the details but her friend had been systematically swindling the office for over a year and, when she was found out and bolted, Lucia had considered it more prudent to face things, and had gone to the office of *Investigaciones*, the detective branch of the police force, to make a declaration. To her surprise and indignation she had been taken into custody pending the arrest of her friend and clarification of the matter. She, like me, was being held incommunicado prior to her court hearing. We talked for a while until the wardress returned and I was locked once more in my cell.

Antonia and Maria brought my supper and again I had the luxury of eating meat, for they were determined to rebuild my strength. They brought me messages of affection and support from the other political prisoners and I learned that there were ten other girls who had been tried and were serving sentences of up to 25 or 30 years.

The next day, Thursday 13 November, was an easier one. As Lucia was transferred, I was allowed out of my cell into the dormitory. I sat by the window and read the Bible and stretched my aching limbs, for it had been many days since I had had a space longer than eight feet in which to exercise.

When Sister Augusta came to visit me I asked if I might see the prison chaplain but she was evasive and said that this was not possible. Separated from the mass and daily reception of the eucharist which had become an integral part of my life, I was saddened and felt unfairly deprived, for surely there must be a priest who came daily to the convent and prison. It was not until I arrived at my final destination of Tres Alamos that I learned that Father Patricio Gajardo, the prison chaplain, had been arrested less than a week before and was himself in detention.

The involvement of so many priests and nuns in the assistance of revolutionaries had so incensed the DINA that a wave of repressive action against the Church had been provoked. The arrest of the prison chaplain and his two assistants seems to have been an act of aggression and revenge against the Church and especially against the Peace Committee, for there was no logical explanation for their detention.

Father Patricio Gajardo with two church workers, Loreto Pelissier and Aura Hermosilla were arrested on 10 November. They were detained by agents of the DINA and taken blindfolded to the Casa Grimaldi. Father Gajardo was interrogated for six hours and the two girls were both tortured with electrical shocks. One of them was raped. I met the girls when I was transferred to Tres Alamos and Father Gajardo when we both gave evidence at the fourth session of the International Commission of Enquiry into the crimes of the Military Junta, in Helsinki in March 1976.

Father Gajardo began his work as chaplain to the Santiago prisons in 1974, and he and his assistants helped the prisoners with a project in which they made handicrafts which were sold to raise money for their families. They worked in collaboration with the Committee of Peace which provided money for the materials, and their arrest was interpreted as an attack on the Peace Committee. A social worker was arrested on the same day and a week later the chief lawyer of the Committee, who had been employed to defend Father Gajardo, was also detained without charges and held in the same cell as his client.

The newspapers made much of the arrest of these church workers and published a photograph of a symbolic embroidery made by the women prisoners with the accusation that this was subversive material. The design showed two women kneeling before a flame, their heads united, and their hands tied behind their backs, symbolizing the unity between the prisoners and the unquenchable fire of their hope.

Although Father Gajardo and the two girls were released from prison shortly before I was, they have left the country because of fear of persecution by the DINA.

The following day, Friday 14 November, I was once more taken to the court to appear before the Fiscal.

39
The Reunion

But you and all the kind of Christ
Are ignorant and brave,
And you have wars you hardly win
And souls you hardly save.

I tell you naught for your comfort,
Yea, naught for your desire
Save that the sky grows darker yet
And the sea rises higher.

Night shall be thrice night over you,
And Heaven an iron cope.
Do you have joy without a cause,
Yea, faith without a hope?
                    G. K. Chesterton
                        *The Ballad of
                        the White Horse*

My third visit to the Fiscal was very different from the
previous ones. My transfer to the Casa Correccional and the
assurance by the Fiscal that I was now under the jurisdiction
and protection of the court had revived my hopes and
restored my sense of dignity as a person. This time I was
taken to the court by the prison authorities and the very fact
that they wore uniforms was somehow comforting after the
terrifying anonymity of the DINA with their machine guns
hidden in suitcases and pistols in underarm holsters. Now
all the world knew I was a prisoner and, escorted by a
wardress and a prison officer with only a small pistol at his
waist, I felt a measure of protection.

When the prison van arrived at the court and they opened
the back door to let me out there was an excited group of
reporters and photographers crowded round the van. I
looked at them with no particular emotion, for after having
been stripped and tortured and deprived of all liberty, the
invasion of privacy caused by the press seemed of no

consequence. Suddenly, among the sea of faces, I recognized the young reporter who had bought me a sandwich and gave him a broad smile. The resulting joyous photograph appeared in all the newspapers that night and I think must have comforted my friends and puzzled the DINA.

As I sat waiting outside the Fiscal's office a group of people came down the staircase that led to the basement office and there, incredibly, walking behind the guards from the men's prison, were three of my companions in crime, the priests who had helped the two fugitives and their wives. Heedless of the guards we hugged each other, and it was then that I realized that they were chained together by the wrists and also by the feet.

Shortly after their arrival I was called into the office. The Fiscal and his two assistants were weary after what had been a long week of hearings but they were as polite as ever, and assured themselves that I was being well treated. After a brief period of questioning I was asked to wait outside. I was told that the ban of incommunicado had been lifted and that I was free to speak.

Hardly able to believe that I was free to communicate with my friends I sat on the desk outside the Fiscal's office and tried to think of people to telephone. I could remember no number but my own and although I found the numbers of two of my friends in the directory they were not at home so, frustrated, I returned to my seat. By now the four priests were waiting outside as Father Carlos had been brought from the penitentiary where he had been held since we last met. Fathers Fernando Salas, Patricio Cariola and Gerard Whelan, who had been directly involved in the finding of asylum for the injured man and his wife, were still under orders not to talk but after a while Father Salas was called to the office and when he emerged he told me that the incommunicado order had been lifted for him too, so we were able to have a conversation.

We stood quietly talking in a corner of the hall. He told me that he and Father Cariola had presented themselves to the authorities the previous day and were now facing charges of hiding the revolutionaries. After a while Father Whelan was also permitted to talk and he told us how he had been arrested on the Sunday morning nearly two weeks before, when I had told the people who were torturing me that he had assisted Gutierrez. He had been held in solitary confinement in Cuatro Alamos since the day of his detention and, like the other two priests, was charged with hiding a revolutionary.

As we sat talking the British consul arrived and for the first time since my arrest I was able to speak to him in private. I told him all that had happened and of my treatment at the hands of the DINA, and also of my fears that if any protest was made it might weigh against my chances of release. We decided, therefore, to say nothing at this juncture in the hope that the court proceedings would soon be over and I would be released or deported. He told me that the lawyer who had been retained on my behalf after our first conversation had been active in trying to ensure that I was treated justly.

After a while he left to report the state of affairs to the ambassador and to cable their latest information about my torture to the Foreign Office. He told me that although he and the ambassador had not fully understood what I meant by 'mains' when we had spoken in the presence of the commandant of Cuatro Alamos, he had nevertheless relayed the full content of our conversation to London the same day. I was told after my return to the United Kingdom that the officials at the Foreign Office had guessed the meaning of my coded message long before they received the official confirmation from the consul.

Soon after Derek Fernyhough had left we had another visitor: one of the priests from San Ignacio. When he found that we had had no lunch he went off and returned half an hour later with an enormous packet of sandwiches and fruit. Never will I forget that meal: in the gloomy windowless hall outside the Fiscal's office we shared our lunch with the embarrassed warders. We sat there laughing and talking like a group of children at a picnic: three Chilean Jesuits, an American missionary priest, a Chilean worker priest and an English woman doctor, none of us knowing if we were going to be freed or given a long prison sentence. We had all of us learned to live for the moment and we rejoiced that we were alive, that the people we had helped were safely in asylum and in this unexpected bonus of being together for a few hours. Our guards, ill at ease, refused our offers of food, but eventually hunger overcame embarrassment and that day the bounty of the cook at San Ignacio and of the British consul fed not only the prisoners but the gaolers as well.

Late in the afternoon the Fiscal called me into his office and told me, '*Doctora*, I am setting you at liberty.'

I could not believe my ears and, standing there stupidly, said, 'You mean that I can go?'

'Yes,' he said.

Still incredulous I asked, 'I can go back to my home?'

He nodded.

'Back to my work?'

He smiled. 'Yes.' He explained that he had decided that I was not guilty of conspiring to hide the revolutionaries and that my only crime was that I had failed to report that I had treated a man with a bullet wound.

Completely dazed and still unbelieving I went out of the office to telephone the consul's home to tell him my news. He was out, but I spoke to his wife and asked if I might come to their house that night. She rejoiced at my news and promised to contact her husband. I explained to her that I had to return first to the women's prison so that I might sign the necessary papers before I was freed.

Jubilant, I returned to my friends outside the office and after we had hugged each other and nearly danced for joy they became serious and told me that I must seek asylum immediately. As I listened to them and watched their serious expressions I realized that I was entering into a new and dangerous state for I would soon cease to be the responsibility of the military court, and the DINA might well not be happy that I should go free to tell what they had done to me. We discussed what I should do. They told me that I must get to the British embassy as soon as possible and that I must not be without ambassadorial protection at any time. I realized the sense of what they said and saw how crazy had been my fleeting pipe-dream that I might return to my home and my dogs and my work.

By that time the priests had been joined by Hernan Montalegre, a young lawyer from the Peace Committee who was to represent them. He joined them in advising me that I must be extremely careful and offered to return with me to the Casa Correccional so that he could be with me until the consul arrived to take me away.

Just before six o'clock the Fiscal finished the day's investigation. Father Salas, Whelan and Carlos were free from the ban of incommunicado but their cases had not yet been resolved and they were led away to Capuchinos, an annexe of the men's prison. Father Cariola was to remain incommunicado and in solitary confinement. Before he was led away he asked for a Bible and that he should be brought communion in the morning. As he walked up the stairs, erect and dignified between the two guards, our bubble of happiness burst, and the crazy situation in which four priests and a doctor were in prison for helping a wounded man became a grim reality once more.

When all the priests had gone to their respective prisons my guards told me that we must return to the women's prison. In view of the fact that I had officially been liberated and that they had no transport they agreed that we should go with Señor Montalegre in his car. As we drove he and I talked in English and he told me that he was one of the lawyers of the Peace Committee and that since the coup over 12,000 people had received legal aid from the Committee's legal department.

I told him of the plight of Antonia who had been held without trial for over three years and he promised to go and see her and help speed up the processing of her case. When we arrived at the prison the consul was there to meet me and as I said goodbye to my new friend I little thought that before many months had passed he also would be a prisoner of the DINA, for he was arrested in May 1976 and held prisoner at first in Cuatro Alamos and later in Tres Alamos for six months until he was released in the amnesty of prisoners in December 1976.

I joined the consul in the prison office where he introduced me to the junior of the two lawyers who had been
retained to defend me. Together we explained to the man in
charge of the office that I had been freed and that I had
come to sign the necessary papers. So great had been my
faith in the Fiscal's authority that I was at first unconvinced
when he said that he had no power to let me go. He explained
that as I had been detained initially under the laws of the
state of siege I could not be released without the authoriza-
tion of the SENDET, the office which was responsible for
political detainees: and it was now seven o'clock on Friday
night and the office would be closed until Monday morning!

It was so absurd that I didn't know whether to laugh or
cry. The lawyer telephoned the Fiscal's office but there was
no reply: they had all gone home. For the next five hours we
sat there, the consul, the lawyer, the prison official and myself and telephoned all over Santiago trying to find someone
with authority to free me that night. At first the prospect of
two more days in this prison seemed intolerable and then
as the night wore on I ceased to care and said that if I was
to be released on Monday morning I didn't mind spending
the weekend with Antonia and the nuns and the ducklings.
The lawyer, however, pressed doggedly on and I think in
retrospect that he must have had some idea of the way the
situation was to evolve; if he knew, however, he said nothing
and reassured me that I would soon be safely in the consul's
house. He rang official after official and as we waited for
some general's aide to ring us back the telephone rang. It
was a friend with the news that there was a United Press
release that I was to be put on a plane at ten the following
morning.

Wearily we sat there but when midnight came my two
companions had to leave, for they must not be found outside
their homes after the one o'clock curfew and it would take
them over three quarters of an hour to drive home. Promising to come the following morning they bade me goodnight
and I followed the wardress to my cell, too tired to weep at
the unfairness of it all.

I was welcomed by Antonia and Maria and Sister

Augusta and we sat in the little room with the ducks while I ate the supper which they had saved for me and recounted the events of the day. Although sorry for me that I had not been freed, Antonia rejoiced that we would have time to talk over the weekend and I began to think that it would not be so terrible after all. It must have been one o'clock when I fell exhausted into bed and I slept peacefully, knowing that it could not be long before this nightmarish episode of my life was over.

The next morning I was allowed to join Antonia and Maria for breakfast. I sat and talked to them while they boiled water for coffee on the little electric ring and restored order to the chaos which the chickens had caused, for they had escaped from the cardboard box in the night and run amok in the workroom. Every now and then one would burst its way out and Antonia would chase it round the room until she had cornered it and, admonishing it severely, put it back in the box.

Breakfast over, I sat there relaxed and happy, listening to the squeaks of the ducklings and reading the reports of my day in court in the previous day's papers. My peace, however, was doomed to be short-lived, for the door opened suddenly to admit the most senior of the prison nuns who told me that I must collect my belongings as I was to be transferred immediately to Tres Alamos detention camp.

40

The Haggard Face of Fear

Help me, O God, when Death is near
To mock the haggard face of fear,
That when I fall – if fall I must –
My soul may triumph in the Dust.
Gerald Kirsh
The Soldier

At once I was possessed by a terror that defied all reason. The warmth and companionship of the previous day and the apparent certainty of release had driven a wedge in my emotional defence mechanism and I was totally unprepared for this new trial. For the first time I had been given an order by someone who did not have a gun in her hand and, frantically stalling for time, I told the nun that I refused to go before speaking to the consul. She asked me to come to the office to speak to the people who had come for me but, knowing quite well that this was the DINA, I stood my ground and told her that she would have to take me by force, and that if she touched me I would scream as she had never heard anyone scream before. I think she saw by the light in my eye that I meant what I said, for she retreated temporarily defeated.

I sat on the floor so that I could not be seen through the window and wondered what I should do. By now I was quite convinced that I was to be returned to the DINA and that this could mean further torture or death, and my mind was filled with crazy ideas of how I could escape. I considered hiding in the garden of the prison but I realized that if they really wanted me they would send an armed search party and that there was nowhere that I could hide. After a while the nun returned and said that the men insisted that I be brought. Near hysteria, I told her that they wanted to kill me and that if she took me to them she would be responsible for my death. Again, nonplussed, she retreated, and the two girls and Sister Augusta tried to console me by saying that probably it was just a formality and I would be released in a couple of days; but they were not really convincing for the procedure was so obviously strange.

After what seemed an eternity I was told that the consul had arrived. Still not sure that I was not being tricked, I followed the 'wardress to the office. There, sure enough, was Derek Fernyhough, and the young lawyer who had worked so hard the previous night to get permission for my release. The arrival of these two men who represented my freedom broke down my last reserves and sitting on an office stool I wept like a child. They tried hard to comfort me but it was obvious that they too were worried by this new development and I was in no mood to cling to faint or false hopes.

For nearly two hours the lawyer telephoned, trying to elucidate what was behind this new detention order when I had been officially freed, but on a Saturday morning in full summer there were few people in their offices and those who were either did not know or refused to say more than that an order had been issued at the highest level and that I was to be transferred to Tres Alamos.

Seeing that there was no way out and afraid that my behaviour would anger the authorities, the lawyer told me gently but firmly that I must pull myself together, because if they saw how frightened I was it would only make them suspicious that I had something to hide and my treatment would be worse. Seeing the logic of his argument I dried my tears, apologized and tried hard to regain my composure.

I was allowed to travel in the consul's car, so we set off, a strange convoy, the consul, two armed warders and myself in one car, the lawyer in his, with a prison vehicle behind, and drove the short distance to Tres Alamos.

I had been told by my fellow prisoners that whereas Cuatro Alamos pertained to the DINA, Tres Alamos was run by the regular police. It was no surprise, therefore, when we arrived at the new prison, to be received by uniformed policemen. We were taken into an office and told to wait. After a few minutes a senior official came out to meet us.

He greeted the consul with the respect due to the representative of a foreign government and assured him that I would
be allowed visitors the following Tuesday and that I was to
be held with all the other women detainees. He then politely
indicated that my escort should leave. I stood there helplessly, once more flanked by men with machine guns, while
my two protectors bade me farewell and promised to come
again as soon as was possible.

Weary beyond belief I sat on a chair while I answered the
prison officers' questions for their ledger. It seemed very
much to be a matter of routine to them, as indeed it was, for
there were over 600 prisoners in the camp at the time of my
detention. When they had finished their questions they sent
for the male nurse, who asked me without any more ado if I
was pregnant or if I had any bruises or wounds. The
answers being in the negative I was taken to another office
where once more I was asked my name, age, address,
profession, while a policeman typed out a record card.

Gradually I relaxed and again the form-filling comforted
me because I knew that people whose names are entered in
ledgers and on record cards are much less likely to disappear
than those who are whisked off at dead of night by men in
plain clothes. Before they had completed my card, however,
another officer came in and told me to follow him. We
returned to the office where they gave me the string bag of
clothes which the consul had brought for me and I was led
outside.

Wondering what the hurry was, and if perhaps the order
for my release had come through, I followed the guard out
into the rain and along the concrete path that led behind the
office. We stopped at a large sheet metal gate. He rang a bell
and after a short delay it was opened by a young man in
civilian clothes with a pistol in his belt. I think that if I had
been the sort of person who faints easily I would have given
an anguished moan and fallen to the ground in a crumpled
heap, for I recognized the man as one of the DINA guards
from Cuatro Alamos.

He seemed as surprised to see me as I was to see him, for
he asked the policeman who was escorting me why he had

brought me, but the reply left neither of us any the wiser. He merely said, 'Sudden order from the Ministry of the Interior,' and handed me over like a postman delivering a parcel.

I stood there completely dazed until, taking me by the arm, the young man led me out of the rain and I found myself once more in the office of Cuatro Alamos.

41

Two by Two

Two by two
four unjust metres
a gift from the four generals.

My solitude knows this world:
Two by two
four square metres in this gaol
is the justice of the generals.
From today on my cell is incommunicado,
prisoner without communication,
a person facing the world
not to be communicated.

Anonymous
From a Chilean prison, 22 September 1973

The ten days that followed were not easy ones. Once more alone, I struggled to maintain my composure, for no one knew what was to happen to me, and I saw only the camp commander and the guards. Day followed day without news. My world was limited by the four walls of my cell and the small patch of dried grass that separated my window from the immense concrete wall that surrounded the barracks.

After the initial shock of finding myself once more in the power of the DINA, I took stock of my situation. This time things were different, for I had a few books and a string bag full of clothes provided by my kind American friends and brought to me by the consul. Sally had made herself responsible for my well-being and as I unpacked the bag I marvelled at her careful thought. One by one I laid my possessions along the top of the other bunk and fingered them lovingly.

Never had I felt so rich and never had simple things seemed so wonderful. There was a hairbrush, a comb, a tooth-brush, toothpaste, deodorant, soap, new underwear, two shirts, a sweater, trousers and pyjamas. It is hard to convey without sounding stupid and sentimental just how much those articles meant to me. Ten days spent without a tooth-brush or a change of clothing had made me appreciate their possession in a way I had never imagined. Each time I was allowed to go to the bathroom I solemnly carried my toilet articles with me, and it was only after a week that I realized that the reason my face was so dry and sore was that, obsessed by the richness of owning a bar of soap, I was washing it too frequently!

Far more than the mere possession of these things was the knowledge of the love and caring that had gone into their collection. Nothing had been forgotten and every time I looked at my riches they spoke to me of the love of the person who had thought so carefully of what I needed.

In addition to the clothes and other things Sally had sent me a Bible in English and a few books. This indeed was riches and I was able to organize my day into periods of study, relaxation and prayer. The officials had been so taken by surprise when I arrived that they had forgotten to take away my watch. Thus I was able to make a timetable of activities so that my day was busy and my life purposeful.

It is, perhaps, one of the great miracles and mysteries of life that people are so resilient in adapting to new ways of life. Once more I established a routine, and I think that the discipline that I imposed upon myself was very important in the maintenance of my morale and sanity.

Each morning I woke to the sound of the men being taken to the bathroom and after I had dressed I stood on the chair beside my bed and watched the sun rise behind the mountains. At first the guards were suspicious to find me positioned thus at the window, but they became used to it and made no comment when they came to let me out to the bathroom.

When breakfast came I sat on my chair, and after a long and ceremonial grace ate as much of the bread as I could manage, keeping half of my tea for later on in the morning when I knew I would be hungry again. The previous day's crusts were then carefully crumbled and put on the window sill for the sparrows. These little birds, fed by successive groups of prisoners, were absurdly tame and would dive down to fetch their breakfast. Like Sally's gifts the sparrows became immensely important to my happiness, for they were the only living creatures with which I had any contact who counted as friends rather than foe.

After breakfast I allotted time to studying the Bible, and for the first time in my life set out to read the Old Testament from the beginning. Sally had given me a very modern, popular translation of the Bible and though I missed the poetry of the old translation I was fascinated by the people and events who, for the first time, became life-sized to me.

Reading the Bible, like praying, required a degree of discipline that surprised me. It was much easier to lie on my bunk and daydream or read one of the two precious novels, but I felt very strongly that there must be an order to my life, and now that I had so much time on my hands I knew as before that I must spend much time in prayer. It was curiously difficult, perhaps because I was too unsettled and frightened, but I had learned long ago that prayer depends on the will and not on the emotions. So I gave my time and my anguish to God and tried to understand what it was he wanted of me.

As before, it somehow became clear that he wanted me to have faith in his plans for me, to be supple in his hands and happy to accept whatever he sent. I knew quite well that this followed on from the decision I had made that day in the retreat house when I lay on the pile of leaves at the bottom of the garden and in my mind and heart wrote out the cheque to God in which the price to be paid was left to the drawer.

Although God was not particularly real to me these days in solitary confinement, my cheque was so real that I could as good as see it. There were moments when the folly of my actions obsessed me, and I would snatch the cheque from the hands that held it so lightly and tear it up. Then slowly I took the pieces and sellotaped them together and once more offered my gift. Again and again I weakened but always there was something that drove me to stoop and withdraw the crumpled slip from the wastepaper basket where I had hurled it, and carefully smoothing out the creases, sign once more to make it legal tender.

Day after day I fought the battle until the crisp slip so boldly signed that day in March was crumpled and smeared with my tears and patched together, but still valid.

Four or five days after my arrival the consul was allowed to visit me again. As before, the interview was conducted in the presence of the prison commander, and we were not permitted to speak in English. Even letters from my family had to be translated into Spanish and read to me in the presence of the officials. It seemed that there was no news and it was hard to be of good heart, though in my more optimistic moments I felt sure that it could not be many days before I was released.

When my two novels had each been read for the second time, and I wearied of the Bible, I delighted in reading the many messages painstakingly scratched on the walls and ceiling of my cell. I wish I had committed them to memory for they were incredibly moving and inspiring. The majority were written for the benefit of others, for they were messages of hopé and encouragement and admonitions not to lose heart for truth and justice would triumph. I recall particularly the ones that were written on the wall by someone sitting on the upper bunk where I spent most of my day: 'Remember that the barbed wire is only a piece of metal.' There was another which read, 'I too have sat in this corner and watched the sparrows. Take heart. At least they do not blindfold us here.'

I marvelled at the courage of these prisoners whom probably I would never know, and tried to be worthy of them, for despair would be a betrayal of the spirit of a people who remained unconquered and unconquerable despite torture, imprisonment and death.

> When they want
> us to keep being a number
> without a soul, destroyed
> they forget

that though everything
may be lost on the way:
homes, goods, so many broken lies
they forget
that the Chilean
is made of oak and luma
never bent by a storm.

They forget
that in the sky
there is an indestructible star,
our star,
which, like that
of two thousand years ago
will always be
our goal, our course and our guide.

Anonymous
Tres Alamos, March 1975

42

Nor Iron Bars a Cage

Stone walls do not a prison make
Nor iron bars a cage;
Minds innocent and quiet take
That for an hermitage;
If I have freedom in my love
And in my soul am free,
Angels alone, that soar above,
Enjoy such liberty.

Richard Lovelace
To Althea from Prison

On Friday 21 November the door of my cell opened and the commander said, 'I've brought you some company.' Javiera and I feigned indifference until the door closed and then fell upon each other and did a sort of Indian war dance in the narrow space between the two bunks. The middle-aged woman who had accompanied Javiera watched us in bewilderment until my friend introduced us: this was Isabel who had been detained a few days previously and had been transferred with Javiera from the Villa Grimaldi.

Javiera was paler and must have lost a stone in weight since I had last seen her sixteen days previously. As always she was in high spirits and gave a whoop of delight when she saw my newly acquired wealth. Over a month had passed since her detention and her clothes were in a worse state than mine. Her enthusiasm reached new heights at the sight of the books but was rapidly dampened when she saw that they were in English.

After the tour of inspection of all my – now our – possessions she pronounced herself well pleased though she berated me for spreading myself over all four bunks in such a disorderly fashion. I hastily tidied up and after she and Isabel had laid claim to their respective bunks we settled down to talk. She told me that after I had been taken away she had

remained alone in the Casa Grimaldi for many days. She
said little of how she had been treated except that it had
been very bad. They had abandoned the *parrilla* as she had
apparently had a cardiac arrest during the first interrogation, and had held her head under water in the bath. I found
this so appalling that it was difficult to believe, but I know
now that this is one of the commonest 'aids to interrogation'
employed in Latin America. Worst of all, they had beaten
her so much that she had lost the two-month pregnancy that
had made her so radiantly happy when I had first met her.

There were now many new prisoners in the Casa Grimaldi, and in the women's dormitory remained an elderly
woman and three girls. Javiera had been there when the
Ganga Torres family was detained, and she told me how she
had heard one of them being tortured and then the next day
had heard the lunchtime news telling of his death in a gun
battle with the police on the outskirts of Santiago. Most
important for her was the fact that Andres was alive and
well, but she was worried because he had not been transferred with her group of prisoners that day. She did not
know if anyone had been able to get word to their families
that they were still alive, for though Francisca had memorized her address we did not know if she had been transferred
yet to Tres Alamos where she would be able to see her family.

After the most urgent exchange of news we tried to
comfort Isabel who seemed very depressed. She was an
auxiliary nurse whose job it was to take blood from the out-
patients in one of the large city hospitals. It seemed that her
only crime had been that she had said to her patients, 'The
left arm, please. The blood is better in the left arm.' This
stupid piece of defiance of the four generals and their regime
had labelled her as an antagonist and she had been arrested
at the hospital and taken to the Grimaldi. She showed me the
burns on her breasts where they had applied the current,
accusing her of being a member of a communist cell. She
was desperate to get a message to her mother who was
elderly and lived alone, so Javiera and I memorized the
address in case one of us was suddenly released.

That night we went to bed exhausted, for we had talked

without ceasing, and I was glad to be able to be quiet and alone with my thoughts.

The next day my two friends donned my spare clothes and washed their own so that the cell began to look like a Chinese laundry. Each day we washed something, not only to keep ourselves clean but also because it meant a little more time away from the tiny cell. Each visit to the bathroom was supervised by an armed guard but, emboldened by my status as a relatively long-stay prisoner, I asked them to leave me alone while I washed. Grudgingly they shifted a little way up the corridor, but the rules were strict, and it was not worth their while to break them. The visits to the bathroom had great importance for Javiera as this was the only place where messages were left. Doors and walls were covered with names or brief messages, poignant in their simplicity: 'I am looking for my brother Mario . . . Aminie Calderón Tapia.' I met the writer of this message when I was moved to Tres Alamos. Her brother is still missing.

Mario Calderón is one of two thousand prisoners who have disappeared since the coup. Just why some people disappeared and others were sent to the detention camps is not clear. Perhaps someone turned the current up too high and they died on the *parrilla*, or perhaps their heads were held under water too long. Perhaps they are hidden in barracks or secret prisons: who knows? What is certain is that the anguish of their families is without end.

In the two days that followed I spent many hours in conversation with Javiera. Isabel joined in from time to time, and then would lie with her back to us sleeping, or worrying about her mother. The intensity of our conversation was due to the fact that Javiera had decided that this was an excellent opportunity to broaden her education and learn the basic truths of Christianity. A deeply committed Marxist, she was in no way wavering from her convictions, but she wanted to know what it was that had made me able to stand up to adversity in more or less the same way as herself.

Her total honesty and lack of all restraint in asking questions was completely disarming. She genuinely wanted to know, and when she found what I told her stupid or peculiar, or if she didn't understand, she said so. Educated at a progressive left-wing school, she knew far more than I did about matters historical or sociological, but religion does not seem to have featured in the curriculum, and her ignorance was almost complete.

Never good at explaining the mysteries of my faith, and greatly hampered by my inadequate command of Spanish, I searched for words to explain the beliefs that were so important to me that I felt prepared to die for them. She was a good listener and so completely open minded that after a while I relaxed and tried to put into language that she would understand my mysterious experience of the existence of God: an experience that could not be explained or shared but which was so powerful that it gave a meaning to life that I longed to share.

Inevitably she asked me if it was true that I planned to be a nun and, incandescent with her love for Andres, asked how I could bear not to marry. The directness of her question caught me by surprise, but she was so honest in her search to understand that I could only answer her as truthfully as I was able. I told her that I had always thought that I would marry and that I had been in love more than once but that in some indefinable way I felt that I was called to serve God as a single person and that at times it seemed bitterly hard and unfair. I tried to explain too that by not giving my love to one man my heart remained open to the love of all men, and that I believed that I would grow and mature in love and compassion as I gave myself freely to God and to man.

If she found me crazy she did not say so, though I did not expect her to understand something which I barely understood myself.

It was easier to talk about the Church in general and I told her of the change in attitude of the Church in Latin America since the Conference of Medellín: a change which demanded a personal conversion and a life of commitment to the oppressed every bit as demanding as her own.

On and on we talked, for with the intensity of her eighteen years Javiera was determined to understand this way of life which she had hitherto thought unworthy of her consideration. In a constant sharing dialogue we found that there was much that we had in common. She was at first surprised that I did not hate the men who had hurt us and who held us prisoner, but when I explained my feeling that it was they who were prisoners rather than us, she agreed. The freedom of spirit which we enjoyed was something that our captors did not possess, and which they could not wrest from us.

Prisoners together in this bare cell, with not even the freedom to go to the bathroom when we chose, we knew quite well that it was the DINA who were in chains. Always busy with the practical things of life, I had rarely given myself to the consideration of the eternal truths. Now, sprawled out on this narrow bunk, I discussed the meaning of freedom and slavery with Javiera. So recently stripped of all our possessions we rejoiced in the freedom of spirit that this violent separation had brought to us and, seeing with new eyes how we had been slaves to our limited wealth, we mourned for the truly rich who lived behind walls so high that their chances of escape were minimal.

Mostly, though, we mourned for our torturers and the men who found the torture justifiable. What sort of lives did they lead, these men? How could they wash the blood off their hands and return to sit with their wives and play with their children? Did they sleep peacefully at night or did they lie awake and hear the screams of the men and women they had hurt?

It is said that many of the people who perform the actual physical acts of violence are drawn from the criminal classes, and it was perhaps understandable that people of low intelligence with a sadistic streak could become accustomed to the systematic infliction of pain. Far more difficult to understand was how the senior officers came to terms with their consciences and whether or not they suffered remorse.

. . . you cannot lay remorse upon the innocent nor lift it from the heart of the guilty. Unbidden shall it call in the night that men may wake and gaze upon themselves.

Kahlil Gilbran
The Prophet

So the days passed, intense and filled with the joy of companionship after so many days alone. I learned many things from Javiera and Isabel, both about them and about myself. It was not always easy to keep the peace between the three of us for Isabel, nearly 35 years older than Javiera, felt that the younger girl looked down on her for her lack of education. This was in no way the truth and I found that while I was pleasant to Isabel out of a strong sense of duty Javiera seemed to have a spontaneous love and caring that made me ashamed of myself.

I was to have my self-centredness exposed by the innate other-centredness of my fellow prisoners again and again in the weeks that followed. I remember particularly one small incident during my time with Javiera and Isabel. The older woman was asleep, a sad figure, her pale face blotched with tears and anxiety, and I was thankful that I was momentarily freed of the responsibility of caring for her. With Javiera, however, caring was not a face that she put on like a doctor's white coat, for she suddenly got up and, whispering that Isabel would catch cold while she was asleep, carefully covered her with a blanket. It was the little acts of kindness such as this that convinced me that Javiera and the other young revolutionaries were motivated by a deep loving care for their fellows and that they obeyed more truly and more instinctively than any Christian I knew the most devastating of Christ's commandments, 'You shall love your neighbour as yourself.'

43
Tres Alamos

The whole group of believers was united
heart and soul; no one claimed for his
own use anything that he had, as everything
that they owned was held in common.

Acts 4:32

Late in the morning of Monday 24 November one of the
guards came into the cell and said with the brusqueness that
was habitual to them, 'Get your things together.' Torn
between the fear of uncertainty and the hope of release I
gathered my books and a change of clothes and, leaving the
rest of my treasures for Javiera and Isabel, hugged them
goodbye and followed him out into the corridor. He led me
into the office and there I found myself with two girls that I
had not met before. They appeared to be in their middle
twenties and were dressed as I was in shirts and jeans. Their
long hair, sadly unwashed, indicated that they had been
prisoners for some time.

The commander was in good spirits as he supervised the
signing of the release forms. Silently we signed the form
which stated that we were being set at liberty in the vicinity
of our houses and that we had been well treated. Their
watches and chains and crosses were returned to them and
the commander was rather peeved to find that he had
forgotten to take mine away from me when I was transferred from the Casa Correccional. Then, shepherding us
out like a small flock of sheep, he led us down the concrete
path until we came to the main office of Tres Alamos. (I
never fully understood the layout of this prison, apart from
the fact that Cuatro Alamos lies completely within the
compound of Tres Alamos, but is surrounded by a very high
wall and is under the administration of the DINA rather
than the police.)

After being handed over to a policeman with the inevitable machine gun we were led across a wide expanse of barren ground to a wooden barracks where we were received by a woman guard. The door of the barracks was opened and, as soon as we passed through, slammed behind us.

I don't know what I had expected to find but this apparently vast sea of smiling faces was totally unexpected. I was hugged and kissed and greeted by name until I was quite exhausted and there, suddenly, among the crowd I recognized Francisca, Magdalena and Esther. They were sunburned and radiant and we greeted each other with the wild joy of friends who had never expected to meet again. They led me to a table and as soon as I had sat down a plate of salad was placed before me and I was told to eat.

Still dazed, I pushed my hair out of my eyes and asked if anyone had a hair grip. Immediately the girl opposite me removed a clip from her own hair and handed it to me. This was the beginning of my introduction to a life where all things were shared, and it was not until I had used this clip for three weeks that I discovered that it was the only one this girl had.

My two companions were seated at another table likewise surrounded by new and old friends and eating the lunch which mysteriously appeared. We had not had a chance to speak to each other but I was told that they were Loreto and Aura, two girls who worked for the Committee for Peace and who had been arrested in the reprisals that followed the Malloca affair. I discovered that they had been in the room next to mine and that it was they who had sung the Hymn of Joy with Javiera and Isabel and me each evening when the guards seemed safely out of the way. It was with them that we had communicated several times each day by banging on the wall, and Javiera had managed to have a brief conversation by whispering close to the window.

After lunch I was taken to my room and again the spirit of the community took me by surprise for they asked, 'Which bunk would you like?' I looked at them and then at the bunks. There were six bunks and each of them was obviously occupied, for the user's belongings were neatly arranged at the foot of the bed or in bags nailed to the wall. Again they asked me 'Which one would you like?' and, still not understanding, I said, 'But which one is vacant?' Then they explained. There were more prisoners than bunks, so that someone would have to share or else sleep on the floor. As I was the newest arrival I was to have a bunk to myself and was given the privilege of choosing where I would like to sleep.

The bunks were made of wood and in tiers of three. Not feeling sufficiently agile to climb to the highest I chose a second-level one. This belonged to Christina and immediately she cleared away her things and stacked them in a corner so that I had somewhere to lie and to put my things.

The bedrooms were very small and were built without windows. They measured 2.5 × 2.8 metres, and were 2.8 metres high, which gave just over one square metre per person. The bunks were made like a ship's bunk and were very narrow. They were unsprung, being constructed entirely of wood, and were so close together that it was not possible to sit up in bed.

The prison provided a mattress and a couple of blankets for each prisoners, and each girl had a pair of sheets from home. One of the girls gave me a clean pair of sheets and together we made up my bed. After nearly three weeks of sleeping in dirty prison blankets the prospect of sleeping between sheets was a marvellous one.

Once my base was firmly established the members of my room took me on a tour of our quarters. It had been purpose built as a concentration camp and the small dormitories were constructed so that they enclosed a square patio. This measured fourteen metres by ten (we measured it a few days before I was released) and there was a wooden lean-to which provided shelter from the sun and the rain along each side of the square.

In the centre of one side of the square was the washroom. It was well constructed, and the girls kept it spotlessly clean. They explained to me that all the prisoners took it in turn as members of either the cleaning squad or the team which prepared the food. There was a row of wash basins along one wall and behind the lavatories two communal showers. As we inspected the washing facilities the girls said, 'You must be longing to have a shower. Why don't you have one now?'

My brand new sense of well-being deserted me. How could I tell these girls that I was a plutocratic self-indulgent bather rather than a spartan showerer and that the thought of a cold shower filled me with horror. I decided that I could only submit with good grace and, trying to look happy, I marched off to the bath house with the communal soap and shower cap and a borrowed towel.

I have never considered myself a prude, but I was educated in an Australian convent school where we dressed and undressed decorously behind our dressing gowns and were not expected to romp joyously together in the changing rooms as is the custom in many schools. Thus it was that at the age of 38 I had my first shower in a communal bathroom. Not so much embarrassed as acutely ill at ease I did my best to laugh my way through it, but fate was not on my side for no sooner had I covered myself in soap than the water ceased to flow because of the people doing their washing outside! After this my trip to the bath house became my private purgatory and inevitably my room mates found out how much I hated it and made it their business to ensure that I didn't miss a day!

Later in the day my new friends explained to me the lines upon which the camp was run. There were at that time 120 women, most of them in their early twenties and the great majority drawn from the professions. Many of them had been in prison for over a year and there were a few who had been there over eighteen months. Because this was a permanent and publicly recognized detention camp conditions were very much better than in Cuatro Alamos although, as I was to experience later, there was much that fell far below the conditions laid down for political prisoners in international agreements.

The greatest problem was the food. The food for all the

prisoners was prepared in a central kitchen, and either because of lack of funds or as a deliberate repressive measure, it was grossly deficient in quality – the same diet, in fact, as we had had in Cuatro Alamos. To maintain the health of their loved ones the prisoners' families (who were allowed to visit twice a week) brought eggs, fruit, vegetables and tinned fish.

In the early days after the establishment of Tres Alamos the prisoners kept the gifts brought by their relations until it was recognized that the families of some of the prisoners were in such straitened circumstances that they were going hungry themselves in order to bring food for their daughter or wife. It was decided, therefore, to pool all the provisions that were brought and redistribute them according to the needs of the prisoners. It soon became apparent that some of the women required a special diet. Several of them were pregnant and as such needed supplements of milk and protein, and some had gastric ulcers or gall bladder disease, making a special diet imperative. Those women who had spent a long time in the Villa Grimaldi or in the Incommunicado block and those who had suffered haemorrhages as a result of torture required special care if they were to regain their health. Attention to the diet of this group of prisoners was doubly important as they were precisely the women who were most at risk of being returned to the Villa Grimaldi if it was thought that more information could be extracted from them. An example of this group of 'high risk' prisoners was Gladys Diaz, a journalist who was also a high ranking member of the MIR, and who spent three months in the Villa Grimaldi on grossly inadequate diet and who was frequently returned there as an act of reprisal when her case was publicized abroad.

The sharing of the food gradually extended to include a sharing of toilet articles among the inhabitants of the different rooms. This made for a much smoother running of the camp, as each group of six or ten girls became responsible for maintaining themselves with sufficient toothpaste, detergent, etc. Clothes were shared, though to a lesser degree. It was soon found that a common pool of clothes was essential as all new prisoners arrived only in the clothes in which they had been detained, and they were always desperately in need of clean ones. Those girls who felt that they had sufficient therefore donated what they could spare to 'the wardrobe', and when someone was released she had to leave what she could spare behind for those who were so surely to take her place.

The greatest triumph in community living was achieved when it was decided to share the cigarettes. Chileans smoke heavily and smokers who live under conditions of great stress feel the deprivation of cigarettes perhaps more acutely than anything else. People were graded according to the need they felt to smoke, and were given a weekly allowance. Chocolates and sweets were shared in a similar fashion, though we were all urged to explain as far as possible to our friends and families that it was better to bring fruit or vegetables rather than inessentials such as sweets.

By some whim of the authorities families were only allowed to bring supplies on one of the two weekly visits, so that in the hot weather there was a considerable problem in preventing the perishable goods deteriorating before the week was over. It was decided, therefore, to reserve one of the two shower areas for the storage of the fruit and vegetables. The bathroom was the coolest place in the camp and anyway there was no room in the tiny cells which each housed six or eight prisoners.

The role of administrator of the food and diets was held by different prisoners in turn. A sixth year medical student was in charge of the overall administration of the food for two months and each week one girl was nominated the 'economist' and was responsible for deciding on each day's menu and which of the fruit should be eaten first. Anyone who was hungry between meals had to ask permission of the economist for a biscuit or other snack and on the one occasion when someone helped herself without asking, the community was deeply shocked.

44

Threads Drawn from the Heart

And what is it to work with love?
It is to weave the cloth with threads drawn from your
    heart, even as if your beloved were to wear that
    cloth.

Kahlil Gibran
The Prophet

Every night we were in bed by eleven for, glorying in the little power given to them, the wardresses were strict in their enforcement of the prison rules. Anyone found out of bed, or talking or smoking, was punished by the suspension of the visit of their family, or if they dared to protest, a day in the *calabozo*, a punishment cell.

As I lay in the dark on the first night and watched the glow of forbidden cigarettes, I tried to digest the experiences of the day and I was thankful that no one could see the tears of self-pity that flowed unbidden down my cheeks. After supper I had spoken at length to Francisca and when I had told her that I was certain that I would only be in the camp for a few days she had shaken her head and told me gently that it was the general opinion that I would be detained for two or three months. I stared at her unbelieving as she told me that they had come to the conclusion that the Chilean government would never risk setting me at liberty until the New Year hearings of the United Nations at Geneva were over. The last hearing, in which the Junta had been publicly condemned for the 'flagrant disregard of human rights', had been given wide publicity in Chile, and my release, they thought, would therefore be delayed until after the next hearing.

Smiling, she told me that three months was a very short time, and that most of them would be in prison for a year or more. Finally, with the seriousness that characterized these youthful world-changers, she said that experience of life in the community would be very good for me as, like all of them, I had much to learn.

I began to experience that night a sense of conflict that was to torment me for the whole of my stay in Tres Alamos, and which even in England does not let me rest. Fêted and loved as the '*gringa*' who had suffered for their cause, and thus accepted as one of them, I longed to be as other-centred and self-disciplined as they, and yet I found myself naturally expecting the preferential treatment, love and respect that was accorded to me. To be told that I could benefit from a period of this spartan community life with the unspoken implication that I had to learn about the war with self-indulgence filled me with an anguish that shamed me because I knew that they were right.

In bed that night I fought the battle which always seems so absurdly difficult: the fight to be reasonable. I knew that I was incredibly lucky to be alive, and that the experience of living with and getting to know these girls was a privilege that money could not buy. I knew, too, that unless something very unexpected happened, I was safe, and that I would ultimately be released. I realized that, much as I liked to see myself as one of this brave band of women, mine was nothing more than a temporary and superficial partici-pation in their situation, for I would return to my country and my loved ones and pick up the threads of my life. Not for me was the anguish of fears for a missing brother or sweetheart or the knowledge that my family was going hungry to keep me alive. For me release would signify per-manent reunion with my family; for my companions it meant freedom but also heart-rending farewells to parents whom they would never see again, as they set off to rebuild their lives in whatever country would accept them. The knowledge of how lucky I was gave me small comfort that night and I could have lain on the ground and screamed like a spoilt child, 'I want to go home.'

Sleep magically reknit the ravell'd sleave of my care, and I rose in the morning resolved to learn all that I could from my new friends. We breakfasted at the long wooden tables which were ranged round the patio and the standard prison breakfast was greatly improved by the addition of Nescafé to the nondescript hot liquid sent from the kitchen and of margarine for the bread. I found myself sitting opposite the girl who had given me her hairclip. This was Lucinda, a girl of rare artistic ability whom I soon grew to love for her deep sensitivity, unfailing good humour and kindness.

Breakfast was served by a team of girls whose turn it was to work that day. There were six or eight of them and, under the direction of one of the older members of the community and the 'economist', they prepared and served the meals and washed up afterwards. It was a good system for, although it meant a day of very hard work, it only came every eight or ten days as everyone took their turn according to the rota.

After breakfast there was quiet activity while beds were made and teeth cleaned then, promptly at nine o'clock, the 'workshops' began. Three of the four long wooden tables were occupied, each by a group of girls doing a different type of craft work. At first I thought this was occupational therapy until it was explained to me that the goods made were sold and each worker was paid a wage after new materials had been purchased. Many of the girls were married and had small children; some of their husbands were unemployed, but a greater proportion of them were also in detention, and some of them had disappeared. The children therefore were cared for by the girls' parents or by their in-laws, and in many cases there was a real need for the small contributions they were able to make by selling their work.

There were five workshops which produced in turn sandals, fine leather goods, articles of crochet, soft toys and embroidered blouses. I learned much from the girls who ran these workshops because shortage of money and materials had taught them to improvise in a way that we, in our affluent society, have forgotten. Most important of all, however, I learned about working in a team. Always inordinately proud of my achievements I like to make things on my own, and 'all me own work' has long been a saying in my family. It was therefore totally alien to me to finish off something begun by someone less skilled, unless, of course, *I* was bountifully assisting *them*. Likewise, I did not like to have someone else touch my work, for if their help was skilled I could not claim the finished article as my own, and if they were less skilled, then I feared that my handiwork would be spoiled.

This attitude was outside my friends' comprehension. Each of them worked happily, apparently uncomplicated by such emotions, doing that part of the work that they did best or which was allotted to them by the team supervisor. Thus in the embroidery workshop my friend Lucinda worked in the design section, inventing and modifying designs to be embroidered on the blouses, while a myriad of other workers painstakingly washed the material, ironed it, cut it out and made the blouses, and then traced the patterns on the fabric. All over the outside patio (for we

Embroidery work at Tres Alamos, 1975

were allowed outside at the discretion of the wardress) girls sat in groups meticulously embroidering the peasant-style blouses with fine brightly-coloured wools. Each Friday morning the finished garments were once more washed and ironed and given to the visiting families so that they could be sold among the tight circle of friends of the families of the detainees. In 1976 many of these blouses were exported and sold at exhibitions in support of the prisoners in different countries. They are a true example of the artistic work produced in bleak detention camps throughout the length of Chile, a flowering in the desert that bears witness to the unquenchable flame of the human spirit.

The urge to create something lovely burned like a fire in all the prisons. Underfed and lonely in the snows of Dawson Island the first political prisoners of the Junta, lawyers, doctors, professors and cabinet ministers produced engraved pendants of a haunting loveliness from the finely polished stones that they picked up from the ground under their feet. Later, the men of Chacabuco, the big concentration camp in the northern desert of Chile, produced copper rings made from the wire that had imprisoned them, and engraved pendants from worthless coins.

Perhaps the most fascinating and original of the prison arts was the work in bone. The Chilean national dish is *cazuela*, a beef stew in which a piece of meat is served on the bone in the stock in which it has been cooked, accompanied by a potato and a piece of pumpkin. The prisoners found that it was possible to work with the dried bones and thereafter families were commissioned to bring in the bones from the Sunday *cazuela* and they were carefully washed and dried in the sun and stored until they were needed. It was a skilled art, requiring much patience. The object to be 'carved' was drawn on the bone and then cut out with a fine saw. This could take an hour or more, depending upon the hardness of the bone and the skill of the worker. It was then filed smooth and finally sandpapered and lastly polished with an abrasive paste made from zinc oxide powder or, if there was none available, toothpaste. Only certain prisoners found this work to their taste, but they produced the most lovely pendants of which the favourite designs were the dove of peace, or the clenched fist that signified the resistance of the Chilean people. I joined the bone carvers and made a number of crosses which I gave away to my friends. The last and most successful I could not bring myself to give away and when I was interviewed at the airport one of the newspapers reported that I was wearing two crosses, one gold and the other ivory!

The art of the detention camps was fired by two deep human needs: the desire to give to loved ones, and the need to express the multitude of feelings of sorrow and joy, anger, despair and an ever-flowering hope. Because of the constant repression there developed a highly symbolic art, and hidden away because of the intermittent raids were drawings and poetry in which the deepest emotions were allowed to cry out. So strict was the self-imposed emotional discipline to maintain morale that no tears were shed or loved ones publicly mourned, but hearts were poured out on paper and anger exhausted in carving symbols of the fight for freedom.

Many of the poems have been smuggled out and they are a poignant testimony of the anguish in which they were composed. The following poem was written in July 1974 in the public gaol in Santiago where men are herded into dark cells where it is hard not to succumb to bitterness and despair:

> There,
> where the light of the sun
> lost itself
> more than a century ago,
> where all gaiety
> is impossible
> and any smile
> is a grimace of irony,
> where the stone stench of darkness
> inhabits those corners
> even the spiders
> have abandoned as inhospitable,

and where human pain eludes
that which can be called human
and enters the category
of the unprintable . . .
There, I am writing.

From the scorched, disused saltpetre mine of the desert camp of Chacabuco comes the cry of a coal miner, over a thousand miles from his wife and children in the green southern town of Lota near Concepción.

I want my bread, I want the air beyond this wall of wire.
I look out into the distance over the white roofs of earth
and can just barely see
cars crossing the nitrous pampa
from north to south and from south to north,
the frontier train on the small tracks
like a child's toy on the hillside . . .
My hope!
I turn to look at everything:
the gay travelling couple,
the son encountering his mother
the father who is returning,
the blind one who is singing for money
and who never sees the combat planes
quickly devour space, soldiers of the air at war.
I want to return to my earth:
to drink in my hand
the water which has surrendered itself
to the tranquillity of raindrops,
to contemplate the forest,
to stretch out on the grasses
to listen to the trill of birds
to kiss the wheat,
to smell herbs freshly nibbled off branches
by the goat on the rocky crag,
to hear the barking of a dog
or the mooing of a cow.
Such joy!
The afternoon arrives whistling tranquil tunes

and singing songs of freedom.
Walking in the streets without concealing my face
I, miner of Lota, with joyous steps,
lift my sooty face
and with my breast warmed by the heat
extracted from the inner recesses of the earth
by my fist and my soul
reach my home
and joyfully encounter my wife waiting at the door
the children catching at her hem
her smile and her awaited kiss
without room for a tear.
May the darkness be not so dark
and may hatred not close our souls.

So much of this poetry is written in blood and tears for children, husbands and wives. This is a message to his children from a man who like so many was imprisoned because he taught that all men are created equal.

SPEAKING WITH THE CHILDREN

It so happens that I won't be home tomorrow either
and I'll continue beneath the night
that eclipses and erodes
the profiles of the world I know.

If it comes to pass
that I get lost during the night
and don't find the road back home,
I want you to know the reasons for my absence.

I have learned and I have taught that a person is free,
and now I awaken to the rattling of irons and bolts,
Because I loved culture
and humanity's inheritance
the flames have fed themselves with my books.

I did not stain my spirit with hatred,
but I have seen the anguish
of the epileptic terror
of naked men being electrocuted.

I returned to the roads the peasants used,
speaking of a life without miseries.
I explained that work brings dignity
that there is no bread at all
without a sheaf of wheat made noble
by the planting of a seed into the earth
by a simple hand.
For this, among other things,
it so happens
that I won't be home again tomorrow either
but continue beneath the night.

Doctors, lawyers, teachers, and all the other professional people who had taught 'that work brings dignity' now turned their hands and their hearts to manual labour, and almost overnight intellectuals became craftsmen. I was fascinated by the sandal workshop not only because the finished products were charming, but because of the improvisation with materials. The soles of the sandals were made from old car tyres, and the designs on the leather drawn with felt pens. Greek designs taken from some old book were adapted and tooled on to the leather and then the colours picked out in brilliant reds and greens. When the pens ran dry they were refuelled with cologne for the girls had found that the spirit was a solvent for the dye.

Although the majority of the prisoners worked, there was no obligation and some of those who had no need to earn money preferred to work on their own. When I had settled in I was delighted at the wide range of crafts, for I have always loved to work with my hands. After years of being too busy either studying or working to be creative I threw myself into a multitude of activities. In the first few days I was severely frustrated by lack of materials, for though I was surrounded by a wealth of fabric, wool and leather, I quickly found that it was all spoken for, and when I pleaded for left-over scraps I found that in this economical society there were no leftovers. The instruments, too, were in great demand, and were jealously guarded by the workshop chiefs against careless or inexpert users. It wasn't until I had proved myself as an able worker in bone and various other materials that I was allowed to borrow the precious leather knives and punches to make miniscule Christmas gifts with the remnants that fell from the cobbler's last.

On my first day as I set up 'house' in the small place alloted to me I made a bag in which to guard my various treasures. It was made in the style of old-fashioned shoe holders, and had several different sized pockets, in the depths of which I repeatedly lost small treasures such as hair grips or pencil stubs. With my name and a large flower brightly if irregularly appliquéd on it I nailed it firmly to the only bare piece of wall and christened it the *guardahuifa*, a name which is really only funny in Spanish, but means a repository for bits and pieces.

As I surveyed my new home I felt a great need for a crucifix. Not usually a devotee of religious objets d'art, perhaps I sensed that my life here would be so full that in my new happiness I risked neglecting the God to whom I had turned so instinctively in my pain.

I set out, therefore, to mark my bunk with the sign of the cross and eventually found two narrow strips of wood which I glued together and stained with dye purloined from the sandal makers; upon it I hung with fragments of red wool a copper Christ fashioned out of a piece of discarded telephone wire. I nailed it firmly to the bottom of the top bunk so that I faced it when lying in my bed.

> You pray in your distress and in your need;
> would that you might pray also in the fullness
> of your joy and in your days of abundance.
>   Kahlil Gilbran
>   *The Prophet*

45

Ready to Greet You

The next day the little prince came back. 'It would have been better to have come back at the same hour,' said the fox. 'If, for example, you come at four o'clock in the afternoon, then at three o'clock I shall begin to be happy. I shall feel happier and happier as the hour advances. At four o'clock I shall already be worrying and jumping about. I shall show you how happy I am! But if you come at just any time, I shall never know at what hour my heart is to be ready to greet you . . . One must observe the proper rites.'

Antoine de Saint-Exupéry
The Little Prince

On Tuesdays and Fridays the women prisoners at Tres Alamos were allowed to receive visitors. The visiting was from three until six o'clock, and for hours before the camp buzzed with activity and anticipatory joy. Lunch was hurriedly eaten and carefully set hair brushed out until it shone. Then, at half past two, dressed in clothes reserved only for these special days, they lined up at the door to submit to the mandatory search before they were allowed outside to join the line of those waiting to be called to the visitors' patio.

Most wore around their necks two or three pendants of bone or other material, carrying them out to give away to friends or families.

I had no idea who would come to visit me but I had heard from Derek Fernyhough who had come the previous day that my friends were eagerly awaiting permission to come. It was therefore with a joyous and full heart that I awaited this reunion with those men and women to whom I had grown so close. Shortly before three o'clock a police officer came down with a list and began to call the names of those who had visitors, for though we were all grouped together those prisoners who had no one to visit them had to stay in the barracks.

I stood there with my heart beating absurdly until my name was called and I joined the long line of girls excitedly waiting to be marched off. At last the list was complete and we were led off to the patio to settle ourselves before the gates opened. Rugs and ponchos were spread on the dusty ground for there were not enough benches, and then the big iron gates were opened and the waiting people let in. They came slowly, for each had to leave their identity card with the guard and be searched to make sure they were not carrying any letters or other forbidden objects. The bag of food which they had brought for the person they were visiting was then left on a long table where it would be searched before being handed to the prisoner for whom it had been brought.

I looked at the crowd of entering people and suddenly there were Frances and Anna. I leaped up and down impatiently while they passed through the check point and soon we were hugging each other delightedly. In a few moments we had been joined by Sally and Rosemary and two other American missionaries. They were laden with fruit and chocolates and a pile of sewing materials and coloured pencils that I had requested via the consul. Lastly, they had brought me two poetry books and a breviary, the book of prayers, Bible readings and Psalms that constitutes the official prayer of the Church and is said by priests and nuns the world over.

After the wild greetings and a few introductions to friends who were sitting next to us we settled down to talk. There was so much to tell. Like a river that has burst its banks I raced through the events of the past three weeks. These were close friends, people with whom I already had a deep understanding and there was nothing I wished to hide from them. Of the torture there was little to say, other than that it had happened, but I recounted the incredible trip through Santiago looking for the house that did not exist, and how I had been forced to lead the DINA agents to the convent. They told me that Helen and her friend had now returned to the USA and with them had gone Margaret, the nun from the provinces who had been staying with Helen when she gave asylum to the revolutionaries. It was many months later that I learned that the three nuns had spent a very frightened few days hiding from the DINA while the American consul negotiated with the authorities on their behalf. They were never offered asylum.

They told me that Fathers Maroto, Whelan, Salas and Cariola were still in prison, as was Father Daniel Panchot, an American missionary who worked for the Committee for Peace. Father Philip Devlin, also an American missionary, who had helped transport the fugitives to asylum, had himself found it necessary to take asylum in the Nuncio's house and was probably to be deported within the next few days. Two Italian priests from the northern city of Copiapo had also been arrested and were being held in Tres Alamos. (At that moment eight Catholic priests were in prison, one in asylum, and three American nuns had been expelled from the country. The scandal was immense, and had been in the headlines daily until the Fiscal had prohibited reporting on the case, saying that it was doing damage to Church–State relations.) The ethics of whether or not a doctor should treat a wounded fugitive, and whether the Church was right in granting asylum to men on the run from the authorities, had been discussed on radio and television, and an open attack on the Church made in a television programme had been answered by a powerful statement from the Cardinal in which the man who had accused the Chilean Church of being infiltrated by Marxists had been publicly told that he could consider himself excommunicated unless he recanted. The following day he withdrew his accusation.

The hours flew. Although we were all packed together under the trees, each girl was absorbed in conversation with her family. From time to time fellow prisoners walked past and I introduced them to my friends. Proud mothers brought me their babies to admire, and as I saw the girls carrying their infants I realized once again that their suffering had a dimension that I would never share nor even begin to comprehend.

The problem of separation of mothers from their children is a complex one and the psychological trauma inflicted upon children who witness their parents' arrest and in some cases their torture, must be enormous. There was a small boy of four who had been held with his mother in Cuatro Alamos for over a week at the time I was there. His parents had been detained together, and although his mother had asked permission to leave her two children with neighbours this had been refused. The boy and his eighteen-month-old sister had been taken first to the Villa Grimaldi where they had heard their father's screams while he was being tortured and then they had been transferred to Cuatro Alamos. Although I did not see the children while I was in solitary confinement I could hear the little boy's voice as he spoke to the guards and I heard the baby cry.

When their mother was transferred to Tres Alamos the children were handed over to their grandparents, who brought them to see their mother on visiting days. At this time the children's father remained 'disappeared' and there were fears for his life. The little boy seemed gravely disturbed by his experiences and knew quite well that the police had taken his daddy away. The use of children as hostages is well documented, and a number of cases in which the children have been tortured in an effort to make their parents speak has been reported to the United Nations. Whilst I cannot personally confirm this appalling accusation I would mention that at the time of my interrogation the DINA agents were very anxious to know the whereabouts of Gutierrez' baby; I can only assume because they wished to pressurize the child's parents.

A little before six o'clock it was announced over the loudspeaker system that it was time to go. As I said goodbye to my friends I saw the tense farewells of many of the women: wives to husbands, daughters to mothers, and, most poignant of all, to their children. For some this was the only visit possible in three months, for many of the families came from outside Santiago, and train fares were too expensive to make frequent visits possible. One of my friends came from the north of Chile and it was a month before her mother could afford to come and bring her two-year-old child. Another woman had a large family and her husband, having been dismissed from his job the day of her arrest, could not afford to bring the children to see her. Again and again I realized that I was very lucky.

Impatient soldiers called us by name and, carrying our rugs and the heavy bags of food and other supplies, we filed slowly towards our barracks, heads ever turning for a last look at friends and families waiting to be allowed to leave.

Back at the barracks, the treasured moment of being a precious individual over, we reformed naturally into a disciplined community. For the first time I saw the pooling of resources, the basis of our economy. Three tables had been arranged as a reception centre, and there was one girl to receive the tinned goods, another the fruit and vegetables, and a third the small luxuries such as cigarettes and chocolate. To my shame I found that it was not easy to hand over the gifts brought for me by loving visitors. It was not so much that I wanted to sit in a corner and eat them all myself, but that I would have liked to share them with my particular circle of friends. I learned much those days about community living and the sharing of possessions, for in giving up my goods I also gave up the pleasure of sharing them as I wished, and I realized how much I enjoyed the act of giving, and that being thanked for what I gave was more necessary to me than I liked to admit. It was hard to get used to the anonymous giving, although I had no problem in eating the salads and fruits that appeared just as anonymously on my plate!

It wasn't until after several weeks of living in Tres Alamos that I really came to understand just how deeply the girls cared about their rule of life. Mr Secondé, the ambassador, brought me a very special gift of a tin of some English sweets. They were of a quality which I had never tasted and I longed to share them with my room mates who were now my close friends. I rationalized that it would be absurd to hand this one tin into the general pool and that half the pleasure of eating them would come from the knowledge that here, in a prison in Chile, we were tasting a special

English delicacy. Feeling a little like Ananias or Sapphira I placed my booty on the foot of my bunk and that night I offered one to Marlena, one of my room mates. At first she refused politely, but I pressed her repeatedly and at last she took one and pronounced it delicious. Thus vindicated I sucked my own and returned to my sewing.

An hour later, however, Marlena told me that she wanted to talk to me so I joined her outside. In the gathering dusk we sat on a bench and she told me that she wanted me to know that she bitterly regretted accepting my sweet. Had she not been so obviously in earnest I would have laughed. As I sat there not knowing what to say she told me that she had betrayed the code of behaviour of the community and that she was deeply distressed. I tried to explain to her how I had wanted her to have the experience of tasting something very special from my country, and that there were not enough to give one to every member of the camp, but she repeated that she had broken faith with the community pledge of total sharing.

Not a little distressed myself, I told her that it was more important for her to accept my gift and understand my desire to share than it was to remain faithful to her pledge. Absurdly, for an hour we argued, and finally, both in tears, we hugged each other in a warmth of deepened understanding and made hurried preparations for bed.

The next morning I gave the sweets to the girl who was in charge of the food, and chalked up yet another lesson learned.

46
Free Indeed

You shall be free indeed when your days are not without
a care nor your nights without a want and a grief.
But rather when these things girdle your life and yet
you rise above them naked and unbound.

                                        Kahlil Gilbran
                                        The Prophet

Gradually I settled into the routine of my new life and in
many ways I was very happy. After more than three weeks
alone and living in a constant state of fear it was happiness
indeed to be with friends and to be allowed to see, albeit
only twice a week, those who were closest to me.

My life took on a new pattern and I found that there
were not enough hours in the day to do all the things I
wanted. I was possessed of a deep peace and joy, which was
something quite apart from the inevitable difficulties of life
in the camp. My sense of the presence of God in the things
around me returned, and I felt as if I had come out of a long
dark tunnel. The greatest difficulty in my new life was
finding time to be alone to pray, for we were 120 women in
as many square metres, and everyone was constantly on the
watch for signs of depression or withdrawal in their fellows.
Every time I walked alone in the outside patio, glorying in
the play of the setting sun on the mountains which seemed
incredibly close, I was joined by someone who thought I
was pining for my family. At last, in desperation, I told them
that I needed to be alone, and when they realized that I was
quite happy they let me sit or walk on my own, gazing at the
mountains which cried out to me as they had done so often
of the immensity and majesty of God.

Knowing how much I cared about the eucharist one of
my priest friends had asked permission to bring me communion but he was refused. The nuns, however, were not to

be defeated and at every visit they brought me the conse-
crated host carefully concealed and wrapped in a handkerchief. Living under conditions of religious persecution, for
the prison chaplains were not permitted to visit or say mass
for us, I dared to reserve the host, and each morning, before
my room mates were awake, I gave myself communion and
prayed for my fellow prisoners and for the men who held us
captive.

The greatest joy of my day was the freedom to do as I
chose with my time. Convinced that it would not be long
before I was released I did not join one of the workshops,
but amused myself by working as the spirit moved. Cristina,
one of the girls in my room, had a loom on which I wove a
small piece of cloth. The greatest enterprise, however, was
my long-thought-out 'operation mouse'.

Christmas was approaching and everyone was feverishly
making presents for their children and families. In addition
each prisoners was asked to make a soft toy to be given to the
children of prisoners who were in such straitened circumstances that they were unlikely to receive gifts from anyone
else. When I was told of this I made a small green mouse.
With large ears lined with flowered material, black whiskers
and a long fine tail he was very handsome, and I gave him
to Francisca as a token of my gratitude for her nursing care
in the Villa Grimaldi. Having parted with this rodent I
embarked upon another and then another. Soon there was a
trickle of visitors and I was asked if I could make a pattern
for it. Happy to oblige I drew a pattern, but before long
there was a waiting list of people wanting to have mice cut
from various scraps of material that didn't correspond to the
pattern. Just before Christmas we had an exhibition of the
toys, and like Hamelin's town in Brunswick there was a
plague of vermin: red, blue, green and yellow, striped and
spotted, plain and flowered, they leered at me until I could
have screamed for the Pied Piper!

The art which most intrigued me, however, was the
making of things in bone. I had done a little wood carving
as a child, and some clay modelling as an undergraduate,
and now this glistening white bone made my fingers itch. It

was not easy to come by but, not easily put off, I eventually located the girl who owned the various tools and who had a supply of bones awaiting carving. She very kindly gave me a piece and I carried it off in triumph to work it. I decided to make a cross and drew with care the largest one that would fit into this particular piece of bone, and set about cutting it out. It did not take me long to find out that bone carving was a lot more difficult than it looked. No longer than five centimetres, the fragment of bone was extremely difficult to stabilize while it was being sawed. It took me the whole morning to cut out the cross and my fingers were sore and cramped. When I had returned the saw to the owner so that it could be lent to the next person waiting for it, I was given a small triangular file and told to smooth down the cut edges. This was easier, though none the less time consuming, but it was a quiet, inoffensive work that could be carried out while talking to friends. I settled myself down with a group of girls who were embroidering and passed a happy afternoon gossiping and smoothing away with my file.

By evening it was considered smooth enough and my instructress passed me a fine bradawl to make the hole for the string. Like the earlier processes this was very slow but by ten o'clock I had a beautiful, simple cross with a neat hole in its upper end, and my teacher, pronouncing her satisfaction, gave me a minute quantity of zinc oxide powder on a piece of glass. Lovingly I polished it, and by bedtime it was finished, and I showed it proudly to my room mates.

The next one, a larger Maltese style cross, was easier, as I worked in a much thinner bone, and by Friday I had two completed to give away to Frances and Anna who had come to visit me. I made five crosses in all and eventually shortened my production time to about five hours, but after the fifth (which I kept myself) I downed tools and went into the leather business instead.

During my bone-working days I made the acquaintance of a fellow carver, Señora Juana, who came from a provincial town in the south of Chile, where she had worked for twenty years in a factory. Her crime was that of political agitation for she had dared to protest when the management of the foreign-owned factory had decided on grounds of economy to withdraw the allocation of hot water with which the women made their tea. A calm, placid lady, with a magnificent sense of humour, she explained to me that most of the women left their homes early in the morning without their breakfast in order to be at the factory by seven a.m. For twenty years they had been given a cup of hot water with which they made their tea which, with a piece of bread brought from home, kept them going till lunch-time.

Since the coup, the workers in Chile no longer have the right to unionize, let alone the right to strike, so that when Señora Juana dared to act as spokesman for her angry workmates she was arrested and imprisoned. She and six other workers were brought to Santiago and held without charges with the other political prisoners. She was released in the Christmas amnesty but in a country with an overall unemployment figure of over 20 per cent it seems unlikely that she would have been given her job back.

As the days passed and I met more and more of my fellow prisoners I realized how right Francisca had been when she said it would be good for me to spend a few weeks at the camp. Each day I made new friends and each day my respect for the people around me deepened.

The majority of them were aged between twenty and thirty although one girl was still not eighteen and one lady was well over seventy. They never spoke of why they were in prison or of what had happened to them before they arrived in '*libre plática*' (the place of free speech), but little by little I learned about some of them and as we became friends asked them to tell me about themselves.

The 'oldest inhabitant', and the best known among the prisoners, was Luz Ayress. A 26-year-old student of cinema, her full name was as beautiful and romantic as her story was appalling. Luz de las Nieves means 'light of the snows' and with her long black hair and brightly coloured clothes Luz made me think of the Red Indian maiden from Hiawatha, though she was in actual fact of Scots descent. Her grandfather, one James Ayres, had emigrated to Mexico from Scotland and his son had gone to seek his fortune in Chile.

During the Popular Unity government Chile renewed diplomatic relations with Cuba, and there was considerable cultural exchange. Luz Ayress was one of many university students who were given a scholarship to study in Cuba and for two years she studied cinema photographic technique.

Early in 1974 she was arrested, as were her father and her fifteen-year-old brother. Her account of her interrogation and torture and her detention in the notorious camp of Tejas Verdes (Green Roofs) is an almost unbelievable tale of brutality and perversion. For a month she was interrogated almost daily and was beaten, hung alternately by hands and feet, stretched on a rack, stimulated with electricity, tortured with live animals and finally made pregnant after multiple rape. She was transferred to the Casa Correctional where she was seen by visiting members of the International Red Cross and a Chilean bishop. Her statement was smuggled out of Chile and submitted to the United Nations and also to the third session of the International Commission for Investigation of the Crimes of the Military Junta, in Mexico City in February 1975.

I had heard of Luz Ayress before I was detained, as the Chilean newspapers gave great prominence to her case after it received publicity in the *Washington Post*. They stated that she had become pregnant in Cuba and had been aborted and as a result was mentally unbalanced. They described her as a 'poor demented creature' who invented horrific stories to justify the sin of her abortion.

Far from being a 'poor demented creature', Luz Ayress was a cheerful, highly intelligent and articulate girl who was always busy in one or other of the various camp activities. Over eighteen months in detention, she was mistress of many trades and her bunk was a brilliant corner in the bare wooden hut, its walls covered with drawings and pieces of embroidery, crochet or weaving. Blessed with a steady hand and an artistic flair she painted in the eyes on the soft toys which were made for sale, and I can see her now, perched on her bed, bringing to life the absurd 'gonks', the shapeless creatures which were one of the major products of the camp.

Luz's father Carlos and her youngest brother (also called Carlos) were both detained in the men's section of Tres Alamos so that Señora Virginia, Luz's mother, came four times a week by bus to the prison to visit her family. It was only every couple of months, however, that Luz was allowed to see her father or brother, as inter-prison visiting was strictly limited. Señora Virginia and Luz sat next to me at visiting times and we soon became good friends, sharing the little luxuries of the day between us. I remember that she often brought ice cream, and how delicious it tasted in the dusty heat of the Santiago summer.

I never ceased to marvel at the faith and courage of this woman who lived only for the four days in the week when she could see her family. A message that she sent me shortly after my release must put into words the indomitable spirit of the families of the detainees: 'With the truth we will always live tranquilly. The faith which animates us is stronger and more powerful than all the guns: here, as always, we are awaiting the new dawn . . .'

The faith of Luz Ayress' mother was great indeed, for her daughter had the distinction of being the only prisoner for whom it was said that there was a special decree that she was never to be released in the duration of the military Junta. Always serene, Luz told me that she was never free of the fear that one day she would meet with a 'convenient accident' or would be 'shot while trying to escape'. It was generally accepted in the camp that she was unlikely to be released, and when after a Christmas amnesty in which 30 women were released the camp commander asked all the prisoners who had been detained for more than a year to step forward, he said to Luz, 'Not you,' indicating that she was in a special category.

In December 1976, however, Luz Ayress was expelled from Chile. What changed the heart of the military authorities will perhaps never be known, but perhaps General Pinochet, wearying of letters and postcards from all over the world, asking for her release, decided that she was more trouble than she was worth.

By a curious coincidence I found myself able one day to

be of some small service to the community which had taken me so warmly to its heart. I have always enjoyed drawing, though I have no illusions that my ability is anything more than slightly above average. It has always been a sadness to me that I have never been able to capture a likeness, but one day as I sat down to sketch one of the girls as she sat cross-legged on the ground embroidering, I found that the simple line-drawing that came from my pen had caught something of the personality of the subject. Encouraged, I tried once more and magically it happened again. As always happens when one draws in public, people came to look over my shoulder and they joined in my delight. Not wishing to part with the original sketch I made a tracing of the drawing and as the lines were bold and simple, was able to reproduce it accurately. Thus I was able to present each 'model' with two copies, one for herself and one for her family, and I became known as the camp 'photographer'. I must have done over thirty life drawings during my stay, but perhaps not surprisingly, they were confiscated when I was released. It seemed almost as though the gift was given for the pleasure of the prisoners, for I have never drawn as well either before or since.

On my first Sunday in Tres Alamos I was called upon to give witness to my faith in a way that I found surprisingly difficult. A group of prisoners approached me and asked if I would hold a service. I was both perplexed and embarrassed for although I was a frequent mass goer I had never conducted a service, let alone a public one in a community in which most of the members were Marxists. I realized, however, that this small group of Christians felt a great need to pray together and that they looked to me as a religious leader. Ashamed at how much it cost me in terms of fear of being laughed at by my non-believing friends I put up a notice informing the camp members that those who wished could join us for prayer in the patio at eleven.

I devised a simple liturgy, choosing familiar and appropriate passages from the New Testament and a few Psalms and hymns. By five past eleven there were more than twenty girls gathered under the trees and we read the passage from the Sermon on the Mount and St Paul's letter to the Romans in which he declares what he had learned to be true:

> 'Neither death nor life, no angel, no power, nothing that exists, nothing still to come, not any power, or height or death, nor any created thing can ever come between us and the love of God'.

Romans 8:38, 39

We prayed for our fellow prisoners, for the families and children of all, and then we broke bread as a symbol of our offering and sharing.

Throughout the whole liturgy we were watched suspiciously by one of the wardresses but when we exchanged the sign of peace I took her hand and for a brief moment the barriers between captors and captives were lifted.

Sunday in Tres Alamos

The following week we held a similar liturgy and, curious to see what happened, nearly fifty people came. Although many were unbelievers they seemed glad to be able to share somehow their longing for peace and to articulate their fears for those who remained in the power of the DINA.

So it was that my days were filled up with activity and friendship, for there was always a group that I could join to talk or to sit quietly while I sewed or drew. Curiously, the only thing that was almost impossible was to read. I was one of the few people who had books, for in the early days the guards were lax in permitting my visitors to bring me reading material. I soon found, however, that there was no place where I could be alone and quiet. For the first few hours of the morning we were confined to the barracks and in each of the rooms there was a group of girls talking. The inside patio was also humming with the noise of busy workers discussing designs, or hammering nails into shoes.

At last I discovered a refuge: Magdalena was a reader rather than a talker and I was offered the hospitality of the top bunk in her dormitory, the owner being otherwise engaged; every morning, therefore, I would retire for a couple of hours to read and to pray, almost invisible as I lay on my stomach like an eagle in its eyric, so close to the roof of the hut.

Lucinda lent me Carlo Carretto's *Letters from the Desert* which had been brought to her by a visiting nun; a very powerful book, written by a man who abandons a busy life to live as a contemplative among the poor in the desert, as a Little Brother of Charles de Foucald. I was deeply and uncomfortably moved by his thoughts on poverty.

Before my arrest I had often discussed with my friends how difficult I found it to live simply, and that I prayed to God that he might help me to separate myself from my house and my dogs and my books and all the things to which I was so attached. When they visited we were able to laugh together when they said, 'Well, he took you at your word, didn't he?'

Now, robbed of my house, my possessions, my friends, my work and my freedom to come and go as I pleased, I knew an unbelievable freedom of spirit. As if with a sword the ties that bound me like Gulliver had been slashed, and I had discovered the truth that:

> Poverty is a liberating and freeing thing, through which, surprise, surprise, the whole world is ours.

Thomas Cullinan, OSB
If the Eye be Sound

47

Bloody but Unbowed

Out of the night that covers me,
Black as the pot from pole to pole,
I thank whatever gods may be
For my unconquerable soul.

In the fell clutch of circumstance
I have not winced nor cried aloud.
Under the bludgeonings of chance
My head is bloody but unbowed.

Beyond this place of wrath and tears
Looms but the horror of the shade,
And yet the menace of the years
Finds, and shall find me, unafraid.

It matters not how strait the gate,
How charged with punishments the scroll,
I am the master of my fate;
I am the captain of my soul.

William Ernest Henley
Invictus

Another prisoner who had become a legend in Tres Alamos was Gladys Díaz. I had heard of her first from Javiera when we were in the Villa Grimaldi, for Gladys had spent three months in the torture centre and had been subjected to a long and systematic attempt to break her spirit. It had failed.

In her mid-thirties, Gladys Díaz was a journalist and the mother of a boy of seven years. She was a member of the MIR, and after the coup had lived in '*la clandestinidad*', the hidden life of the committed revolutionary. My knowledge of her is fragmentary, gleaned from the few personal conversations that I had with her, from what other people told me, and more than anything, from living at close quarters with her for five weeks when we were imprisoned together in Tres Alamos. She impressed me as an intelligent woman of a remarkable integrity and of a physical bravery that is rare in either men or women. Most of all she possessed to a high degree that quality to be found in revolutionaries, martyrs and saints: she was consistent with her beliefs.

The courage to die for their beliefs is given only to those who have had the courage to live for them. The final victory over their terror of pain and physical death is the last of a thousand victories and defeats in the war which is fought daily and hourly in the human mind and soul: the war in the overcoming of self. Dissected and examined in detail this is a most unglamorous battle and to the outsider seems absurd; but it is the constant denying of the natural human urge to stay in bed longer than necessary, to eat or drink more than is justifiable, to be intolerant of the stupid, and to accumulate more than a fair share of this world's goods, that makes possible the gradual freeing of the human spirit.

The achievement of this freedom is a slow and acutely painful process, and it cannot be achieved by those who have no light to follow, no banner under which to stand. I have seen this freedom in those who have surrendered their being to the most powerful force in the world: LOVE. Love of God, and love of man, which, if that love is whole and true, are different sides of the same golden coin, is what drives men and women to die to themselves so that they and others may truly live.

The universal truth that the grain of wheat must die if it is to bear fruit is expressed with a rare power and beauty by the Lebanese poet and prophet Kahlil Gibran:

Then said Almitra, Speak to us of Love.
And he raised his head and looked upon the people, and there fell a stillness upon them. And with a great voice he said:
When love beckons to you, follow him,
Though his ways are hard and steep.
And when his wings enfold you yield to him,
Though the sword hidden among his pinions may wound you.
And when he speaks to you believe in him,

Though his voice may shatter your dreams as the north wind
lays waste the garden

.   .   .   .   .   .

For even as love crowns you, so shall he crucify you.
Even as he is for your growth, so is he for your pruning.

Even as he ascends to your height and caresses your ten-
derest branches that quiver in the sun,
So shall he descend to your roots and shake them in their
clinging to the earth.
Like sheaves of corn he gathers you unto himself.
He threshes you to make you naked.
He sifts you to make you free from your husks.
He grinds you to whiteness.
He kneads you until you are pliant;
And then he assigns you to his sacred fire, that you may
become sacred bread for God's sacred feast.

All these things shall love do unto you that may you know
the secrets of your heart, and in that knowledge become a
fragment of Life's heart.

The fact that Gladys Díaz maintained her sanity under
prolonged and brutal torture and inhuman living conditions is a confirmation of the conclusions reached in a
recent paper on torture presented at the xxist International
Congress of Psychology in Paris: 'According to the information we have gathered, it seems that the extent to which one
can resist torture and face death is closely related to one's
ideological formation.'
I have written in some detail of the *parrilla*, the application
of electric current to a victim bound naked, gagged and
blindfolded to a metal bunk. This appears to be a standard
interrogation technique in the countries which use torture
as an aid to interrogation. Much simpler is the immersion of
the head in contaminated water until the subject is near to
drowning and is forced both to swallow and inhale. Simple,
too, is hanging by the wrists from a hook in the wall or from
the bough of a tree. Straightforward beating of a man or a

woman, sightless and unclothed, so that each blow takes
them unawares, is common practice, and is a frequent cause
of severe internal injury. It is not for nothing that the DINA
maintains a special clinic where urgent resuscitation and, if
necessary, surgery can be performed; I know personally one
young revolutionary who had to have surgery because of a
ruptured liver, and world publicity was given to the case of
Guillermo Herrera who died in his father's arms of an internal haemorrhage after he had been brutally beaten in
his own house.

Gladys Díaz was lucky because broken ribs heal without
treatment, and she knew enough to ask a fellow prisoner to
tear up a dress to bind around her chest to stabilize the
fractures.

Much is written about inhuman prison conditions, and
dark cold cells and inadequate toilet facilities are indeed
hard to bear, but in a different category indeed are the
'rabbit hutches' of the Casa Grimaldi. I did not see them,
but Gladys and others described to me how cages were
built in the base of an old water tower and how the prisoner
was forced to enter on all fours, and then either sit with her
knees drawn up or stand, for there was no room to lie down.
Anyone who has travelled a long distance in the back of a
small car will understand the agony produced simply by the
limitation of movement in this way. In common with other
prisoners who have been kept in 'the tower', Gladys
suffered from spinal problems.

Even in the darkness of the tower the flaming spirit of the
prisoners could not be extinguished. They discovered that it
was possible to communicate with other prisoners by speaking through the water pipes, and each smuggled a piece of
newspaper when he visited the bathroom and, holding the
paper to a crack which admitted a shaft of light, read the
latest news to fellow captives. Visits to the bathroom were
made in chains, and at times when the other prisoners were
shut away out of sight.

Well known in Latin America for her writing and television work, Gladys Díaz received considerable publicity,
and on a number of occasions she was removed from the

relative security of Tres Alamos and returned to the Villa Grimaldi. She said, laughingly, that whenever her name appeared in a foreign newspaper they would take her to the Grimaldi in exasperation and revenge. These reprisals, however, were a small price to pay for the knowledge that her death would not pass unnoticed, and ultimately the unflagging efforts of thousands of people in the free world were rewarded, for in December 1976 she was released from prison and expelled from Chile.

Although the length of time over which Gladys Díaz was tortured was exceptionally long, I found that there were many other girls who had received equally harsh treatment. As a rule no one ever spoke about her torture except in a matter of fact way, when describing something or relating some funny incident. Knowing that it was likely that I would be released, I asked certain of them to tell me how they had been treated, and it was these conversations that confirmed the reports that torture was the rule rather than the exception in the interrogation of political prisoners in Chile. The majority of my fellow prisoners had been subjected to beating and a certain degree of sexual abuse as well as at least one session on the *parrilla*.

A number of the women who had been thought to be concealing information had been subjected to more sophisticated and brutal combinations of the use of hanging and the application of electricity. This is no place for a study of the psychology of the torturer, but I was left in no doubt that much of the treatment of the women was gratuitous sadism, and the use of live animals and frequent rape are evidence of the appalling degradation of these men.

The bravery and composure of those who had been tortured was impressive. They related what had happened to them in a controlled way, without any apparent exaggeration, and I had no reason to disbelieve what they told me. Too many accounts tallied with my own experience and with what I had heard from other people to leave me in any doubt as to the truth of this widespread and cold-blooded infliction of pain.

That the coup unleashed a latent hatred and brutality

in many members of the armed forces is well documented, for the violence of the behaviour of large numbers of troops throughout the country cannot be explained in any other way. Just how many people have the latent capacity for agression and violence, and how deeply this force is buried and what are the factors which unleash it is a question for sociologists and psychologists. Far more disturbing and of relevance to every thinking and caring person is the ethics of the cold blooded systematic use of torture.

There are certain questions that must be asked, however embarrassing and unpleasant the answers. Who manufactures the machines for the infliction of electrical torture? Who trains the military personnel in the use of this equipment? Anyone who cares to read the testimony of political prisoners who have been tortured in the right-wing military dictatorships of Latin America will be immediately impressed by the similarity of the testimonies. The factor which seems constant in the testimonies of torture received from Latin America is the use of electrical stimulation.

The use of torture is prohibited in the Universal Declaration of Human Rights and in many similar agreements. It is therefore of importance that, if the victim is to return to society, he should not be able to prove that he has been tortured. Beating leaves bruises, burns leave scars, as do pins passed under the finger nails. Electric shocks, however, unless strong enough to cause a local burn, leave no mark. In this way very severe pain can be repeatedly induced in a controlled way, and yet there are no scars.

I have heard it alleged while in Chile, in France, in England and in the United States, that torture methods are taught in special schools. In Chile there was frequent reference to a United States 'counter insurgency' school in Panama where it was said that Chilean military officials were sent for training. The Amnesty International delegation that visited Chile after the coup was informed by prison guards within the National Stadium that Brazilian police had assisted in interrogations there and had also given a course in techniques of interrogation at the Ministry of Defence.

It is too easy for civilized people in Europe and the United States to express horror and incredulity at the barbaric cruelty inflicted by Latin Americans upon their fellow countrymen. Every man and woman living in a democratic state should ask themselves whether the torture techniques used in totalitarian dictatorships are taught in *their* military academies and whether this expertise is handed on to personnel from other countries.

The efficacy of torture is two-fold: it is, in most cases, a rapid and simple way of 'persuading' a man or woman to divulge information against their will, and it is a powerful repressive weapon for use on the population as a whole. The fear of physical pain and death is a universal one and people do not lightly undertake activites which may land them in this situation.

My own case is different for although I knew quite well that if I was caught treating Nelson Gutierrez I would be expelled from the country, it never crossed my mind that the authorities would dare to torture me. That I thought in this way is a measure of my ignorance of Latin American police policy, for an English priest, Father Michael Woodward, was tortured to death after the coup, and in September 1974 the Reverend Fred Morris, a North American Methodist missionary working in the north-eastern Brazilian town of Recife, was brutally tortured over a period of several days. He had not engaged in any political activity but was a friend of Dom Helder Càmara, the Brazilian archbishop who is consistently outspoken in his condemnation of the breaches of human rights in Brazil.

Although the majority of the population are afraid to speak against the government or take part in any activity which could incur the suspicion of the intelligence forces, there remains in all the Latin American dictatorships a hard core of young men and women who are prepared to run this risk. In the full knowledge that, if caught, they will be tortured and possibly killed, they work for the restoration of liberty in their country. These are not desperate, oppressed peasants, but university students or young professionals from middle class families. They have no material need to work for revolution: the life of the middle class professional in Latin America is a far more comfortable one than that of his counterparts in Europe or in the United States.

Let us consider for a moment a few of the better known revolutionaries of Latin America: Ernesto Che Guevara was a doctor; he was an Argentinian and yet, crippled by severe asthma, he died in combat fighting with the revolutionaries in Bolivia.

Camilo Torres, a Roman Catholic priest, and son of a well-to-do Colombian paediatrician, laid aside his cassock and a successful career as professor of sociology, not for the love of a woman, but because he believed that Christian love demanded that he joined the armed revolution. In his message to the Christians in January 1966 he said: 'I have given up the duties and privileges of the clergy, but I have not ceased to be a priest. I believe that I have given myself to the revolution out of love for my fellow man'. A month later, on 15 February, he was killed in combat.

Nestor Paz, a Catholic medical student and ex-seminarian, left his wife to join the Bolivian National Liberation Army, and died of starvation with the guerillas, the day before his 25th birthday. His diary is a poignant testimony of his three consuming loves: for his wife, his people and his God. On Saturday, 12 September, a little less than a month before his death, he wrote in his diary:

My dear Lord: It's been a long time since I've written. Today I really feel the need of you and your presence. Maybe it's because of the nearness of death or the relative failure of our struggle. You know I've always tried to be faithful to you in every way, consistent with the fullness of my being. That's why I'm here. I understand love as an urgent demand to solve the problem of the other – where you are.

I left what I had and I came. Maybe today is my Holy Thursday and tonight will be my Good Friday. Into your hands I surrender completely all that I am with a trust having no limits, because I love you. What hurts me most is perhaps leaving behind those I love the most –

Cecy and my family – and also not being able to experience the triumph of the people, their liberation.

We are a group filled with authentic humanity, 'Christian' humanity. This, I think, is enough to move history ahead. This encourages me. I love you, and I give to you all that I am and all that we are, without measure – because you are my Father.

Nobody's death is useless if his life has been filled with meaning, and I believe ours has been.

Ciao, Lord, perhaps until we meet in your heaven, that new land that we yearn for so much.

My dear love: Just a few lines for you. I don't have the energy for any more. I have been tremendously happy with you. It hurts me deeply to leave you alone, but if I must, I will. I'm here till the end, which is Victory or Death.

I love you. I give you all that I am, all that I can, with all the strength I have. I'll see you soon – either here or there. I'm giving you a big kiss and protecting you in my arms.

This was no violent fanatic but a young man of flesh and blood who longed to assuage the hunger that was killing him and to be with the wife whom he loved, but who knew that he had been true to his God.

The list could go on and on: Miguel Enriques of Chile, doctor; Bautista van Schauwen, doctor; but it is enough to show that a high proportion of the revolutionaries of Latin America are seeking to change a system which is unjust, not to themselves or to the class from which they come, but to the dispossessed of their land: the underfed, poorly housed, under-educated majority of their fellow countrymen.

For five weeks I lived with over a hundred women who had given themselves to this struggle. For five weeks, night and day, I shared their food, their clothes, their anguishes and their hopes. For five weeks I watched their behaviour, listened to their conversation, and asked them questions, and I formed my own judgement of them.

The conclusions I came to were these: that they were

women who were motivated by love for the underprivileged
of Chile, of Latin America and the world. They were pledged
to join in the world-wide struggle against fascism and were
prepared to live and if necessary to die in the fight to libe-
rate the oppressed. A small minority were atheists, some
were non-practising believers, and others were committed
church-going Christians. The majority believed that armed
struggle was the only path by which the oppressed of their
continent could be freed. Disillusioned by the bloody massacre that had ended Allende's 'peaceful road to socialism',
they believed violence was now the only course to be
adopted by clear-thinking revolutionaries.

How difficult it is for the majority of people living in
democratic Europe or the United States to understand the
young revolutionaries of Latin America. Perhaps it is not
possible for those who have never lived in a situation where
extreme wealth and subhuman living are bedfellows to
understand the anger that this generates in the souls of
caring people. True, this anger most readily finds expression
in Marxism, but people who have come to know Latin
American revolutionaries personally, know that not all
those who profess to be Marxists are believers in atheistic
materialism. Disillusioned by a Catholic Church that has
for centuries sided with the rich élite, they have found in
Marxism a constructive plan for the building of a better
society.

The Latin American Church of the 1970s, however, is
very different from that of fifty, twenty, or even ten years
ago. Since the Second General Conference of the Latin
American bishops at Medellín in Columbia in August 1968,
the Catholic Church has pledged itself to the service of the
dispossessed of that continent. Painfully aware of the previous lack of adherence to the gospel message, the bishops
proclaimed: 'We have seen that our most urgent commitment must be to purify ourselves, all the members and
institutions of the Catholic Church, in the spirit of the
Gospel. It is necessary to end the separation between faith
and life, because in Christ Jesus . . . only faith working
through love avails.'

Throughout Latin America Christians are reading their Bibles. These are not beautiful leather-bound volumes in which a 400-year-old translation is printed so small that it requires a magnifying glass. No: these are cheap paperbacks, earmarked, underlined and battered, in which the teachings of Jesus Christ are related in a language that ordinary people can understand. What is lost in poetry is gained in understanding, and Christians are discovering that

> We were given a Gospel that was a wild tiger, we tame it and domesticate it into a pussy cat.
>
> Thomas Cullinan, OSB.
> *If the Eye be Sound*

The magnificent words of the Prophet Isaiah are a sample of the call to justice and love that runs like a golden thread throughout both Old and New Testament.

The 'Good News' of Jesus Christ (and 'Gospel' means 'Good News') is that God became man in order that we should have life, and have it more abundantly, and that we must love our neighbour in the same measure that we love ourselves.

For five weeks I found myself in a paradoxical situation, for I witnessed a day-to-day living of the Christian message of love, sharing and sacrifice by people whose professed ideology was opposed to Christianity. Never, before or since, have I had the privilege of living in a community of people who were prepared to live and die for their beliefs, and whose day-to-day behaviour made me think again and again of Christ's message to His disciples:

> By this shall all men know that you are my disciples, if you have love, one for another.
>
> *John 13:35*

48

The Cold Outside Your House

This Speaker
was not born within your fold,
supported by your grace,
held fast, never
to turn from you his face.

Hear the voice of those who in all honesty
feel bound to choose
the cold outside your house.
Nevertheless,
they still believe in you,
although they may not know it,
for are not you the truth?
And these people both
speak it (and in your own phrase)
do it.

You are beauty
and pure eyes remaining childlike
still look wonderingly
on your earth's loveliness.

You are goodness
and I find
you in people who do not confess
you. They lack your body
but speak your mind.

Helder Càmara
The Desert is Fertile

As the weeks passed and I became integrated into the prison
community I made many friends among my fellow captives.
As we sat sewing in the outside patio or walked the well-
worn exercise path in twos or threes, we talked.

For all of us this was a time of direct, almost naked
communication. People stripped of all they possess, deprived of their liberty and threatened with death, do not
spend their time in small talk. The preoccupation of all was
the oppression reigning in Chile. Although outraged at their

own torture they were far more concerned for the safety of those who were still in the hands of the DINA and for the suffering of their families and the people of Chile as a whole.

They had good cause for concern, for there were few who did not have a husband, a lover or a brother who had disappeared since detention. Many of them had been in the Casa Grimaldi or other torture centres with both men and women prisoners who had been taken away never to be seen again. Risking retaliation from the DINA, several girls had given evidence in court that they had been detained with persons whose disappearance was now being investigated.

There was much conversation, too, of a philosophical nature, for the confrontation with death inevitably has an enormous impact and forces people to examine what they believe. That I was an committed Roman Catholic was universally known and there were many of my companions who were interested in discussing religion. The depth and range of these conversations was considerable, for the beliefs of the girls ranged from atheism through agnosticism and tepid faith to profound commitment to the Christian message.

Not once did anyone attack my beliefs and neither did I seek to convert, but we tried to understand each other a little better. I tried, in particular, to understand why Christianity and the fight for social justice appeared incompatible to the Marxists, because as I understood Christ's message it called for just that liberation of the oppressed and the establishment of a just society that these women were fighting for.

I have never studied Marxist teaching, nor for that matter any other political theory, and I did not seek to now. I sought only to understand why people that I loved and respected hated the Church that meant so much to me. The answer was never completely clear, but what emerged was that this hatred had a historical rather than an actual basis. All the abuses practised in the Church over the centuries: the abuse of power and privilege and the accumulation of wealth of which I had heard vaguely, but conveniently ignored, were placed before me.

In the Latin American context the hatred of the Church by the revolutionaries stems from the fact that since the arrival of the Conquistadores the Church appeared to align itself with the ruling élite. In the country in particular the priest was paid by the landowner and it seems that here religion was truly the opium of the people, for they were told to accept patiently their conditions of living and work because this was the will of God for them.

The exasperation and anger of two Chileans from peasant families burst forth into song.

Violeta Parra, who is perhaps Chile's best known folk singer and composer, and may be regarded as the forerunner of the Chilean protest singers, sang:

> *Por qué los pobres no tienen*
> *en este mundo esperanza?*
> *Se amparan en la otra vida*
> *Como una justa balanza.*
> *Pobre . . . las procesiones*
> *La vela y las alabanzas.*
>
> *De tiempos inmemoriales*
> *se ha inventado el infierno*
> *Para asustar a los pobres*
> *Con sus castigos eternos*
> *Y el pobre que es inocente*
> *Con su inocencia creyendo.*
>
> *Y para seguir la mentira*
> *Lo llama su confesor*
> *Le dice que Dios no quiere*
> *Ninguna revolución*
> *Ni pliegos ni sindicatos*
> *Que ofenden su corazón.*

Why do the poor not have
Any hope in this world?
They seek protection in the after life,
To balance this life's misery.
Poor . . .
In candles and praises.

From time immemorial
Hell has been invented
To frighten the poor
With its eternal punishment.
And the poor who are so innocent
Believe what they are told.

And to continue the lie
They call the priest
Who says that God does not wish
Revolution
Nor petitions nor trade unions
Which offend His heart.

Violetta Parra
Porque los Pobres No Tienen

A generation later, in 1966 Victor Jara wrote:

Al pobre tanto lo asustan
para que trague todos sus dolores
para que su miseria la cubra de imágenes
la luna siempre es muy linda
y el sol muere cada tarde

Por eso quiero gritar,
no creo en nada
Sino en el calor de tu mano con mi mano

Por eso quiero gritar,
no creo en nada
Sino en el amor de los seres humanos.

They frighten the poor so much
So that they will swallow their suffering,
So that they will cover their wretchedness
With images of saints.

The moon is always beautiful,
The sun dies every evening,
And that is why I want to shout,
I believe in nothing
But the warmth of your hand in mine.

I want to shout
I believe in nothing
But the love of human beings.

Victor Jara
La Luna siempre es muy linda

Listening to the description of the old Church in Latin America it was not hard to understand why young people in search of justice and freedom turned away from it in the hope of finding another brighter light to follow; small wonder that they cried

I believe in nothing
But the love of human beings.

A committed Christian only in the last two years, this Church was a stranger to me. The Church I knew and loved worked and fought for the poor and underprivileged. Believing passionately in the intrinsic dignity of the human person and his inalienable rights, the Church I knew, far from saying that God did not believe in trade unions, had pledged itself to be the voice of those who had no voice.

The Bishops of Latin America had declared at Medellín that they were committed:

– to inspire, encourage and press for a new order of justice that incorporates all men in the decision-making of their own communities;
– to promote the constitution and the efficacy of the family, not only as a human sacramental community, but also as an intermediate structure in the function of social change;
– to make education dynamic in order to accelerate the training of mature men in their current responsibilities. (As late as 1950 a large farm just north of Santiago had a church for its workers but no school.)
– to encourage the professional organization of workers, which are decisive elements in socio-economic transformation;
– to promote a new evangelization and extensive catechesis that reach the élite and the masses in order to achieve a lucid and committed faith;

– to renew and create new structures in the Church that institutionalize dialogue and channel collaboration between bishops, priests, and religious laity.
– to co-operate with other Christian confessions, and with all men of good will who are committed to authentic peace rooted in justice and love.

Archbishop Helder Càmara of Brazil, prophetic voice of the new Latin American Church, was one of the prime movers at the conference of Medellín. A man who works for peace with all men of good will, he has heard and accepted the accusations against the Church:

> We Christians in Latin America have been, and are, seriously responsible for the situation of injustice that exists in this continent. We have condoned the slavery of Indians and Africans; and now are we taking a sufficiently strong stand against the landowners, the rich and powerful in our own countries? Or do we close our eyes and help to pacify their consciences, once they have camouflaged their terrible injustice by giving alms in order to build churches (very often scandalously vast and rich, in shocking contrast with the surrounding poverty), or by contributing to our social projects? In practice, don't we seem to have vindicated Marx, by offering to pariahs a passive Christianity, alienated and alienating, justly called an opium for the masses?
>
> Dom Helder Càmara
> *From a lecture given in Paris,*
> *25 April 1968*

Dom Helder goes on, however, to explain that Christianity demands a structural revolution in Latin America and indeed in the whole world, and speaks of the change of attitude among Christians expressed at the Conference of Medellín. Living as he does in one of the most oppressed countries of Latin America, Dom Helder knows well the spirit and idealism of the revolutionary. In *Spiral of Violence* he speaks of the three forms of violence which result one from the other. Basic to this theory is the understanding of the concepts of peace and violence. Peace does not exist just because there is an absence of fighting, 'a peace based on injustices – the peace of a swamp with rotten matter fermenting in its depths' (Camara) cannot be called peace. 'The egoism of some privileged groups drives countless human beings into this subhuman condition, where they suffer restrictions, humiliations, injustices; without prospects, without hope, their condition is that of slaves. This is *established violence.*'

This 'established violence', the situation in much of Latin America, attracts the second violence, 'the violence of *revolt*', either from the oppressed themselves, or of youth, firmly resolved to do battle for a more just and human world.

A friend of all his people, Dom Helder speaks out for the young revolutionaries. 'The young no longer have the patience to wait for the privileged to discard their privileges. The young very often see governments too tied to the privileged classes. The young are losing confidence in the churches, which affirm beautiful principles – great texts, remarkable conclusions – but without ever deciding, at least so far, to translate them into real life. 'The young are turning more and more to radical action and violence.'

I have quoted extensively from Helder Camara not only because he explains so lucidly what fires the young revolutionaries, but because, although he loves and respects them, he does not share their view that violence is the only course of action that remains to bring about the necessary changes in Latin American society. He is convinced that the armed struggle of the revolutionaries brings about the third violence: the violence of the repressive military dictatorships to whom the internal security of the state is more important than the rights of those who live in it. Regimes which maintain people in subhuman living conditions breed revolutionaries, and they in their turn bring down the wrath of the regimes they are trying to overthrow, who retaliate with a violence of terrifying proportions.

Like Martin Luther King and Mahatma Gandhi, Dom Helder is a 'pilgrim of peace'. In a lecture on violence given in Paris in 1968 he spoke of the difficulty facing those men of peace who live in a climate of violence:

It is difficult not to speak of violence if it is either to condemn it out of hand, from afar, without bothering to examine its various aspects or seek its brutal and regrettable causes; or if it is to fan the flames from a safe distance, in the manner of 'an armchair Che Guevara'.

What is difficult is to speak of violence from the thick of the battle, when one realizes that often some of the most generous and able of one's friends are tempted by violence, or have already succumbed to it. I ask you to hear me as one who lives in a continent whose climate is pre-revolutionary, but who, while he has no right to betray the Latin American masses, had not the right either to sin against the light or against love. . . .'

This then, is his personal position:

I respect those who feel obliged in conscience to opt for violence – not the all too easy violence of armchair guerillas – but those who have proved their sincerity by the sacrifice of their life. In my opinion, the memory of Camilo Torres and of Che Guevara merits as much respect as that of Martin Luther King. I accuse the real authors of violence: all those who, whether on the right or the left, weaken justice and prevent peace. My personal vocation is that of a pilgrim of peace, following the example of Paul VI; personally I would prefer a thousand times to be killed than to kill.

Helder Camara
Paris, 25 April 1968

Difficult it is indeed to speak of the rights and wrongs of violent revolution in Latin America. I did not seek to treat Nelson Gutierrez, nor did it occur to me to refuse him treatment when I was asked. I did not seek the company of Marxist revolutionaries during my four years in Chile, nor, when I was put amongst them, did I spurn their friendship. My deepening commitment as a Christian and my increasing vision of Christ in all men has opened my heart so that I can say simply and in all honesty that I hate no one.

I have tried to relate honestly the story of my encounter with a group of young Latin Americans whose ideology and actions make them misunderstood and feared if not hated by a large section of the Christian world. I am not a Marxist but I would be committing a grave injustice if for fear of being thought one I did not speak the truth, as I understood it, about the people with whom I was in prison. I respect them for their integrity, I admire them for their selfless courage, and I love them, quite simply and unashamedly, because they are my friends. I share their longing for the restoration of democracy in Chile, and although I feel a profound duty to do all within my power to bring an end to the violation of human rights, I do not feel called to join their political and revolutionary struggles.

Like Helder Camara and Martin Luther King I have the audacity to believe that

> . . . one day mankind will bow down before the altars of God and be crowned triumphant over war and bloodshed, and non-violent redemptive goodwill will proclaim the rule of the land. And the lion and the lamb shall lie down together and every man shall sit under his own vine and fig tree and none shall be afraid. I still believe that we shall overcome.

Martin Luther King
Nobel Prize Acceptance Speech

49

Christmas

Birth or Death? There was a Birth, certainly,
We had evidence and no doubt. I had seen birth and
  death,
But had thought they were different; this Birth was
Hard and bitter agony for us, like Death, our death.
We returned to our places, these Kingdoms,
But no longer at ease here, in the old dispensation,
With an alien people clutching their gods.
I should be glad of another death.

T. S. Eliot
Journey of the Magi

Far from home I looked forward to Christmas in a way that I
had not done since I was a child, lying in bed and dreaming
of Christmas trees and carols, of parcels and tinsel, and most
of all of roast turkey and Christmas pudding. I could imagine so well my family doing last minute Christmas shopping
and the happy chaos of children wrapping carefully chosen
gifts and running covetous, inquisitive fingers over mysterious packages labelled 'To Lucinda from Granny', or 'To
Peter from Daddy'. Every time the wardress entered the
compound I thought they had come for me and that I would
be whisked away and put on a plane for England.

So it was that when on 23 December we heard on the
lunchtime news that '*La Doctora* Cassidy' was to face further
charges, the nature of which had not been disclosed, I broke
down and wept.

In a little while I pulled myself together and tried to put
on a brave face. I knew perfectly well that I was being extremely childish and self-centred, for I knew now that it was
only a matter of time before I gained my liberty, whereas for
my fellow prisoners it would be many months or even years.
The possibility that some of them might even meet their
death 'accidentally' was too terrible to think about.

The atmosphere in the camp was unusually tense, for word had come through that there was going to be a Christmas amnesty, and everyone was struggling to maintain their outward calm, while hoping against hope that their names might be on the list. All day there had been speculation as to who would be released, and those who had been held for over a year sat discussing intently whether the fact that they had been held so long made it almost certain that they would be released or if, conversely, it meant that they were considered dangerous and would be held even longer.

Suddenly, at about six o'clock there was a cry, '*la Lista! la Lista!*' and we ran to where a group of girls were crowded round a small transistor radio. The reading had already begun: 'Aranda, Gloria; Araya, Miriam; Araya, Juan; Ariztia, Margarita; . . .'. They were reading the names of the men as well, and we listened intently, for many of the girls had husbands or lovers or brothers in the men's section of the prison. Every so often there would be a scream of delight followed by cries of exasperation as some lucky person gave voice to her delight, and thereby drowned the name of the next person on the list. I was sitting on the ground next to my friend Marcia when her name was read; she was not expecting to be released and when she heard her name there was a breathless gasp of joy and disbelief. We hugged each other and listened for the next of the names.

When the list ended pandemonium broke loose. There were thirty girls on the list and they rushed frantically to organize their things, for it was the custom to release people without warning so that they could not smuggle messages out. Hurriedly precious pieces of embroidery or crochet were packed, and friends sped across the courtyard with tiny mementoes made of leather or wool or whatever was at hand. All spare clothing was hastily given away, for it was an unwritten law that anything that could be spared was left behind, for many of the prisoners were very poor and those who arrived from the torture centres had only the clothes in which they had been arrested, and after several weeks worn both day and night these were usually in a sad state.

It was not long before the door of the compound opened and the camp commander appeared. We were called on parade and then he read out the list of those who were to go. They were sent to fetch their things and while we stood to attention they were escorted away to the main offices. There were no final hugs or goodbyes, for the girls had learnt that such 'disorderly' behaviour resulted in suspension of visits from relatives, or a day in the *calabozo*, the underground cell which was used for punishment.

When the excitement of the departure was over we re-settled ourselves. It was a relief in many respects, for we had been 120 women in a camp built to hold 80, so the departure of the 30 meant that there would be a bed for everyone and an end to sleeping on the floor. The dramas of the day were not over, however, for the door opened again and Georgina came in carrying her new baby daughter. She had gone into labour two nights previously and had been taken off to hospital, but now that the delivery was over she returned to prison to share a room with five other girls. The joy of the girls knew no bounds and Susanna, who was a midwife, proudly took the tiny Javiera in her arms and displayed her to the assembled group.

At last things were quiet, and we busied ourselves wrapping up our presents. It had been decided that each girl should make one present and that these would be collected and redistributed during the party on Christmas Eve, so that everyone would receive a present. I had made leather pendants from scraps left over from the sandal 'workshop' and I gave one of these. When I had exhausted my leather supply and admired the row of completed pendants and key rings for my friends whom I hoped to see on Boxing Day I looked around the bare compound and wished I had something to give it a festive air. Materials, however, were always at a premium as we had all of us become expert in making gifts or ornaments from scraps of wool, cloth, wire or bone.

Separated as I was from the traditional English Christmas and from all forms of religious support, for no priests or ministers were allowed to hold services in the camp, I

longed especially to make some Christian sign to mark the
coming feast. I considered making a crib but again there
was the problem of lack of materials, so I decided upon a
poster and borrowing a Christmas card from one of the
members of the Peace Committee set about copying the
design. The card had come from the Catholic bishop who
was a co-founder of the Committee, and who had been a
frequent visitor to the prison in the days before he was conveniently transferred to the far north of Chile and visits
from the clergy were suspended. Carefully I copied the card
and on a large piece of shelf paper drew the figure of the
Christ child holding on his lap a large, fat dove, the symbol
of the peace for which we all longed. There was no paint to
colour it, but I had a felt pen and shaded in a blue background. The pen was nearly dry but I replenished it as I
had been shown with cologne (necessity being truly the
mother of invention) and it painted on, if a little paler. The
result was a rather pleasing mottled effect and I fixed it to
the wall with some stolen pins.

Christmas Eve dawned and as soon as breakfast was
cleared away the girls began to prepare for the party. For
weeks they had hoarded cans of *manjar*, the delicious spread
which the Chileans make by boiling cans of condensed milk
for hours, and other goodies. Now they gathered their resources together to make a pudding for 80 people. I watched,
fascinated. They took two tin trays and covered them with
broken biscuit; then came a couple of cans of peaches and
the *manjar*. My thoughts went guiltily to the two Harrods
tinned Christmas cakes which the British ambassador had
given me and which I had refrained from handing in to the
common pool because it seemed such a waste. I stood there
and battled with my conscience and eventually honour (and
the knowledge that no one would join me in a secret feast)
triumphed and I brought them along and presented them
to the cake-makers. I could not resist making it very clear
that these were very expensive, very special English cakes,
the like of which was not made in Chile, but they were used
to my inability to be an anonymous member of the community and thanked me suitably. Deprived of alcohol as we

were, the very smell from the opened tins made us giggly
and I stood by while the rich dark product of some secret
Harrods recipe was stirred sacriligeously in with the biscuits
and condensed milk.

As I stood watching the final touches being made to the
pudding I was called by the wardress and told that the camp
commander had graciously allowed the army chaplain to
celebrate mass and as I was the most vocal of the Christians
(I had frequently done battle with the colonel to try to persuade the imprisoned priests to say mass for us) I was deputed
to prepare.

Delighted, I gathered a band of helpers and we carried
a table out into the exercise yard. Someone had a clean
sheet and we arranged a Christmas altar bedecked with

'Choir practice' in Tres Alamos

branches pulled from bushes in the prison yard. I pinned my poster on to the front and laid out the crucifix with the Christ made in copper wire that I had made the day I arrived at the camp. Determined that the service should both give glory to God and solace to the prisoners I conferred with Beatriz, who had been allowed to have her guitar for Christmas. We made a list of hymns that most people knew and the 'choir' went into one of the rooms to practise. As they sang I sat on the floor and sketched them, perched on the top bunk together.

At about twelve the priest came and we sat on benches and on the ground in what shade we could find, for the sun was very hot, and joined with the priest in the prayers of the mass. Seldom have I participated in a more moving act of worship, for we were joined, Christians and Marxists, believers and atheists, in praise and thanksgiving and desperate asking to our God or whatever force drives the universe. There were many tears as we sang familiar hymns and especially the 'Song of Joy' which has become like a protest song in Chile, for it speaks of the day when all men will again be brothers. At the communion Georgina carried her baby to the altar with her and I think there was no one who did not see in Javiera the defenceless babe of Bethlehem.

In the afternoon we prepared the compound, arranging the tables in one corner for the food and the benches around the walls. The prison kitchen made no gesture for the festive season but no one bothered to eat the tasteless soup because we knew that there were trays and trays of open sardine sandwiches and delicious little biscuits with cheese or hard-boiled egg. Everyone dressed with care, for the lack of menfolk was no excuse for depression, and at eight o'clock the compound was full of elegant ladies happily drinking fruit juice and talking to their friends. Even the perpetual feud which raged with a small group of informers in the camp was temporarily suspended. At nine o'clock the 'pudding' was produced and it was as though the miracle of the loaves and the fishes had been repeated, for the ambassador's two small cakes fed the eighty of us with some to spare. After supper Beatriz played her guitar and we all sang with a rare joy, for even singing had been prohibited for months in an effort to lower morale.

Then at exactly ten o'clock came the most moving ceremony I have ever witnessed, for it was the hour which had been set to sing for the benefit of the men, so near and yet so far, in their compound a hundred yards away. Standing on tables and benches so that their voices would carry further the girls sang as if their lungs would burst and their hearts would break. Their song filled the night air and rose towards the star-filled sky as they sent their Christmas message of love and hope to their menfolk and to those who had no one to love them behind the high concrete wall. On and on they sang, finishing with the mighty chorus of the song written in prison: '*Animo, Negro José* – Take heart, Joe my love.'

Suddenly the order was given to be silent and we waited with breath held. I found the tears rolling down my cheeks

'*Carols at Christmas*', *Tres Alamos 1975*

as faintly on the wind I heard the answering song of the men.

After the singing we danced and, resplendent in a dreadful T-shirt with a black-habited nun riding a motor bicycle and the legend 'Nun Power' emblazoned across my bosom, I rocked and rolled as I had not done for twenty years. (The shirt was a gift from an American friend and so pleased my fellow prisoners that I was made to wear it.)

As I flung myself in gay abandon round the compound the girls drew to the side and clapped, for my dancing was so enthusiastic and funny that it had become a cabaret turn. Delighted to be a source of entertainment I gyrated until I was so dizzy that I could no longer stand and collapsed in a breathless heap on the ground.

Then, at five minutes to eleven, we fled like Cinderellas to our bunks and as I lay exhausted in the darkness looking at the familiar glow of the last illicit cigarette in the opposite bunk I knew that this would be the Christmas that I would remember with the greatest nostalgia of my life.

50
Goodbye to Chile

How shall I go in peace and without sorrow? Nay, not without a wound in the spirit shall I leave this city.

Long were the days of pain I have spent within its walls, and long were the nights of aloneness; and who can depart from his pain and his aloneness without regret?

Too many fragments of the spirit have I scattered in these streets, and too many are the children of my longing that walk naked among these hills, and I cannot withdraw from them without a burden and an ache.

It is not a garment I cast off this day, but a skin that I tear with my own hands.

Nor is it a thought that I leave behind me, but a heart made sweet with hunger and thirst.

Kahlil Gibran
The Prophet

On Boxing Day Derek Fernyhough, the consul, and his wife Grace, came to visit me and England seemed immeasurably closer as I ate ravenously of the cold turkey and ham that they brought me, and heard the news that I was probably to be released the following Monday. Many of my friends had come and we laughed and talked together like children. There were so many people to whom I wished to speak in private that they took it in turns to walk up and down the prison yard with me while the others sat under the tree and talked among themselves and to the other prisoners.

Though filled with a wild joy at the thought of my imminent release I knew that this could well be the last time that I would see those friends who had been so close to me during the past year. My friendship with them had changed my life; I knew there was no going back and yet how was I to go forward without their inspiration and their help?

This little group of American nuns and priests had

taught me the truth of Christ's promise to his disciples: 'And everyone who has left houses or brothers or sisters or father or mother or children or lands, for my name's sake, will receive a hundredfold, and inherit eternal life.'

Matthew 19.29

Theirs indeed was the folly of the Cross: they had freely left loving families, comfortable homes, promising careers and the right to marry and beget children so that they might follow Christ. They had found him, just as he had been 2000 years ago, poor and vulnerable, living in a stable amongst the dispossessed, despised and rejected, hunted like an animal, mocked and spat upon, stripped and scourged and done to death by men who knew not what they did.

Through their eyes, and walking at their side, I too had found him, and like the three wise men I feared that upon returning to my Kingdom I should no longer be at ease.

> . . . in the old dispensation,
> With an alien people clutching their gods.

T. S. Eliot
The Journey of the Magi

I had yet to learn that amongst the alien people I would find again the babe of Bethlehem and the Man of Sorrows, and that there would be willing hands to guide and support me as I stumbled on in my search.

All weekend I lived poised in anticipation that I would receive official notification of my release, but there was none. I listened avidly to the news bulletins, and heard again and again that I was to leave Chile on the four o'clock British Caledonian flight on Monday, 29 December. Without official confirmation it was difficult to believe. We none of us felt sufficiently secure to have any kind of farewell celebration. Late on the Sunday night, however, we gathered in the inner patio and Beatriz played the guitar while the others sang for me the songs that I loved most. One song had become my favourite and I had taken the words of a rejected lover for my own:

> *Perdonaría todas las ofensas*
> *Pero olvidarte jamás, jamás.*

I shall forgive you the wrongs you have done me,
But forget you? Never! Never!

On Monday morning there was still no news, but I packed my few belongings in two shopping bags and tried to contain my mixture of excitement and anxiety. Ten o'clock, eleven o'clock, twelve o'clock: the morning wore on until suddenly we heard the familiar harsh words of the wardress '*Todos a formar.* – Everyone on parade.'

Inside each one of us there remained a deep fear of the unknown, a legacy of days of torture and sudden journeys to unknown destinations made with eyes sealed with scotch tape. Worried and expectant we lined up and faced Colonel Pacheco, the prison commander. Without explanation he gave the order: 'Everyone to the visitors' patio.'

As we moved in the direction of the central office building fear heightened, for there had been a rumour that the military authorities were planning a gigantic farce, a staged 'attempted escape' in which it would be proved that the prisoners had dug tunnels from their encampments to beyond the prison wall. It was said that this was to be the excuse for the murder of many politically important detainees and that many hundreds of the people in the surrounding *población* would be rounded up and then released in a spectacular 'amnesty'.

When I first heard this rumour I found it too incredible to believe, and then I recalled the unmistakable sounds of digging which we had all heard behind the hut in which I slept, and how I had often woken at night to hear movement behind the building. Remembering the careful staging of the evidence in the case of the 119 disappeared prisoners, in which two foreign magazines had been printed especially as evidence, it was not so impossible to believe. The thought was terrifying and I wondered suddenly if this was the moment and I would never see England again.

As we moved away, Señor Pacheco called roughly to me: 'You, stay here.' I stood still and my companions moved out of sight until I was alone in the empty barracks with the commander and two wardresses. Although I knew this must mean my release, fear and uncertainty were strong within me. Brusquely he told me that I had three minutes in which to pack my bags, and one of the wardresses accompanied me to supervise my preparations.

Quickly I dressed in a pair of jeans that Sally had given me and an embroidered blouse made in the camp, and I was ready. Even in five weeks I seemed to have accumulated a lot of possessions and the wardress helped me to carry my poncho and bag of books as we walked towards the central offices. We passed behind the building along the concrete path that led to the men's section and to Cuatro Alamos and then stopped suddenly at a door that I had never noticed. It led to a cellar where there were obvious signs of building, and to my horror I was motioned inside.

Immediately I was filled with the anguish of the earlier days. Could it really be that they meant to kill me now at this eleventh hour? Was I to be buried under the concrete in this cellar and my friends told that I had gone to England? Terrified, I clasped my home-made crucifix which I had brought with me and went down the steps into the darkness.

My fear was mercifully short-lived, for after a few minutes' waiting a door opened and I was told to go up into the building. I realize now that this was a manoeuvre to ensure that my companions did not see me again. Perhaps the prison authorities were afraid of emotional farewells, or just wished to deny us the pleasure of saying goodbye. Whatever the reason behind it they were successful, for I left the girls with whom I had shared so much without even a glance of farewell.

Once in the building I was taken into the large waiting room where I had often seen the consul and, my fears gone, I relaxed and stood sadly by as they searched my belongings and confiscated little mementos made for me by the other prisoners. By some miracle I was allowed to keep the Bible which the Red Cross had given me, which had been signed by all the prisoners, and a few other gifts which bore no evidence that they had been made in prison. All my drawings were confiscated, and I too was searched but as I carried no clandestine papers there was no incident.

After the search was completed I was taken to one of the offices where I signed my release papers, cyclostyled forms in which I declared that I had received humane treatment and that I was in sound health. Then I sat down to wait.

As the minutes passed I began again to be afraid. When I had been brought from the barracks I had been told that I must hurry because the ambassador was waiting, but now that two hours had elapsed I knew that they had lied. By three o'clock, when I was convinced that it was all part of some nefarious plot, I was told that my transport had arrived.

The ambassador had promised me that there would be someone from the embassy to accompany me to the airport for he knew that I was very afraid, but I met only a tall young man who told me that he was from the CIME (in English the ICEM, the International Commission for European Migration). I had never met him before and, quite unbelieving, accused him of being a DINA agent. He assured me that he wasn't and that it was his job to get me on to the plane, and that his car would follow mine until we arrived at the airport. Only marginally comforted, I climbed into the black limousine with three armed men and we set off.

As I sat tensely in the back they tried to make conversation with me, and finding me unforthcoming asked if I did not trust them. I replied that I had learned to trust no one and said I thought they belonged to the DINA. Their indignation was genuine enough to be reassuring and after a long circuitous drive I realized that we had arrived in the vicinity of the airport.

I knew that there would be many people to see me off, for the time of my departure had been so publicized, but the driver told me that he had instructions to wait outside the airport until fifteen minutes before the plane was due to take off. Then I realized that my departure had been organized so as to allow the minimum of time for goodbyes. The authorities wanted me to leave the country with as little publicity as possible and they were quite determined that there were to be no dramatic farewells.

As we sat in the car on the outskirts of the airport I thought sadly of Sally, Rosemary and all the other friends who would be waiting in the visitors' gallery on the roof. Then, at a quarter to four, an airport vehicle appeared and I was told to get into it. We entered the airport from a side entrance and sped across the tarmac to the passenger lounge where I was told to get out. In the brief time that it took to alight from the van and enter the lounge I saw a sea of faces and turned to wave.

Inside were Mr Secondé the ambassador and Derek Fernyhough. They gave me my ticket and a temporary pass·port and after a rapid goodbye I went with Derek and the man from the CIME to the airport bus. Unable to contain my excitement and joy at seeing my friends I waved madly to the crowd on the balcony. My two escorts urged me on but I stood my ground for long enough to pick out the faces of at least some of the crowd who had come to bid me goodbye.

Luckily I did not know that many people have been re-arrested even at this late stage, and I did not understand why the consul was so worried. I learned much later that Mary Ann Beausire's brother William had been picked up by the Argentinian police at the airport in Montevideo and returned secretly to Chile where he had been seen in various centres of interrogation.

Once on the airport bus I found an open window and managed to put out my arm to wave a final goodbye. As we drove towards the plane the faces blurred and I could see only a sea of waving arms. Slowly I climbed the ramp and at the plane door said goodbye to Derek Fernyhough who had been so good to me during the past two months. I have not read the code of behaviour laid down for guidance of consuls in dealing with foreign nationals in trouble but it is difficult to imagine that it includes the provision of handkerchiefs for weeping, novels, Bibles, food, clothing and the care of the subject's dogs while he or she is in prison!

Once in my seat I pressed my face to the window and through the thick glass and my own tears saw only a blurred image of the people and country that I had come to love so much; then the engines revved and we taxied out of sight. As the plane became airborne I looked down in sadness and longing at the long narrow strip of land that is Chile: at the land where war and peace, riches and destitution, hatred and love live side by side, and where paradoxically, in losing my life I had found it again.

Epilogue

ADIOS A LA DR SHEILA CASSIDY

La fuimos a despedir el lunes 29 en una radiante tarde de sol. Sólo la divisamos a través de los cristales de las puertas de Pudahuel; luego subió feliz al bus que la acercó al avión. Entre otros bultos negros subió las escalinatas del gigantesco aparato, blanca figura recortada sobre el horizonte de la lejana ciudad. De una jaula en otra, por los huecos libres que encontraba, sacaba su largo brazo y mostraba su alegre risa para responder a la afectuosa despedida de sus amigos. Agitaba al aire la misma mano que tocó tantos cuerpos enfermos en nuestra Policlínica de la Zona Norte, donde tantos la conocían y querían, mano abierta y franca, incapaz de doblez y de violencia; lo sabemos muy bien.

Su última jaula fue el inmenso pájaro de acero que la tragó generoso. Cuando se elevaba entre el fragor de las turbinas, pareció que el majestuoso pájaro llevaba prendido en la proa una inmensa rama de olivo.

† JORGE HOURTON
Vicario Zona Norte

FAREWELL TO DR SHEILA CASSIDY

We went to see her off on Monday the 29th, a glorious sunny afternoon. We only managed to catch a glimpse of her through the glass doors at Pudahuel; then she happily got into the 'bus that took her to the aeroplane. Amongst many black forms she climbed the stairway of the enormous machine – a white figure outlined against the horizon of the distant city. From one cage to another, through any gap she found, she waved her long arm and smiled gaily in answer to the affectionate farewell of her friends. Now she was waving the same hand that had touched so many sick bodies in our Policlinica of the Northern Zone, where so many had known and loved her – an open, honest hand, incapable of deceit or violence, as we all well knew.

Her final cage was the vast steel bird that swallowed her whole. As the majestic bird took off amongst the roar of the turbines, it seemed that it carried in it's beak an immense olive branch.

BISHOP JORGE HOURTON
Vicar of the Northern Zone

(Published in *Comunidad Cristiana*, weekly supplement of *Iglesia de Santiago*, 11 January 1976)

Acknowledgements

Acknowledgement is gratefully made for permission to include the following works or extracts from them:

Gibran, Kahlil: extracts from THE PROPHET (Heinemann, 1972).

Neruda, Pablo: poem from VICTOR JARA, HIS LIFE AND SONGS (Elm Tree Books, 1976).

Amnesty International: extract from a report on Chile (Amnesty International, 1974).

Quoist, Michel: extracts from PRAYERS OF LIFE (Gill & Macmillan, 1965).

Covert Action in Chile: 'Hearings before the select committee to study governmental operations with respect to intelligence activities of the United States Senate' Vol 7, 1975.

Jones, Christopher William: extracts from LISTEN PILGRIM (Darton, Longman & Todd, 1968).

Camara, Helder: extracts from THE DESERT IS FERTILE (Sheed & Ward, 1974).

'Speaking with Children': from CHILE – POEMS AND SONGS OF CAPTIVITY (Office for Political Prisoners and Human Rights in Chile).

Kipling, Rudyard: 'If' from DEFINITIVE EDITION (Hodder, 1940).

Cardenal, Ernesto: 'Why have you left me?' from PSALMS (Search Press, 1977).

The ITT Corporation Subversion in Chile: A Case Study in US Corporate Intrigue in the Third World (Bertrand Russell Peace Foundation, 1972).